THE 54th INFANTRY BRIGADE, 1914—1918

TO
OUR OLD COMRADES,
THE
OFFICERS, NON-COMMISSIONED OFFICERS
AND MEN
OF THE
54TH INFANTRY BRIGADE,
WHO FELL GLORIOUSLY DURING OUR FOUR YEARS' SERVICE,
1914–1918,
TO WIN THE FINAL VICTORY,
THIS LITTLE RECORD OF THEIR ACHIEVEMENTS
IS DEDICATED.

THE 18TH DIVISION MEMORIAL IN TRONES WOOD, WHERE THE 54TH BRIGADE HAD SOME HEAVY FIGHTING (SEE CHAPTER V). On the right is an enlargement of the inscription.

Frontispiece.

Printed for private circulation only

THE
54th INFANTRY BRIGADE
1914-1918

Some Records of Battle and Laughter in France

AUTHOR'S FOREWORD

THE above heading is quite misleading. There has been no author—or, rather, there has been no *one* author, for this book is made up of the stories and recollections of all ranks. If it fell to one fellow's lot to collect the stories and pass them on to the printer, that was simply his excuse for sitting and smoking in his billet whilst the rest of the Brigade were out on " salvage " during these last months in France.

The fact that the book is to be regarded as written by the Brigade itself, and not by any individual, explains why you will find, " We went forward here," or " We dug in there," on so many of the pages, as though the writer had been present on every occasion when the Brigade went into action. You must imagine this book written by the Spirit of the Brigade, which shared every tour in the line, went over with each battalion behind every barrage, and never missed a parade.

But even the Spirit of the Brigade has its limitations. Some who read this book will turn to a particular chapter and say, " Why, they've missed one of the best incidents in that fight " ; or, " A very funny thing happened in that sector—pity it's been left out." Well, that's where it is better to drop all this talk about an omnipresent Spirit of the Brigade, and confess that we are only human, and that we could only put into this book the material that was received. Goodness knows we worried everyone we could get at for stories and recollections, and goodness knows everyone we worried was patient and kindly beyond words, and did his best to supply material for these pages. If we failed to get hold of what you believe to have been the best story of the whole campaign—well, sorry ! Better luck next war !

One or two omissions have been unavoidable. Certain portraits should have been in this book, and every effort was made to get them, but up to the moment when the last pages had to go to press they had not been received. Also, it had been fully intended to print a full list—and it would have been a long and splendid one—of all the honours and awards gained by officers, non-commissioned officers, and men while serving with the Brigade. Unhappily, the rough-and-tumble of service in the field sometimes makes the keeping of full and exact records impossible, and while some units furnished the lists required, others were unable to do so. In these circumstances it seemed better, rather than publish an incomplete record, to publish none at all.

There is nothing more to say except to thank all those of all ranks who have so good-naturedly assisted in compiling these pages, and have borne patiently with the writer when he has pestered them to fight their battles over again for our common information.

E. R.

HEADQUARTERS,
    54TH INFANTRY BRIGADE,
        FRANCE.
March, 1919.

CONTENTS

	PAGE
CHAPTER I	
EARLY DAYS IN ENGLAND	1
CHAPTER II	
FIRST EXPERIENCES IN THE TRENCHES	11
CHAPTER III	
FURTHER EXPERIENCES IN THE TRENCHES	20
CHAPTER IV	
THE SOMME—JULY, 1916	31
CHAPTER V	
TRONES WOOD	43
CHAPTER VI	
THIEPVAL	51
CHAPTER VII	
SCHWABEN REDOUBT AND REGINA TRENCH	68
CHAPTER VIII	
BOOM RAVINE	75
CHAPTER IX	
THE GERMAN RETREAT OF 1917	85
CHAPTER X	
CHERISY	96
CHAPTER XI	
THE YPRES SALIENT AND GLENCORSE WOOD	105
CHAPTER XII	
HOUTHULST FOREST	117

CHAPTER XIII
THE MARCH RETREAT 126

CHAPTER XIV
THE DEFENCE OF AMIENS 141

CHAPTER XV
ALBERT 154

CHAPTER XVI
THE BRAY-CORBIE ROAD 161

CHAPTER XVII
THE PASSAGE OF THE ANCRE-COMBLES 171

CHAPTER XVIII
THROUGH THE HINDENBURG LINE 178

CHAPTER XIX
LE CATEAU AND THE ARMISTICE 189

APPENDIX A
BRIGADE COMMANDERS, BRIGADE MAJORS, STAFF CAPTAINS, COMMANDING OFFICERS 201

APPENDIX B
VICTORIA CROSSES 204

LIST OF ILLUSTRATIONS

THE 18TH DIVISION MEMORIAL IN TRONES WOOD, WHERE THE 54TH BRIGADE HAD SOME HEAVY FIGHTING *Frontispiece*

	FACING PAGE
BRIGADIER-GENERAL L. DE V. SADLEIR-JACKSON, C.B., C.M.G., D.S.O.	32
MAJOR-GENERAL T. H. SHOUBRIDGE, C.M.G., D.S.O. ...	33
MAJOR-GENERAL W. C. G. HENEKER, C.M.G., D.S.O. ...	48
LIEUTENANT-COLONEL C. C. CARR, D.S.O.	49
LIEUTENANT-COLONEL A. E. SULMAN, M.C.	49
LIEUTENANT-COLONEL A. E. PERCIVAL, D.S.O., M.C. ...	80
THE LATE LIEUTENANT-COLONEL G. R. RIPLEY	81
LIEUTENANT-COLONEL R. TURNER, D.S.O.	81
LIEUTENANT-COLONEL THE HON. C. M. HORE-RUTHVEN, D.S.O.	96
MAJOR E. G. MILES, D.S.O., M.C.	96
CAPTAIN G. F. J. CUMBERLEGE, D.S.O., M.C.	96
LIEUTENANT-COLONEL G. PRITCHARD-TAYLOR, D.S.O., M.C.	97
MAJOR CAMPBELL, D.S.O., M.C.	97
MAJOR G. LEDGARD, M.C.	128
THE LATE MAJOR G. BREMNER, D.S.O., M.C.	128
THE LATE CAPTAIN C. F. PAVITT, M.C.	129
CAPTAIN E. M. WEST, M.C.	129
THE 54TH INFANTRY BRIGADE BATTLE FLAGS	144
BATTLE FLAG OF THE 11TH (S.) BATTALION ROYAL FUSILIERS	145
BATTLE FLAG OF THE 7TH (S.) AND 2ND BATTALIONS BEDFORDSHIRE REGIMENT	176
BATTLE FLAG OF THE 6TH (S.) BATTALION NORTHAMPTONSHIRE REGIMENT	177

THE 54th INFANTRY BRIGADE, 1914—1918

Chapter I

EARLY DAYS IN ENGLAND

IT is a far cry from the early days of the war, when " Kitchener's Army" was shaking down—with much fun, much faith, and much fervour, but little else in the way of uniform or equipment !—to later days when the Service Battalions won their spurs and made glorious traditions for brigades that were as new and free from tradition as themselves. It is a story of hard work on the training ground and in the line, of cheery steadfastness through the darkest days, of a splendid contempt for pain and death, of hardship which none can realize except those who had it for their common round and daily task, but all brightened by so much fun and good comradeship that none who knew those days will look back on them without kindly memories.

It is the story, among so many others, of the 54th Infantry Brigade.

Throw your mind back for a moment to those earliest days. At least one officer, happily a survivor of the Old Originals, has a vivid recollection of his first introduction to the 7th Bedfordshire Regiment. He arrived on an afternoon in the autumn of 1914 at Liphook Station, and met one of his men on the platform. He gasped—I am not sure that he did not try to bolt, but he is silent on that point—for the man was radiant and happy in scarlet tunic with no belt, corduroy trousers, buttoned boots, and a black bowler hat. It hardly mattered, after that, that he had a civilian overcoat on his arm. And yet, I wonder whether we should not cheer, rather than laugh ? The men who could face the small boy in the street or the red-tabbed General alike in that fighting kit was not likely to have any unwholesome dread of the Germans ; and, after all, it was the men who rushed to join up in those early days, when rifles could not be had and uniforms had to be improvised, who were the salt of the New Armies. The world knows now that it is unsafe to provoke a nation that can be gaily grim and martial in a scarlet tunic and a bowler hat.

More than four years later, on a cold, wet December day at Serain, on ground torn by the shell-fire of the last victorious push that ended the war, among the graves and débris of battle, the 54th Brigade, its fighting days done, paraded with the rest of the 18th Division for the last time. The Divisional Commander, Major-General R. P. Lee, C.B., afterwards published the following Order of the Day :—

> I was more than pleased with the review of the Division to-day, and congratulate all ranks on the turn-out and the admirable precision which marked all the parade manœuvres. It was a reflection of their glorious deeds.
>
> The Division has taken part in most of the great battles, from the Somme in 1916 down to the Armistice—*i.e.*, " The Somme," " The Ancre," (both autumn and spring), " Arras," " Flanders," " The retreat from the Oise," " The Defence of Amiens," and lastly, " The Hundred Days' Victory."
>
> Throughout these historical operations the Division has proved itself equally strong both in attack and defence, and has earned a reputation second to none through the courage, resolution, and achievements of the officers, non-commissioned officers, and men that it is, and has been, my pride and privilege to command.
>
> I take this opportunity of again thanking you all for your unfailing loyalty, and of expressing my admiration for your gallantry and devotion to duty.

That Order sketches, in a few words, the long story that lies between the early days of the Brigade in England and its last fight on the edge of Mormal Forest, just before the Armistice. The story as it is told in these pages is necessarily the work of many memories, and all ranks have contributed their recollections and stories. Perhaps at times the fun of the long campaign rather than its tragedy may seem to predominate. There are many reasons for that. There are scenes and experiences that men will try to forget—certainly they will never sit down in cold blood to recall them—and perhaps one may best describe this story by slightly altering some lines of Kipling :—

> " We have written the tale of our life,
>   For a sheltered people's mirth,
> In jesting guise ; but ye are wise,
>   And ye know what the jest is worth."

The 54th Brigade was formed in September, 1914, under the command of Brigadier-General H. Browse-Scaife, and has ever been a part of the 18th Division. No finer Division ever left England, for it had a long and careful training under its first

Commander, Lieut.-General Sir Ivor Maxse, C.B., C.V.O., D.S.O., one of the most famous trainers of men in the Army.

The early period of training was spent at Colchester, first at Reed Hall Camp, and afterwards at Middlewick, out by the Rifle Range. The Brigade at first consisted of the following Service Battalions :—

> 10th Royal Fusiliers.
> 11th Royal Fusiliers.
> 8th Royal Sussex Regiment.
> 12th Middlesex Regiment.

After a few days the 10th Battalion Royal Fusiliers was replaced by the 6th Battalion Northamptonshire Regiment, and in February, 1915, the 8th Battalion Royal Sussex Regiment was made a Pioneer Battalion, and became Divisional troops, being replaced in the Brigade by the 7th Battalion Bedfordshire Regiment. As it completed its training and proceeded overseas, the Brigade thus consisted of :—

> 11th Battalion The Royal Fusiliers.
> 7th Battalion Bedfordshire Regiment.
> 6th Battalion Northamptonshire Regiment.
> 12th Battalion Middlesex Regiment.

The following units have also formed a part of the Brigade throughout its history, and their officers and other ranks have ever been a part of the same cheery, " full o' heart " comradeship :—

> 80th Field Company, Royal Engineers.
> 54th Field Ambulance, R.A.M.C.
> 152nd Company, Royal Army Service Corps.

The only other alterations to be recorded—and they will be dealt with at the proper time—are the merging of the 7th (S.) Battalion Bedfordshire Regiment in the 2nd (Regular) Battalion when the latter joined the Brigade in May, 1918 ; and the disbanding of the 12th Battalion Middlesex Regiment early in 1918, when Brigades in France were reorganized on a three-battalion basis, and the junior battalions, after much good and gallant work, had to go. If such battalions did not live to see that day when the old front line swept forward, and our troops re-entered Mons at the dramatic end of the Hundred Days' Victory, at least they will go down in history as having done their bit through the long, hard days of preparation to win those last battles.

Only with great difficulty was order evolved from chaos. The 12th Middlesex Regiment started with a draft of 500, which arrived at Colchester at 11 p.m. on September 4th. Telegrams had been received from the War Office, warning the Brigade of the probable arrival of 500, and ordering them to put up a camp and issue blankets. But the 10th Royal Fusiliers also received a telegram warning them of the arrival of 500 on the same day, and ordering them to find food and cooking utensils. So when the 500 arrived in the pitchy darkness, one can imagine the confusion between two groups of officers, both claiming the men. The matter could not be amicably settled until the next day, when further telegrams were exchanged with the War Office, and a ruling was obtained that the men were to be Middlesex. Further complications had meanwhile arisen, as it was discovered that the conducting N.C.O. had disappeared during the night with the only nominal rolls.

The history of the Brigade's early training is a history common to all New Army formations—much keenness and earnestness and fun, but also much ignorance, which was cheerfully recognized and tackled in the best of spirits. There were days when musketry seemed a hidden mystery, and to " form squad " on the move was to melt into a riot of distracted men. The officers were in many cases in worse plight than the men. Some already had experience in Yeomanry, Territorials, Public School and University Corps, but many had to pick up drill and musketry from the beginning, as the men had, and, in addition, had to puzzle out the mysteries of map-reading, compass work, and minor tactics. Very often, and especially on night operations, the best-laid plans went west, and an unhappy platoon commander would lose himself and his platoon, or march doggedly in a circle till the luck of the British Army or a rural policeman set him on the right road again.

Even the most ingenious plans for meeting all difficulties had a knack of developing on lines that the wildest dreams of fun never anticipated.

There was, for instance, the bright idea of a certain Adjutant — an idea which has never been tried in actual warfare to this day, so conservative are we. The battalion had to make a night advance on a certain position in line of platoons in fours—an operation in which it is notoriously difficult to keep direction. Accordingly this officer stretched a rope from the centre of his battalion to the centre of the objective, and, to make doubly sure, stationed a man with a bicycle lamp at the enemy end of the rope. Every student of war will see at once that this was quite a new idea in minor tactics, and all would have gone well had not the Colonel, and everybody else whose good opinion was worth having, fallen over the rope in the darkness. Otherwise all went well ; the platoons walked cheerfully up the rope, and if there had been a real enemy, and they had been sporting enough to ignore the man with the cycle lamp sitting in the middle of their line, the thing must have been a huge success. But—except so far as this can be regarded as a serious military textbook—the idea has never been taken up warmly in training manuals.

Two more night manœuvres come to mind. In one, the battalion concerned had to do an approach march along a white tape. Unfortunately, a man of the " point," laying out the tape, unwittingly got his foot caught in a loop, and then the most weird marching and counter-marching began. In and out round and round they went, until eventually the foot came out of the loop, whereupon the battalion deployed and did a beautiful attack—but due S. instead of N.E. as had been intended.

In the other manœuvre the 54th Brigade unluckily selected the same ground for a night attack as two battalions of another Brigade. The inevitable happened, and the fight when the opposing forces met was worthy of a mêlée of mediæval warfare.

In those days, so far as one remembers, the Brigade had only three " regulars " as regimental officers — Captain L. A. Newnham, Middlesex Regiment (our first Staff Captain, and at the time of writing Major on the General Staff of the XIII. Corps) ; Major M. Scarbrough, also of the Middlesex Regiment, killed at Thiepval ; and Captain P. Meautys, of the Bedfordshire Regiment, killed in June, 1917, in front of Arras, when Brigade-Major of the 53rd Brigade. Of N.C.Os. who had been " regulars " there was but a handful. If premature grey hairs were their only immediate reward, as they toiled to set our feet in the right paths, and to impart some instinct for discipline, one can but hope that they were not ashamed of their pupils when the Service Battalions got to work in France.

The selection of N.C.Os. was one of the earliest difficulties. " Take the case of the 12th Middlesex " (writes Major Newnham, in sending some interesting notes on those days). " Scarbrough and myself were the only two regular officers—in fact, the only officers for ten days—and there were 1,100 men to tackle, with only three N.C.Os. who had been regulars.

" I went right through the battalion, asking each man what he had been. If I found a boy who had been in the Gordon Boys' Home, then I automatically found an N.C.O., for he at any rate knew how to number off a squad and form fours. One man I remember I made a Corporal at once for two reasons only—(1) That he could keep himself clean, and (2) that he had been a hawker of fish near Billingsgate, and consequently had an excellent voice, and was likely soon to get a good word of command ! And he did, and was an excellent N.C.O.

" I wanted a physical training N.C.O.—nothing easier. A look round revealed the fact that ' The Lunatic Bakers ' from the ' Halls ' were in one company, and, after two days' instruction, a fully fledged P.T. N.C.O. was mine."

The fact that, though we were all comrades in a good cause, one does not hail a General by his nickname, and try to make him feel at home, took a little grasping. One wonders, for instance, whether any one has ever dared to remind Sir Ivor Maxse of a certain day when he was holding a " pow-wow " during some field operations. He was surrounded by his Staff and all the Brigade and Battalion Commanders, when a hot and dirty private, towing a very bored-looking mule after him, pushed through the group, selected Sir Ivor himself out of the crowd, and demanded, " Where's the Bedford's transport ?"

The General has some reputation for rising to the occasion, as an orator, when the situation demands, and one fears that, if the transport driver and his mule had faithfully followed the instructions given them, they would not have reached their own transport lines to this day.

The same famous General seems to have had bad luck when it came to mules. At that time every Commanding Officer had two horses, and one day each battalion received orders that the C.O.'s second charger was to be sent to Brigade Headquarters at an hour stated. A certain transport officer—with that delightful gift for doing the wrong thing if it would make a good story which cheered the Kitchener battalions on their way—jumped to the conclusion that it only meant that one horse was to be withdrawn and sent to another unit. He saw in this a Heaven-sent chance to get rid of his worst mule—a tripod rather than a quadruped, for only three of its legs really worked—and personally dragged the unloved and unlovely animal to Headquarters at the appointed time. There he learned, to his horror, that each battalion was to parade an animal for Sir Ivor Maxse to select a second charger for himself. Before the mule could be dragged away, or shot and thrown down the nearest drain, the General appeared, and was confronted by the proposal that he should consider the claims of the three-legged beast to become his spare mount. I have never quite got out of the hero of the story what the General really did say—he has tried, but confesses himself unable to do justice to the purple patches.

There is an old cobbler in a village near Colchester who had the surprise of his life while some of the R.A.S.C. train attached to the Brigade was billeted in the neighbourhood. A very new and very keen young officer had just arrived, and decided to have a look at the regimental saddler's shop. The gods of mischance—who, as I have already said, did so much to cheer us in those early days—sent him in error to the tiny shop where the village cobbler sat at work.

The officer bounced in, said, " All right, my man, don't trouble to get up "—the cobbler had certainly shown no signs of doing so—and added, " Seems rather stuffy and untidy here ; still, I suppose it's all right—carry on !" and bounced out again. It was not tactful to mention village cobblers to him after that, if you wanted a pass or a drink.

Most people will mention Middlewick Camp as a very draughty spot. On November 11th a real East Coast gale blew over the countryside. Tents were blown down right and left, canteen tents especially catching it badly, and the whole camp was flooded out. The Brigade Headquarters marquees were wrecked, and all the precious papers were blown all over the camp, thereby considerably easing the " returns " problem. The bill for damaged tentage came to about £1,500, and the next day orders were received to go into billets in Colchester.

The first casualty in the Brigade was a man in the 11th Royal Fusiliers, who was badly wounded on January 18th, 1915, whilst walking over the entrenching area behind the butts of the rifle range at Donyland. A stray went over and hit him so badly that he died the following day.

On February 21st, 1915, the Brigade first experienced the Bosche and his " hate," a German aeroplane coming over and dropping bombs on Colchester.

There came at last a day in this Colchester period when uniforms and equipment were complete. The wonderful scarlet and blue uniforms, with headgear which varied from glengarries and golf caps to bowler hats, gave place to khaki. And —one was always learning new things of military importance— one learned that uniform might really fit without spoiling a man's efficiency. Hitherto, for some obscure reason which has baffled the scientist, a tall man always got a dwarf's outfit of the workhouse garb in which we began our military careers. But now all had real khaki, and real equipment, and real rifles. It was a proud moment ; officers and men alike now felt that Heaven was possible but unnecessary.

Then began more strenuous days. Equipment had to be fitted and packs packed—do you remember the feeling, when you had all the Christmas tree on, including full pack, and thought you could hardly walk across the room ? And when all was ready, the Brigade set out on " field work " in real earnest. There was the Ipswich-Woodbridge-Hollesley Bay trek, for instance, in full marching order, covering always twenty-five and sometimes thirty miles a day, with tactical schemes thrown in— advanced guards, outpost, attacks—in which you did " short rushes," with periods of repose flat on your face in ploughed fields in between, and all the rest of the fun. It was hard work, but they were jolly days, trudging along the roads, with home-made marching songs to swing the tired legs and take the mind off the blistered heel or the heavy pack.

There was one song of that period—how many good fellows who sang it will rest for ever behind the old line in France !— which will be remembered by all who tramped those roads by the East Coast. Set down now on paper, in cold blood, it doesn't look very inspired or inspiring, but those who survive will remember how we roared out the " Hollesley Bay Song " :

> " There's a place down in Suffolk called Hollesley Bay,
> We 'ad orders to go there and walk all the way.
> Twenty odd miles we marched every day,
> And that's how we got down to Hollesley Bay.
>
> *Refrain :*
>
> " Hold yer row ! Hold yer row !
> We ain't said a word about half what's occurred.
> Hold yer row ! What d'yer say ?
> We knew every milestone to Hollesley Bay.
>
> " Now, while we were stationed at Hollesley Bay,
> The sick they paraded in scores every day,
> And the doctor when he saw them cried in dismay,
> ' 'Ow on earth did yer manage to walk all this way ?
>
> " While we were stationed at Hollesley Bay,
> We went to a church about ten miles away,
> And the people who saw us they all ran away,
> For they'd heard what we'd said about Hollesley Bay.
>
> *Refrain :*
>
> " Hold yer row ! Hold yer row !
> We ain't said a word about half what's occurred.
> Hold yer row ! What d'yer say ?
> We learned some new swear words at Hollesley Bay.

On March 19th the Brigade had its first ceremonial inspection, by Sir Archibald Murray, then Sub-Chief of the Imperial General Staff. A snowstorm swept over the ground while the battalions awaited his arrival, and there was a bitter cold wind, but the men were quite steady on parade, and all went off well.

Early in May, 1915, the Brigade moved by road to Hertford, a three days' trek, and there entrained for Codford, on Salisbury Plain, where the rest of the days of preparation in England were spent. There " intensive field days " set in with more severity than ever, and the days of hard marching and great expenditure of blank, both ammunition and language, around Stony Hill and other training areas were things to remember.

Sport was not neglected, and the 54th has ever been a good sporting Brigade. Many will remember that great cross-country run on the Plain on May 29th, 1915, when Lieut.-Colonel (then Captain) A. E. Percival, of the Bedfordshire Regiment, was the first officer home, and Sergeant Rickard, of the same battalion, the first of the other ranks. Sergeant Rickard, unfortunately, was killed in the Brigade's first big show, the capture of Pommiers' Redoubt, at the opening of the Somme offensive of July 1st, 1916. There were 500 starters per battalion. The Bedfordshire Regiment won first place as a team (each team was a trifle of 500 strong), and the Northamptonshire Regiment was second. The first 300 home of each battalion counted for points, one for the first man, two for the second, three for the third, and so on, and 2,000 points for every man who did not finish within twenty minutes of the winner, the team with the fewest points winning. Major Newnham, who organized the race, sat up till the early hours of the next morning getting out the results. The final calculations ran into millions. Try it for yourself.

At this time bombing was a new, or rather a revived, art in the British Army, and there were some hair-raising moments when the Brigade settled down to master the art and to conduct their own experiments. The idea was to fill a jam-tin with old nails and bits of horse-shoe (the latter, possibly, in the pathetic and ill-founded belief that it would bring luck), and to learn by rule-of-thumb how best to explode it with as little inconvenience to yourself and as much annoyance to your hostile " opposite number " as possible.

There were moments when the luck-bringing properties of the bits of old horse-shoe did not " function " properly, and the bombing officer, with his enthusiastic N.C.Os., were men to be avoided. They would mix and experiment till it seemed as though the explosives had been trained to feed out of their hands, and then suddenly some long-suffering chunk of gun-cotton would protest with much flame and noise. One day Lieutenant Smith, Brigade Bombing Officer, was mixing some chemicals together, with the rapt enthusiasm of a mediæval alchemist scrounging for the philosopher's stone, when the whole thing went up. Just why the spectators—Corporal Twiggs (now Sergeant, and wearing the D.C.M. for a bombing affair in the trenches), who was sitting on a box of gun-cotton, and Corporal Turner, who was kneeling on a case of detonators— did not go up too is a part of the history of the everlasting luck of bombing enthusiasts.

No empty jam-tin was safe from the conspirators. It might be your most prized possession, but if you left it out of your sight for a few moments, you would return to find it filled with explosives and rusty nails, complete with fuse. The home-made " hair-brush " bomb was a special joy. On a " hair-brush " of wood was lashed a slab of gun-cotton, with primer and detonator in the centre. Demonstrations were given in the evening, and these became quite smart affairs, to which officers brought their wives, knowing that there would always be plenty of fun and excitement.

So the cheery days went by—darkened only by the fear (how fantastic it seems now !) that the war would be over before the Brigade could get out—till at last the eagerly awaited orders came ; and on July 26th, 1915, the Brigade landed in France, to begin a fighting career that was to last well over three years.

Even the mules came over, though they developed conscientious objections at embarkation, and caused harassed transport officers to apply vainly on the quayside for transfers to the Flying Corps, or any other branch of the service where mules are unknown. Captain Browning, of the Bedfordshire Regiment, was then transport officer to his battalion, and through the sunny hours of a July afternoon his mules persisted in sitting down in the gangway. Hot and tired men, in a hurry to get to the war, reminded those mules of their blotted pedigree and tried to shame them into embarkation, but the mules only sat and smiled. At last, after three hours' exertion, the last mule had been pushed and heaved on board, and all was ready for the opening of the great adventure.

A niche in the Temple of Fame must be found for the celebrated billeting party that came over to France with the Brigade. It consisted of an officer from each battalion, and the Staff Captain, and all were mounted on motor-bikes. How the bikes were smuggled across is another story, and quite unfit for the pure ears of any high authority who may some day find this book in a dentist's waiting-room. As a hint for the next war, let it be said that one bike was " stripped " and concealed in the battalion transport, a wheel in one limber, the engine in another, and so on. Captain Newnham's posed as a signal's machine. But the party landed safe with motor-bikes, and got on with the good work,.

Chapter II

FIRST EXPERIENCES IN THE TRENCHES

WHEN the Brigade arrived in France, in the summer of 1915, things were by no means comfortable or rosy. People in England, who saw the New Armies training on every countryside, and pouring overseas, might talk gaily of peace by Christmas; and the old men, or the men in comfortable jobs, might cry stoutly, " Go on, boys, give 'em hell!" But the boys who knew most about hell knew what a very one-sided hell it was while we were waiting for guns and ammunition.

The situation at that time was well summed up by " Ian Hay " in a lecture to American troops some years later. Speaking of the arrival of the first Brigades of the New Army in France in mid-'15, he said :

" True, we now had the men, but we had not the munitions. All we could do for the present was to stick our toes in, play for time, and harass the enemy, while back at home behind us the factories were being erected and the machinery laid down, and men and women—more especially women—were working night and day, Sundays, weekdays, Christmas and holiday time included, to turn out the tale of guns and shells for our purposes, until at last we could say as a nation, ' We are ready ; full speed ahead.'

" Out on the Western Front we had to wait a long time for that message. In the summer of 1915 it never came at all. All during that summer the trenches were held, grimly and doggedly, by men who, a year previously, had been peaceful farmers, or mechanics, or miners, or clerks—men with no military tradition to uphold them. Our supply of gun ammunition in those days was limited to three or four shells per gun per day, and the guns themselves were not plentiful. If the Hun shelled our front-line trenches, as he did at least twice a day, and the parapet began to fly up in the air, and you got to the wire and telephoned to the artillery behind for retaliation, too often the answer came back : ' Very sorry, nothing doing till to-morrow.' The best we could hope for was to save our scanty supply of ammunition during a few quiet days, and then indulge in a real good outburst of retaliation—say, on Saturday afternoon. For the rest of the time we sat at the bottom of our trenches and wished for happier days. It was not a pleasant experience ; but all the while we were learning and learning, and finding our feet, and acquiring the priceless art of playing a poor hand."

The first few months of the Brigade in France were devoted to this learning, and then came long months of holding on grimly while the Germans treated us to those " hates " which we had neither the guns nor the shells to return.

Training was carried out at first in the Corbie area, and late in August came instructional tours in the line, the battalions being attached to Brigades that had already served their apprenticeship in the trenches.

The first day, and more especially the first night, in the line is a turning-point in a man's life. He finds that, as regards being really scared and jumpy and downright uncomfortable, previous experiences do not count. He has come up against one of the great tests of his manhood. If he can stand up to his job cheerfully, fight down fear, and carry on with a smile and a jest, he has passed his entrance examination, and may look to the next ordeal, " going over the top," with any sense of pleasurable anticipation he can muster.

There are still many who recall the Brigade's first experience of the line, before they had learned those arts of making themselves nearly comfortable and almost safe which distinguish the seasoned battalions. One of them will remember to the end how far he felt from home and hope and help when, just before midnight, a Scottish officer took him to what appeared the weakest and loneliest spot in the whole line, and said : " There, laddie, you'll be on duty from twelve till four. This is the front line, the Germans are very close, and a mine's going up at dawn." Exit Scottish officer, leaving behind him one British officer complete with " wind up."

Instructional tours being over, the Brigade took over a sector of the line early in September, 1915, opposite Fricourt. The Brigade front was divided into two sectors—D.1 on the right, and D.2 on the left. At first D.1 was held by the Fusiliers and the Northamptonshire Regiment, and D.2 by the Bedfordshire and Middlesex Regiments. This arrangement held good till the end of November, when battalions changed over, the Bedfordshire and Middlesex Regiments going to D.1, and the Fusiliers and Northamptonshire Regiment to D.2.

Great places for " wind up," those front line trenches in the early days of the new battalions, when all was strange, and every shadow was a German attack. Imagine the discomfort of the Bedfordshire Regiment company commander to whom a patrol reported the discovery in No Man's Land of a trap-door leading to an underground tunnel, from which sounds of mining could be heard. It was the battalion's first tour in the trenches ; appreciation of Hun ingenuity ran high, and there were visions of a surprise attack from the mystery shaft. After some consultation the bombing officer and his corporal were sent for, and, without any undue display of delight at the job, went out to investigate. After throwing several bombs at the "trapdoor," they withdrew for assistance. Finally, the spot was reached, and the origin of the scare was found to be nothing more alarming than the top of an old tin can! And, believe me, there were times when a certain patrol got almost tired of hearing about mysterious trap-doors in No Man's Land.

It was in the same part of the line, and at about the same period, that a certain intelligence officer, who possessed that vivid imagination which is supposed to make for success in modern war, reported one day, "Smoke seen issuing from enemy trench at ———." The next day he reported, "Sound of oil-engine in enemy trench at ———," adding: "It is thought this may be connected with the smoke seen yesterday, and indicates enemy mining." This was sheer genius, almost too delicate and rare for the rough-and-tumble of trench warfare, and when the intelligence officer had sufficiently impressed the idea that the Germans were motoring underground to outflank us from below, a raid was organized to cut out the supposed engine. It is just here that the story breaks away from the Jules Verne or H. G. Wells touch and ends on the dull fact that the raiders found no trace of any engine, and the intelligence officer ceased to attach any importance to the smoke of German trench cookery.

Two other instances of funny remarks in intelligence summaries come to mind. In one, "Smoke as from a cooking fire" was reported. The reasoning by which smoke from a cooking fire could be distinguished from smoke from any other fire was not included in the report. The other instance was the quite famous report (from the Bedfordshire Regiment, I think) that a pigeon had been seen "flying in a suspicious manner" over Fricourt!

There was full reason to watch and listen carefully for any signs of underground activity, for mining was a constant feature of this part of the line, especially in the D.1 sector.

The rocking of the ground, the caving-in of one's firmest and best revetted trenches, the confusion in the darkness and shelling, the hasty digging and building up with sandbags, peering into the depths of the new crater and seeing the blue flickering of gas-fumes at the bottom, all help to make that form of warfare very easy to remember.

Never a week passed without a mine going up, and one week the measures to drive away boredom and dull care included the blowing of five mines, so that at last No Man's Land was nothing but a huge crater. They were exciting and ticklish days, for one never knew when the trench underfoot would go up, as it was known that while the French held this part of the line the Germans had been mining and tunnelling in all directions.

The following extracts from a diary show how frequent these mine episodes were :—

October 3, 1915.—Enemy blew up a trench mine opposite 82 (Bois Français). Some of our parapet damaged, and seven casualties by subsequent rifle and shell fire. Otherwise quiet day.

October 5.—Enemy blew mine opposite trench 77. About 40 yards of parapet knocked down. Two officers and eight men gassed above ground ; five miners killed below ground.

October 7.—We blew a mine in D.1 which turned out a much bigger explosion than had been expected. It is thought that a German mine must have been exploded by ours, as a red flame went up, usually noticed in German mines.

October 8, 5.30 *p.m.*—Enemy blew up a mine opposite trench 79. Buried two of our mining officers and destroyed 50 yards of a new shaft. 7 *p.m.*—We blew a large mine opposite 81. Very little damage to our parapet.

October 13.—Enemy fired mine in D.1. No damage and no casualties.
October 14.—Enemy blew a mine in C.2. (Sector on our right.)
October 20.—Enemy blew a mine in D.1. No damage.
October 23.—Enemy blew a mine in D.
October 24.—Enemy blew another mine in D.1 (opposite 80.B).
October 25.—Enemy blew mine in D.1. Little damage, but one killed and three wounded when making sap out to crater-edge.

Those brief matter-of-fact jottings give some idea of a " quiet " month in the sector.

November 1st was another cheery day. In the middle of the morning the enemy blew a mine in D.1, and brought down a good stretch of our parapet. Our turn came just after dusk, when, says the diarist :—

" We blew three mines (large ones) in D.1. They formed two large craters. Considerable damage was done to our own parapet, but still more must have been done to the enemy's." [Can't you see the cheery philosopher sitting among the ruins of his own trench, laughing to think that the Germans were probably having an even worse time !] "Northamptonshire Regiment immediately reconnoitred the new craters, which were about twenty yards from our front line, and then occupied the near edges and dug themselves in very successfully. Casualties, one officer and one man killed, four men wounded. The night was dark and wet, and the trenches extremely muddy, besides being blocked by fallen parapets, so that this operation was not an easy one, and reflected great credit on the battalion."

While on the subject of mines, another little experience, at a later date, is worth telling here. A mine was to go up under the German front line at about 4.30 p.m. on January 18th, 1916, and Lieutenant Sherwell and 2nd-Lieutenant Driver, of the Bedfordshire Regiment, who were then in the line, were detailed to inspect and report on the damage done.

They were each accompanied by a party of bombers, and were instructed to proceed to the mine crater as soon as it was formed, one party working round the right and one round the left. It was quite dark, but the crater was located, and eventually the two parties met on the farther side of the lip, and a council of war was held. In view of the fact that the crater had been formed in No Man's Land, some twenty yards from the Bosche wire, it was decided to push on to the Bosche trench and see if the explosion had done any damage. Thereupon two very windy officers, followed in single file by the bombing parties, with great difficulty scrambled through the wire, only to find the enemy trench undamaged and deserted immediately opposite the crater.

Orders were then given (and smartly obeyed) for the return trip. All got back safely across the wire except 2nd-Lieutenant Driver, who was unable to extricate himself from the entanglements which held him in a very uncomfortable position, and with no one to help. To add to the unpleasantness, the Germans began to return to their deserted bit of trench, and started putting up light. He was at once spotted, and the Bosche lost no time in taking pot-shots at him. He had lost his revolver and used up all his bombs, and thoroughly disliked his position, but managed to get away unscathed by slipping out of his bomb-jacket and leaving it and portions of his clothing attached to the wire. He was later on wounded in the arm by a bullet, which also killed an officer (2nd-Lieutenant Whatmore) next to him.

Though the mine had not gone off in the right place, the Bedfordshire Regiment consolidated that night the left- and right-hand lips of the crater, and thus the night's effort was not altogether without success, for we could now see by day and night into the Bosche lines.

On October 6th a platoon of the 7th Oxfordshire and Buckinghamshire Light Infantry had a bad time while attached to the Bedfordshire Regiment for instruction. They arrived while the enemy were having a " hate " with heavy trench mortars at some houses in the rear of the trenches near Fricourt. The cellar into which they were put was struck, and most of them were buried. Men of " C " and " D " companies, Bedfordshire Regiment, promptly began to dig them out, but were themselves buried by a second hit on the same house. The casualties were eight killed and twenty-six wounded, of whom seven were Bedfordshires.

Dr. Cecil Powell, then Medical Officer of the Bedfordshire Regiment, went to the rescue, and was about to begin digging out the survivors when a man buried up to the neck in bricks and mortar looked at him and gasped : " Gawd Almighty ! it's Dr. Powell, the man I most want to see." The man was one of his former patients, and lived near his surgery in England. Neither of them had known that the other was in France.

The " nervy " conditions of trench warfare, especially for a new battalion, when every man had a bullet or bomb for every unexpected shadow, led to some unpleasantly narrow escapes from one's own comrades. Colonel Percival, of the Bedfordshire Regiment, had an experience of this in October, 1915, when, as a company commander, he was going round his trenches at night. He turned into a sap to visit a listening-post ; but the post had been moved, and through some blunder he had not been informed. So he sat down and listened, but his meditations were rudely interrupted by Lieutenant Kingdon, who, knowing nothing of his presence, whispered hoarsely : " Private Williams and Private Jones will make a bombing attack down the sap, while Private Pink and Private Bundy will cover the exit of the trench with Lewis gun fire." It was at this point that a rather perturbed captain cancelled the whole show.

Tell that story in any gathering of officers of the Brigade, and one at least will cap it with a somewhat similar story of the same sector. Between two companies was a very bad piece of trench. One night the left sentry of the right company reported to the officer on duty that he had fired at a figure which had disappeared into the aforementioned trench. The officer at once seized some bombs and went off in search of the figure, which sprang up and made off in the opposite direction, hotly pursued with bombs. The next morning an officer who had only arrived in the line the previous day came across to see the company commander, and explained that he had tried to keep in touch the previous night, but had met with considerable opposition !

As already hinted, shortage of guns and shells put us on rather uneven terms with the Germans at this time. They would have a big " hate " with hundreds of shells, and all we could do was to nurse our annoyance till our next lot of shells came up, and then let him have two, if not three !

During a lull in a big strafe, when Jerry had been knocking our trenches to blazes with all sorts of stuff, one of our officers shouted across, " If you don't stop that, we'll throw over at least two bombs !"—and for some unknown reason the Germans soon afterwards stopped. Perhaps the game was getting too one-sided even for them.

Once while the Northamptonshire Regiment was in the line, a German trench mortar had been giving them a deal of trouble and causing a lot of casualties. Captain Beacham, then adjutant of the battalion, took a runner with him one afternoon and went up to the front-line posts to try and locate this trench mortar, and have it knocked out by artillery. He succeeded in locating the place, and sent the runner back to the telephone dug-out with a message to the gunners to fire one round, giving the map reference as near as possible. Soon afterwards the shell came over. " Go back and tell the gunners to fire another round a hundred yards right," said Captain Beacham ; and back the runner went to the telephone dug-out. After the second shell was fired, the adjutant again sent back a message to the artillery to lengthen their range fifty yards. Over came the third shell, but it was not quite on the spot. " Tell them to fire another round twenty yards right, and we've got it," said the adjutant. Back went the runner with the message. Then came the reply over the wire : " Is this really necessary, as we have only two more rounds to last until Friday ?" This answer was duly delivered to the adjutant. " For God's sake tell them to keep them !" he replied ; " we might have a S.O.S. to-night !"

It is only fair to say that, in spite of their handicaps, the gunners did some fine work with their few precious shells. On September 13th, 1915, we had a good little show with the artillery covering our front. A certain snipers' post and big hump of clay in the " Bois Allemand " were very worrying to us. One night an 18-pounder was brought up to within 300 yards of the front line and emplaced. The next evening at dusk the thin emplacement in front was suddenly broken down, and the gunners fired forty rounds of high explosive, point-blank range, as fast as they could. The snipers' post went up in clouds and worried us no more. The gun was hauled back quickly into a quarry before the Bosche could gather what was happening, and later that night was horse-drawn away, with no casualties.

So a second winter came down on the trenches, bringing new discomforts and dangers and new tasks to the men who held the line. What it meant was well summed up in Sir Douglas Haig's despatch, dated May 19th, 1916, in which, describing those months, he wrote :

" The maintenance and repair of our defences alone, especially in winter, entails constant heavy work. Bad weather and the enemy combined to flood and destroy trenches, dug-outs, and communications. All such damages must be repaired promptly, under fire, and almost entirely by night.

" Artillery and snipers are practically never silent, patrols are out in front of the lines every night, and heavy bombardments by the artillery of one or both sides take place daily in various parts of the line. Below ground there is continual mining and countermining, which, by the ever-present threat of sudden explosion and the uncertainty as to when and where it will take place, causes perhaps a more constant strain than any other form of warfare."

And here is another vivid little picture, from the pen of my friend Phillip Gibbs :—

" The New Armies were learning. They were bearing the hardships, the cruelties, the brutalities of war, and had to suffer and ' stick ' it. They were learning the craft of modern warfare in trenches, mine-shafts, and saps, behind field-guns and ' heavies,' and they had to pay for their lessons in blood and agony. . . . Dead bodies were heaped there, buried and unburied. They dug into corruption when they tried to dig a trench. Men sat on dead bodies when they peered through their periscopes. They ate and slept with the stench of death in their nostrils. Below them were the enemy mine-shafts. Beyond them were our own mine-shafts. It was a competition in blowing up the tumbled earth, and men fought like devils with bombs and bayonets over mine-craters which had buried another score or so of men."

It was in such conditions as these that the 54th Brigade carried on through their first winter, and if the story I tell dwells on the humour—the rather forced humour, perhaps—of this period, it is because the men who endured those days seem to remember rather the funny side of that grim tragedy. Phillip Gibbs, whom I have just quoted, attempts an explanation :—

" They cultivated cheerfulness as the first law of daily life, and they succeeded wonderfully in spite of the filthy trenches, the rats and vermin, the ice-cold water in which they waded up to the front line during the long months of a Flemish winter, the trench feet which for a time—till rubbing-drill was adopted—drained the strength of many battalions, and the enemy's shell fire and mining activities, which took a daily toll of life and limb. Many of them found a gruesome humour in all this, laughed at death as a low comedian, guffawed if they dodged its knock-about tricks by the length of a traverse, and did not go very sick if it laid out their best pal. ' You know, sir, it doesn't do to take this war too seriously.' So said a sergeant to me as we stood in a trench beyond our knees in water. It was a great saying, and I saw the philosophy which had kept men sane. Without laughter, somehow, anyhow, by any old jokes, we should have lost the war long ago. The only way to avoid deadly depression was to keep smiling. And so, for laughter's sake and to keep normal in abnormal ways of life, there was a great unconscious conspiracy of cheerfulness among officers and men."

The first Christmas in the line passed off quietly. The Northamptonshire and Middlesex Regiments were in the trenches, having relieved the Fusiliers and Bedfordshire Regiment on Christmas Eve. The Middlesex Regiment held their Christmas festivities on December 22nd, before going into the trenches ; and the Northamptonshire Regiment on January 2nd, 1916, on returning from that tour.

The entry in the Brigade diary for December 25th is :— " Christmas Day. Very quiet. Enemy showed no signs of wishing to fraternize. If they do, troops have orders to fire at once. Our men in billets had special Christmas dinners, etc."

But the days that followed were by no means quiet or uneventful. Says the diarist on Boxing day : " Our artillery carried out a fairly extensive bombardment of enemy front-line trenches and houses in south end of Fricourt. We withdrew men from left half of front trenches during bombardment."

The occasion was the first appearance of some heavier guns on our part of the line. The staff from all neighbouring formations gathered to witness a strafe, which resulted, at the end of an hour, in Fricourt boasting one or two houses less—but only, as we were to find to our cost, at the expenditure of the whole of the next week's supply of ammunition.

The Germans retaliated the next evening, hammering trenches 86 and 89 in D.2 Sector (held by Nos. 4 and 5 Platoons of the Northamptonshire Regiment) until they were almost flattened, and also sending over a lot of tear-gas shells. After a while the fire was lifted from these trenches and put down on support trenches in rear, and also on trenches on either side. This "box barrage" isolated a part of the Northamptonshire Regiment's front in the region of the sunken road running from the station, which we held, into Fricourt itself. A party of about twenty Germans then came over, bombed out some cellars near the station, and marched about sixteen of our men back. Three of our men, including one wounded by a bomb, did not leave the cellars, and, escaping attention, managed to reach the rest of their battalion.

The whole affair was a chapter of accidents. The officer commanding the platoon which suffered was absent, bad weather in the Channel having delayed his return from leave. The platoon-sergeant had just gone on leave that day, and a lance-sergeant left in charge had gone to see his company commander, and had been gassed on the way back. The day sentry post had been knocked out, and in the absence of a responsible leader all the nineteen men took refuge in a cellar without leaving a sentry at the spot where the Germans entered. The platoons on the right and left stood to when the bombardment opened, and as soon as it was known that Germans had come over bombing parties were sent out. One German who had apparently lost his way was found in our trenches and dealt with.

This was the Brigade's first experience of a trench raid; indeed, it was the first on the Divisional front, and the use of tear-gas shells was also a novelty to us, accounting for a good deal of confusion. It was noted that the German raiders wore gas-helmets of what were then called the "snout" pattern.

The old year passed away without further excitement, the days from December 31st to January 6th being recorded as "very quiet." So the first months in the trenches ended, and the Brigade entered on the eventful year of 1916.

CHAPTER III

FURTHER EXPERIENCES IN THE TRENCHES

ONE of the earliest events of 1916 was the opening of the first course at the Brigade Bombing School (on January 3rd) under Lieutenant Smith, of the Bedfordshire Regiment, with Major Newnham as a very active and inventive spirit.

With these two officers as chief conspirators, bombing was one of the Brigade's leading shows, and all through the autumn of 1915 experiments had been going on, and a bomb factory set up at Meaulte. This passion of toying with insecurely harnessed forces, which marks the bombing enthusiast, makes him shunned by his fellows and drives him from the haunts of men. When these outcasts first arrived with the Brigade in France, they set up the making of jam-tin bombs in a pigsty at Talmas, from which the pig very gladly withdrew.

Experiments in the line were largely concerned with catapults and other devices for delivering our latest samples of bombs in the Bosche lines. The catapult, home-made with elastic on tall uprights, and released by a trigger, was a treacherous affair, for you never knew when it would develop pro-German mania and lob its bomb gently among the group of British spectators. Demonstrations were frequently given, especially when the bombing officer had a new idea to test, and German snipers were promptly located and reported to him by pleasure-seekers of the Brigade.

Only one success by the catapult is recorded, and that was at the expense of a German sniper opposite D.2, who entered into the fun of the thing, and had a pretty wit which it was a pity to spoil. When the bomb had been duly slung over, this German would signal an " inner " or an " outer " with a spade. At last the catapult evidently scored a bull, for the spade went up with the other débris of the explosion, and the signals were made no more.

One of the first D.C.Ms. awarded in the Brigade went to Sergeant Twiggs, then bombing sergeant of the Bedfordshire Regiment, as a result of the catapult's vagaries. A ball bomb had been placed in it, but the trigger failed to act, and the bomb was due to go off in two or three seconds. There was a pretty general scamper round the traverse, the general feeling being that the catapult deserved all it got ; but Sergeant Twiggs picked out the bomb and threw it over the parapet just in time.

As the catapult had too little discipline and a great deal too much initiative, experiments were made by Major Newnham at the Brigade bomb factory at Meaulte, which resulted in the production of the rifle grenade much as we know it to-day. It may be that others were experimenting on the same lines at the same time, and it is claimed that engineers at G.H.Q. also evolved the idea ; while a Mills patent dated some months earlier described a means of firing a hand-grenade from a rifle by means of a rod-attachment. But no results from these ideas had arrived anywhere near the troops in the line at the time I am writing of, and the rifle-grenade as used by the Brigade was the home-made affair invented by Major Newnham.

First experiments were made in October, 1915, by inserting bodily a No. 1 G.S. "Fishtail" hand-grenade in the barrel of a 1½-inch Véry pistol, both the light and the grenade being projected. Further experiments were made, which included screwing a wooden shaft on the base-plug of a Mills bomb, the lever being held within the muzzle, so that it was not released till the bomb had been projected. With this device a range of from 80 to 100 yards was obtained.

In November demonstrations were given at Meaulte before a number of general officers, including General Allenby (then commanding the Third Army), General Morland (then commanding the 10th Corps), and our own Divisional Commander, Sir Ivor Maxse. All were very interested, and Sir Ivor urged that experiments should be continued, but with a service rifle instead of a Véry pistol.

Accordingly the now familiar rod was fixed to the base-plug of the Mills grenade, and the Brigade factory began turning out 100 a week. The number may have been small, but no other rifle grenade of similar properties was then to be had in the Division, and the troops were delighted with this means of getting on more even terms with the Germans and their stick-bombs.

The Brigade bomb factory was a great centre of activity, and there the enthusiasts gathered for their deadly work and worship. It was run by a sapper in the 80th Field Company, R.E., lent for the purpose, who fixed up lathes, forges, etc., and did excellent work. An old motor-engine, lacking a magneto, was looted from Albert. An old magneto was "borrowed" from a despatch rider, who duly reported it "lost," and the bombing staff voted it a jolly good war.

The West-gun afforded some excitement, and both Major Newnham and Sergeant Twiggs will remember some experiments when they were trying to improvise some method for using it to fire No. 1 "Fish-tails."

The grenade under experiment was a percussion grenade, whereas the West-gun (an arrangement of springs) was primarily intended for firing time (ball) grenades. They did not allow sufficiently for the pressure produced by the jar of the springs, with the result that the moment Sergeant Twiggs pressed the firing lever the grenade exploded in the cup, luckily only injuring him slightly.

Others have reason to remember the West-gun also, for it gave them many bright moments in the trenches. Admirers said the gun only wanted expert handling; its best friends never claimed that it was fool-proof, and its early trials in D.2 in September, 1915, nearly spoilt the war for the experimenters.

Some practice was attempted at the Bosche trenches at a point where they were 170 yards away. An officer who was present has supplied the following record of the results:

1st Shot.—Bomb fell 20 yards short.

2nd Shot.—Went off backwards, and burst about 50 yards in rear of our own trench.

3rd Shot.—Bomb hit the parapet and fell on the fire-step, where it was discovered just before it burst.

And the faithful recorder of these experiments adds : " Thank God, our West-gun was destroyed by fire a week later !"

A new officer just joining a battalion of the Brigade while it was out at rest at Morlancourt was startled to see a heap of turnips with fuzes attached. Had our resources fallen so low, he asked anxiously, that we were reduced to turnips as bombs ? The explanation was a great relief to him. It was another idea of the Brigade Bombing Staff (there was no Brigade Amusement Officer in those days), who hollowed out a turnip, and put in a small charge of powder and a fuze. These were used in practising trench warfare, one team against another in a dummy trench, and all men hit by a piece of turnip when the charge went off were counted casualties.

About this time one of the present officers of the Brigade, then a bombing instructor at that place of many memories, the old " Bull Ring " at Etaples, had an exciting experience.

The " Bantam " battalions were then coming out, and each man was given a short bombing course, which included the throwing of three Mills, before being sent up the line.

The " Bantams " were very keen, but owing to the numerous accidents that had occurred with improvised bombs, and the fact that the popular name for bombing instruction was " joining the Suicide Club " a certain amount of nervousness was shown. For instructional purposes a party of about a hundred would be under the shelter of a breastwork, whilst the man who was going to throw was in a trench breastwork at a safe distance in front with the sergeant-instructor. When the bomb was thrown, all the party in rear had to duck when the N.C.O. in charge shouted " Down !" It should be said that the bombing-ground was on the dunes, where the dry sand makes running very difficult, as one's feet sink ankle-deep at every step.

The keenness of the " Bantams " showed itself in their desire to retain the split-ring and pin of the first Mills bomb each man threw. One man came along, strapped on the old-fashioned bombing-apron, with its small pockets in front, and three Mills bombs were placed in the pockets. Following the rule then in force, he was made to take one out, assume the throwing position, draw the pin, and await the order to throw. All this he did ; but on the order being given, the unexpected happened— he actually threw away the pin, and placed the grenade back in the pocket of his apron. The pocket was just loose enough to allow the lever of the bomb to fly back and release the striker, and there followed a scene which would have been extraordinarily funny had the result not been so tragic.

The sergeant grabbed at the pocket, but the lever of the bomb prevented its withdrawal ; he then dragged the man away from some more boxes of bombs which were alongside, and, seeing the impossibility of recovering the bomb in time, got round the other side of the trench breastwork. He was promptly followed by the human bomb, who apparently did not realize that he was the cause of all the trouble.

Then ensued a ghastly game of hide-and-seek, the two people concerned being engaged in dodging round the trench breastwork for what seemed like an eternity, but in reality was only about two seconds, until the sergeant suddenly ran into the open, ploughing with difficulty through the soft sand, followed by the poor fellow carrying the bomb in his apron. This mad chase did not last long, and, being impeded by the apron, its wearer was outdistanced by the sergeant, fortunately for the latter. It is a pity that one cannot conclude by stating that the grenade was a " dud," but unfortunately it was not.

After that, " This practice must cease " was translated by bombing instructors into much stronger language when checking the tendency of recruits to retain safety-pins as souvenirs.

During the early tours in the trenches a prize was offered by the Division for the first piece of German wire brought in. One's own wire being a rather jealously guarded treasure, this was not an easy job. One officer set out with a patrol of three, and all got safely to the wire. There one of them had a bad fit of coughing, which lasted half an hour. Lying out there crouching flat on the ground, with faces pressed into the mud, it seemed to have begun in the dawn of the world, and to be going on for all eternity. At last it ceased, and without stopping to get any wire, the little party returned sadly, and in a very bad state of nerves, to their own trench.

Another attempt was made by some Bedfordshires from the D.1 sector, an officer creeping out with his platoon sergeant— the latter an excellent fellow named Lewin, who had been a policeman. He seemed to have no sense of fear (which was rather unlucky for the officer who accompanied him), for, on reaching the German wire, he shook it, and said in what he may have thought was a whisper : " That's ——— good wire !" He made a dickens of a rattle with the wire, but would not take the first piece, creeping among it till he had selected six good specimens. They got back safely, and the specimens were duly sent to Division, but the expected prize did not turn up. Whether it was forgotten, or whether it had already been won by another Brigade, is not known to this day.

This Sergeant Lewin had a man in his platoon whom he used to run in as a poacher in the old " civvy " days. They were great pals now, and used to go out on patrol work together, doing good work, to which their experiences of poachers and poaching no doubt contributed.

Mud was an unpleasant feature of the Brigade's first winter in the trenches. (It must be very disappointing to the Germans to know that, if you ask any of the Old Originals about those early days, they remember the rats and the mud much more vividly than the Bosche strafes.)

One night in January, 1916, a man stuck in the mud for five hours in a very bad part of the line, and was fed on rum, to keep him cheerful and amused, until he could be got out. It may be only a coincidence that the next night seven men stuck in the mud in the same place ; but the rum treatment was discontinued, and further spread of the epidemic stopped.

The D.1 sector was on higher ground than D.2, and drained into it, an interesting fact of which the occupants of D.1 took full advantage. On one occasion the battalion occupying D.2 built a dam to stop this drainage scheme, and as a result a large sheet of water formed between the two sectors, cutting off all communication.

A Northamptonshire officer had a trying experience while the battalion was in D.2 sector. He went out in No Man's Land on patrol, and arranged to give on his return an imitation of a bird-call as the password. Having said " Pee-wee !" several times, till the sentry had the idea correctly, he set off. Unfortunately, while he was away the posts were changed. On his return he said " Pee-wee !" in what he fondly believed to be life-like fashion. But it was a new sentry, who gave the imitation a cold reception, remarking : " Yes, if you don't stop that —— ' Pee-weeing,' I'll —— well ——" etc., etc. A very indignant officer, feeling very unloved and far from home, was kept lying on his face for half an hour out in No Man's Land, till a sergeant who knew about the " password " turned up and let him in.

Happily, life was not entirely a question of " sticking it " in the line, and the spells in billets, when you had been relieved by the other battalion, made a pleasant change. There was Morlancourt, for instance, where the Northamptonshire Padre (Captain Bennett) rigged up the old church as a canteen (he could always get a crowd when patching the roof), and ran boxing competitions and concerts, as well as a very popular Sunday evening service. " Morlancourt will always be a name to revive pleasant memories " (writes a Northamptonshire officer, while these pages are being prepared), "whether they be of the little orange girl who stood at that very corner we were afterwards [in 1918] to fight for, or maybe the less romantic, though certainly not less humorous, recollection of our practising with turnips for that bombing attack from D.1 which was to have cut out Fricourt, but which, fortunately for those who were to have taken part, never materialized."

During this period the difficulty of getting change for use in the canteens led to an interesting experiment in the 11th Royal Fusiliers. Mr. S. C. Turner, a well-known business man in the City, who made his office the headquarters of all efforts for the good of officers and men of the battalion, decided to issue a special paper currency. This was in the form of books of "tear out" franc notes. The men were paid partly in these, as they wished, and the notes were always good for their face value in the canteen. Indeed, they won such a good reputation among the French people, that local shops, in some of the places where we were billeted, were willing to accept them, knowing that they would be duly honoured.

This was only one of countless ways in which Mr. Turner, at the head of the friends of the battalion at home, cared in practical fashion for the men of the 11th Fusiliers, showing a practical interest in the welfare of the men and their families.

Of quiet days out of the line, the Middlesex Regiment probably remembered January 7th as well as any. Lieutenant-General Sir Ivor Maxse came over to inspect them, and they were drawn up on parade, feeling very good, and hoping that the Divisional Commander would think as well of them as they thought of themselves. when the Germans began to take an interest in the proceedings. They shelled the parade with such enthusiasm and accuracy that the show broke up rather hurriedly.

Indeed, the Germans took a great deal too much interest in our shows when we were out at rest. The following entry in the Brigade diary for January 11th is too good for further comment :—" Quiet day. Enemy fired about a dozen 5·9 shells into Meaulte at 3 p.m., possibly intended for a football match then in progress."

Talking of shows, who remembers the munition workers who visited us about this time to see what we wanted shells for ? Some of them were conducted into the front-line trench by the Brigade Staff, and everything was done to give them a good show. A stolid north-countryman, invited to look at the German line through a trench periscope, was startled to have the top of the mirror shot away while he was peeping. He returned to England much impressed, and the Brigade Staff were very interested in his vivid description of this periscope incident in a local paper. And one of our own fellows, stationed with a rifle a few bays away, with orders to shoot away the top of the periscope as soon as it appeared, was quite proud to find himself described in print as a German sniper of uncanny skill.

Much of January was devoted to putting the sector into good trim for handing over. Thanks to a spell of fine weather, and some good work by the Sussex pioneers on the communication trenches, everything was in splendid condition when we were relieved by the 20th and 22nd Brigades early in February. A big wiring scheme was also carried out during the month. On the night of January 10th two companies of the Northamptonshire Regiment put out 400 yards of new wire along the centre of D.2. There was some rifle fire, but no casualties. The method of putting up the wire had been practised for some days previously in the billeting area.

Before leaving this part of the line, one would like to mention the 174th Tunnelling Company, commanded by Major Stokes. They ran the whole of our mining very sympathetically and extraordinarily well. When we took over this sector several portions of trench could only be patrolled, and never held by sentries. Within a few months the whole situation had been changed—all our trenches were perfectly safe, and we were able to " camouflet " the Hun when and where we liked. The Brigade owed a great sense of security entirely to this tunnelling company and their own mining fatigues.

It should also be recorded here that in his despatch dealing with the winter of 1915-16 Sir Douglas Haig remarks:—

" While many other units have done excellent work during the period under review, the following have been specially brought to my notice for good work in carrying out or repelling local attacks and raids." Then follows a list of battalions, which includes the 7th Bedfordshire and the 6th Northamptonshire Regiments.

Having been relieved in the line, the Brigade marched back to the Lahoussye area, and by February 5th all the battalions were billeted there—Brigade headquarters, the Bedfordshire and Northamptonshire Regiments in Lahoussye itself, and the Fusiliers and Middlesex Regiment in Franvillers. Training was actively carried on.

On February 12th the 54th Brigade Machine Gun Company arrived from England (4 officers and 141 other ranks), and was billeted in Franvillers. The company remained with the Brigade until the forming of the Machine Gun Corps, when the 54th Brigade Company was incorporated in the 18th Machine Gun Battalion, attached to the 18th Division.

On March 1st the Brigade moved to the Corbie area, thence to the Bray area, and a few days later took over our new sector of the line A.1 and A.2 in front of Carnoy. It was during their reconnaissance of this sector that Colonel G. R. Ripley and Captain R. W. Beacham, of the Northamptonshire Regiment, were wounded, a stray shell getting them as they were walking across from Bronfay Farm to Billou Wood. Colonel Ripley was in England for three months as a result of this bit of hard luck, but insisted on returning in June, while still only marked for Home Service, in order that he might " lead his boys in their first offensive."

It was in this sector, and at about the same time, that the Northamptonshire Regiment came across some unusual " trench stores," in the shape of two cows, who, though not in the prime of condition, seemed to promise a change from tinned milk.

It was decided that a change of air would be good for them, and early one morning the Adjutant's batman, who had been a milkman before the war, set out to drive them from the line back to the pastures of Bray. Daylight came, and they were still in sight and range of the enemy's guns, but for once the German was a sportsman or a humorist, for he let the strange procession proceed.

But the experiment was not a success. Perhaps the cows had a sentimental attachment for their old billet in Carnoy, although that village received too much attention from German guns to please most people. At any rate, they seemed to pine, so one day they were driven back, and took up their quarters with the company in reserve at Carnoy. There at each relief they were duly taken over as " trench stores."

The centre of our front boasted five saps, varying from 80 to 200 yards in length, running out to old mine craters in No Man's Land. These saps were held by posts which, on several occasions, owing to their isolated positions, were the scene of lively little encounters with Bosche patrols. It was in one of these duels, between a German sniper and Captain Burrows (Northamptonshire Regiment), who was trying to bomb him at 25 yards range, that the latter was killed.

This part of the line was the scene of a determined raid by the Germans in the early hours of April 13th.

After a heavy bombardment, which practically flattened out our trenches, four separate raids were made—one in A.1 Subsector, and three in A.2 Sub-sector. In A.1 they met with some success, the Middlesex Regiment being unlucky enough to lose ten of their number as prisoners.

In A.2 the Northamptonshire Regiment, profiting by their experience in the previous raid in December, put up a good show, and threw the Germans out, keeping four prisoners as souvenirs and recovering a number of dead. They had thirteen killed and forty wounded, the killed including six of a special wiring party chosen from volunteers for a particularly tricky bit of work among the craters. These men were cut off by the German barrage, and tried to return to our lines through the right company, but were unhappily mistaken for Germans. The leading spirit in the defence that night was the late Major (then Captain) Podmore, commanding the centre company. In spite of bearing practically the whole of the casualties, his men clung on desperately to the battered remnant of their trench, thanks to his fine example. For that night's work he won the first D.S.O. awarded in the Division. Later he commanded the 12th Middlesex Regiment, and met his death in an unfortunate accident at a trench-mortar demonstration on December 31st, 1917.

The Brigade had its revenge for this raid just a fortnight later, when the Bedfordshire Regiment carried out their first raid in the early hours of April 27th. This was led by Captain (then 2nd-Lieutenant) H. Driver, who was awarded the D.S.O. for the affair. He has been good enough to jot down the following account of the proceedings :—

"I had just returned to the battalion after being wounded for the first time, and I was secretly informed by my company commander, Captain T. E. Lloyd, that our company had been selected to carry out a raid during our next tour of duty in the line, and that I was to be in charge.

"We managed quite easily to get volunteers for the raid, and I proceeded to train them at Bray. It must be understood that these were the early days of raids, and none of us expected to get back from the Bosche line even if we succeeded in reaching it. However, we marked out (with the aid of aeroplane photos) a facsimile of the Bosche trench to be raided, and practised raiding it by day and by night until we thought we all knew our own particular job. In addition, I was ordered to take a few men up to our actual front each night, and take them out into No Man's Land to get them accustomed to being there. I disliked this part of the preparation intensely.

"The fateful day approached, and I was interviewed by the Brigadier (General Shoubridge), who was a very cheery man and inspired one with confidence. He told me that at last we had some wonderful artillery, and the raid was to be supported by wonderful 9·2-inch howitzers and 8-inch guns. He added that he expected us to do our job well, in view of the fact that the shells to be fired would cost the country a prodigious sum of money, and the country was looking for something in return. I came away duly impressed.

"The next day the Bedfordshire Regiment took over the line again, and the raid was to take place the same night at 2.30 a.m. The raiding party and myself by this time felt we were all to soon face something we would have gladly handed over to others, and we tried hard to appreciate the grim jest that if we were successful we should immediately go on leave.

"During the evening the raiding party foregathered in a dug-out near the point in our trench from which we proposed to start. We all blackened our faces and hands so as not to show up in the dark, and prepared our bombs. The party was kept very cheery by one of its members, Corporal Lancaster, more familiarly known as 'Alec.' He was quite a wonderful fellow,

and has, fortunately, come through the war safely, though he
has several times been severely wounded. As the evening wore
on a special rum issue was produced, and the men were asked
whether they would like it before or after the raid. They were
unanimous in deciding not to take the risk of not having it at
all. As 'Alec' pointed out, 'There might be no coming back.'

"We settled down about 10.30 p.m. for a four-hour wait,
having completed our preparations. I tried to work up some
sort of appetite for dinner. Suddenly at 11 p.m. (not in accordance with our plan) a heavy bombardment of our trenches
was opened by the Bosche. The next battalion on our right
sent up the S.O.S. signal, and very soon our artillery replied
vigorously. We were naturally rather alarmed, and began to
wonder if the Bosche had any knowledge of our intended raid.
Anyhow, after about half an hour the strafe died down again,
and the rest of the time passed without further incident—
except that my batman informed me that he had packed up
my kit as he expected me to be wounded !

"At 2.15 precisely thirty-four black-faced ruffians, each
heavily laden, climbed over the top, and lay down in No Man's
Land in accordance with our plan. Suddenly at 2.30 we saw
a vivid flash behind us, followed by a terrible crash. It was
the opening of our barrage. I had to shout in the next man's
ear before he could hear what I said. Our spirits went up enormously, for we thought that nothing could live in that storm of
fire. I kept looking at my luminous watch, knowing that at
2.40 the barrage would lift, and we must then be ready to jump
into the Bosche trench.

"Fortunately, I found the exact point at which we were to
enter it, and, with the aid of Corporal Dunkam, soon cleared a
gap in the enemy's wire. I then signalled to my party with a
flashlight, and was quite bucked to see them loom out of the
darkness and walk up in quick time in proper formation. The
leading man carried a ladder, which was put in position, after
someone had first of all taken the precaution of lobbing a bomb
into the trench. All this time the noise of our shells bursting
a little distance in front of us was simply deafening.

"Everything now went like clockwork. One party descended
the ladder and went to the left. A second party went to the
right, while a third remained on guard at the point of entry.
We also knew that by this time a fourth party was out in No
Man's Land laying a white trail (with chloride of lime) to guide
us back over the two or three hundred yards of pitch-black space
we had crossed.

"The few stray Bosches found wandering about the trench
were summarily disposed of, but the chief difficulty lay in dealing
with those who had sought refuge in their deep dug-outs, which
at this part of the line were found about every 10 yards. One had
to descend about a dozen slippery steps in order to get into a

dug-out, each being lit up and containing about a dozen or more Huns, who had thought themselves perfectly secure. There was no time to haul them out and take them back as prisoners, and we had brought 368 bombs (15 bags, each containing 20 bombs, and 2 emergency bombs each in our pockets) ; so, having failed to get the Bosches to come outside the first dug-out, we decided to use a bag of bombs for each dug-out.

" It was fairly simple to roll these bombs down the stairs, and deal with the dug-outs systematically in this way. Unfortunately, owing to misunderstanding, one of our men was accidentally wounded, but we managed to get him home safely. All went well up to a point, and the party that went to the left returned to the point of entry at the appointed time. But there was no sign of the right-hand party, and it is difficult to realize our feelings as we waited on top of the Bosche trench for quite twenty minutes, during which time we fought a battle with some Bosche reinforcements trying to come along the trench from the left. All our bombs having been used, we carried on with rifles and revolvers.

" At last the right-hand party began to arrive, and eventually they all turned up, although some of them had been wounded, and in one case a wounded man had to be carried. It was now nearly dawn, and the Bosche was showing searchlights, but we soon recrossed No Man's Land, and the whole party got home safely, with the exception of one man who lost his way, but who, owing to an error, had been reported as having returned.

" Sergeant Mills got a D.C.M., Corporals Lancaster and Joyce got Military Medals, and every man got a ' Parchment ' from General Maxse, Commander of the Division. They all took the next train for leave. Thus ended our first raid, and I was thankful to cross over to Blighty in a hospital ship.

" Sir Douglas Haig reported our raid in his daily communiqué in the following terms : ' Last night a successful raid was carried out by men of the Bedfordshire Regiment, who entered the enemy's trenches near Carnoy, and, after fierce hand-to-hand fighting, forced them down into their dug-outs and bombed them there, inflicting heavy casualties. Only a few of our men were wounded, and the whole party successfully returned to our lines.' "

Chapter IV

THE SOMME—JULY, 1916

WHEN you were on a fatigue or a working party, it was easy to believe that yours was the only platoon or company doing any real hard work in the whole of France, and, further, that the job had been organized merely to annoy you. So it was that few people, even among those on the spot, doing their own little share of the job, realized how great were the preparations necessary for such an undertaking as the Somme offensive of July, 1916. In his despatch on these operations Sir Douglas Haig gave a vivid picture of the tasks involved :—

"Vast stocks of ammunition and stores of all kinds had to be accumulated beforehand within a convenient distance of the front. To deal with these many miles of new railways—both standard and narrow gauge—and trench tramways were laid. All available roads were improved, many others were made, and long causeways were built over marshy valleys.

"Many additional dug-outs had to be provided as shelter for the troops, for use as dressing-stations for the wounded, and as magazines for storing ammunition, food, water, and engineering material. Scores of miles of deep communication trenches had to be dug, as well as trenches for telephone wires, assembly and assault trenches, and numerous gun emplacements and observation-posts.

"Important mining operations were undertaken, and charges were laid at various points behind the enemy's lines.

"Except in the river valleys, the existing supplies of water were hopelessly insufficient to meet the requirements of the number of men and horses to be concentrated in this area. To meet this difficulty many wells and borings were sunk, and over 100 pumping plants were installed. More than 120 miles of water-mains were laid.

"Much of the preparatory work had to be done under very trying conditions, and was liable to constant interruption from the enemy's fire. The weather on the whole was bad, and local accommodation totally insufficient for housing the troops employed, who consequently had to content themselves with such rough shelter as could be provided in the circumstances. All this labour, too, had to be carried out in addition to fighting and to the everyday work of maintaining existing defences. It threw a very heavy strain on the troops, which was borne by them with a cheerfulness beyond all praise."

As far as this Brigade was concerned, preparations began as far back as May 4th, when the battalions were relieved in the line by the 21st Brigade (30th Division), and were engaged for nearly two months on work in connection with the long-anticipated offensive.

The Fusiliers were in camp at Bois Celestine (just north of Chipilly), employed chiefly on road mending; the Bedfordshire Regiment in billets at Bray, working under the 30th Division; the Northamptonshire Regiment in billets at Frechencourt and Querrieux, building railways; and the Middlesex Regiment at Grovetown, Bray, also on railway work.

The following, quoted from a diary kept by a Fusilier officer, will give a general idea of how the next few weeks were spent by all the battalions :—

> " Huts had to be erected by the score, roads to be made and others repaired, barges unloaded, ballast procured from quarries, and many other arduous tasks carried out. The parties on hut-building soon began to see some result of their labours, and before many days a snug little town had sprung up under the shadow of the budding trees.
>
> " The valley of the Somme was indeed superb. In the early morning you would awaken to the song of birds in the trees above you; dragon-flies, at least six different colours, which drift noiselessly through the air, and beautiful butterflies, made every moment of the day really enjoyable.
>
> " In Chipilly village there were some baths alongside the canal, and our men had a hot bath and a change of underclothing, and a hundred yards away was an open-air swimming bath, where our men splashed about.
>
> " There were magnificent views of the Somme and the lagoons from the woods, and some of the officers got a boat and rowed from one lagoon to another to Sailly Lorette. On the way some indulged in a swim, while the others prepared tea in picnic style. For the men we arranged cinema shows, concerts, and football matches."

Among the work to be done on the front from which the great offensive was to be made was the preparation of Russian saps. These were tunnels under No Man's Land, leading to within about six yards of the German lines. They were filled with tons of stores of every kind, and when the attack had been launched, all that was necessary was to blow out the end, and a way was made for carrying parties to get rations, water, ammunition, etc., to the advanced troops.

There were two of these saps on the front on which the Brigade attacked, and the digging of one of them led to an exciting moment. Work was going ahead in good style, when, to the general consternation, they broke through into a German

Photo: Elliott & Fry] [London, W.

BRIGADIER-GENERAL L. DE V. SADLEIR-JACKSON, C.B.,
C.M.G., D.S.O.,
Who Commanded the Brigade from October, 1917, to March, 1919.

To face page 32.

Photo : *Speaight*]   [*London, W.*

MAJOR-GENERAL T. H. SHOUBRIDGE, C.M.G., D.S.O.,
Who Commanded the 54th Infantry Brigade, December, 1915 to March, 1917.

To face page 33.

dug-out. Luckily it was unoccupied at the time; the hole was carefully patched, and apparently the Germans never knew of our visit.

During this period Brigade headquarters were at Oissy, where Brigade Machine Gun, Trench Mortar, Bombing, and Signalling Schools were instituted. These schools were visited by Sir Douglas Haig and Staff on May 12th.

June came, and with it more active preparations. On the 9th the Fusiliers and Northamptonshire Regiment began digging near Picquigny trenches which were an exact facsimile from aeroplane photos of the enemy system opposite Carnoy, which they were to attack three weeks later. By the 11th Brigade headquarters and all battalions had arrived at Picquigny, and practice attacks over the facsimile trenches were actively carried out.

By the 23rd preliminary training had been finished, the whole Brigade was moved to the Bray area, and on the following day took over the front on which we were to attack.

> "On the way up from Bray," says the Fusilier officer from whose diary I have already quoted, "we were delighted to see guns of every calibre dug in—it seemed everywhere. In fact, the whole ground seemed alive with them, and in every valley behind the line was a very hot-bed of destruction to spit at the enemy.
>
> "A good deal of our time was now occupied in cutting steps in and erecting bridges across the assembly trenches. The steps were to be used by us for quickness when we left the trenches to attack, and the wooden bridges by reinforcements who would come up across the open."

Before the great day came the Brigade carried out two or three successful raids for the purpose of information.

One of these took place on the night of June 25th, when Private W. Crowe, a Middlesex scout, did some fine work, for which he was afterwards awarded the Military Medal. According to the official account, "he was in the screen which preceded the raid. After this screen had been pushed forward from our trenches, a heavy enemy barrage was put down between it and the main body, owing to the division on our left letting off smoke, which alarmed the enemy. Crowe returned through this barrage in the dark, and guided the main body through it up to a position in rear of the scout screen. On the return of the raid, he also displayed great courage in collecting wounded men who had lost their way, and bringing them back to our trenches."

On the night of the 27th-28th 2nd-Lieutenant W. R. Howard took over thirty Fusiliers and raided Austrian trench and Austrian support. The party proceeded along about 250 yards of the trench, but was held up by the enemy at Austrian junction. Valuable information was gained as to the damage done by our bombardment, and the party withdrew safely, suffering a few casualties, but no men being killed. For this good work 2nd-Lieutenant Howard was awarded the M.C.

On the night of 29th-30th about 100 Middlesex men, under 2nd-Lieutenants Chase, Restall, Garstin, and Card, went over and penetrated as far as Emden Trench. A number of Germans were killed, several dug-outs searched, and much useful information gained. The raiders spent two hours in enemy territory. Unfortunately, 2nd-Lieutenant Chase was badly hit just before reaching our lines, and died of wounds.

The German reply to our preliminary bombardment caused a certain amount of trouble. Two brief quotations from diaries will give some idea of what this meant.

A Fusilier officer writes : —

"One morning, about 1 a.m., I had a party of sixteen men working in Hyde Road, when the Huns suddenly directed their fire on Park Lane. As it was impossible for the men to continue their work, I withdrew them towards Piccadilly [these are all names of trenches] ; and as we moved, so did the shells, for they followed us, and it was with great difficulty my men got under cover. Being under cover does not always mean safety, for five of my party who had taken shelter in a dug-out in Piccadilly Circus were wounded, the dug-out being blown in. Wherever we were we seemed to be running into shells, and time after time we were warned by men, shovel in hand, who were digging out some unfortunate comrade, to keep our heads low and get by as quickly as possible, as the spot was a marked one."

It was near the same spot that the Bedfordshire Regiment had a very bad bit of luck, having all the officers of one company killed or wounded only a few days before they were due to go over in the big show. Captain Doake, one of the survivors, gives the following account :—

"On June 26th ' C ' company, in support, had a bad time from enemy bursts of fire. The officers' mess in a dug-out in Piccadilly got a direct hit, while all the officers were having supper, about 9 p.m. All became casualties, as well as some eight servants and other ranks who took refuge. A 4·2 howitzer shell struck the entrance and burst inside. The doorway was filled up, and the smoke and fumes almost suffocated the survivors. Luckily a passing man saw my arm, which had been pushed through a hole, and after a little labour Major (then Captain) Clegg and I were got out. But Lieutenants Baden and Hasler were killed, and Lieutenant Johnson died of wounds. The companies suffered severely that day from bursts of fire, which were very well directed and quite thorough."

The rescue of the buried officers was carried out by Private H. W. Fish. He at once began to dig, and, although the air was thick with gas and he was nearly choked, he refused to be relieved till the job was finished. This same man did some gallant work before Pommiers Redoubt on July 1st, crawling up and bombing a machine gun that was holding up our advance. For these actions he was awarded the D.C.M.

A great deal of rain fell during these days and nights of waiting for the big event, and trenches got muddier and muddier. But in spite of hard work and discomfort, the men were amazingly cheerful, and full of heart. The worse the conditions, the better their spirits seemed to become.

By 2 a.m. on July 1st all units were in their battle positions, as follows :—

> The assaulting battalions (11th Royal Fusiliers on the left and 7th Bedfordshire Regiment on the right) in the forming-up trenches.
> The supports (6th Northamptonshire Regiment) in bivouac in Carnoy Valley.
> The reserve (12th Middlesex Regiment) in dug-outs in Carnoy.

The 54th Machine Gun Company had two guns with each of the assaulting battalions, four ready to go forward behind the Northamptonshire Regiment, two guns in the Russian saps, and six guns to bring indirect fire to bear on the German lines from Caftet Wood.

The newly-formed 54th Trench Mortar Battery had eight guns in position for hurricane bombardment.

There was nothing to be done now but to sit down in the trenches and wait. This was worse than fighting, really a very trying ordeal. Just before dawn most of the companies had tea sent up to them, and this was very welcome, for everyone was thoroughly chilled, and a fine rain was falling. When daylight came our shelling increased in volume, and by 5.30 a.m was a deafening roar, to which the Germans were replying hotly. About 7 a.m. everything became wrapped in a thick mist, but this luckily cleared off just before the start.

The minutes ticked on. Officers were looking at their watches, and the minutes went by—but so slowly, it seemed, when anything would have been better than this ordeal in the assembly trenches, which the enemy's shells were knocking to blazes. At last it was 7.30, and officers blew whistles, but the men at their elbows could not hear them in that hell and hail of shells. But all eyes had been on the officers and N.C.Os. for the first sign of a move, and as the hands of the watches touched the fateful minute it was " Over the top, and good luck to you !"

The two assaulting battalions got well away, and within ten minutes Emden Trench was taken. But it had been a costly ten minutes. The two leading companies of the Bedfordshire Regiment had already lost all their officers, but the N.C.Os. had the waves well in hand. Machine guns had checked the advance from Austrian Support, but these were quickly dealt with, one of them being rushed and captured with great dash by Lance-Corporal A. Payne, of the Fusiliers. Between Bund Trench and Pommiers Trench there was a check, owing to some uncut wire, but a mixed party of twenty Bedfordshires and twenty Berkshires (the latter in the 53rd Brigade) completed this task under heavy shell fire in a most methodical and fearless manner.

The Germans took advantage of the check to make a small counter-attack from the direction of Mametz on the left flank of the Fusiliers. 2nd-Lieutenant Parr-Dudley at once got hold of his platoon, wheeled it half left, and charged, using bullet, bayonet, and bomb to such good effect that not one of the enemy escaped. Unfortunately, the gallant officer himself was killed.

Twenty minutes after the start Pommiers Trench was assaulted and captured, the Fusiliers taking a machine gun. Here, according to programme, there was a forty minutes' halt. But it was a busy time. There was much hand-to-hand fighting, especially at the junction with Black Alley, and a number of dug-outs were bombed out. Some good work was also done along Black Alley by a Fusilier bombing party while the waves were going forward to Pommiers Trench.

" The men were by this time quite cool and collected, and apparently very happy," wrote an officer a day or two later. " Several of them were holding little sing-songs, while others were very energetically shaking hands and wishing their officers good luck.

" During our halt in this trench we have time to realize more than ever what the din of battle is like ; for the roll of the French 75's, the crack of our 18-pounders, the blast of the 60-pounders, the deafening roar of the heavies, the whizzing of bullets and bursting of shells, and the painful cry of the wounded, remind us vividly that we are taking part in the world's greatest battle."

On the way to Pommiers Trench there has been many instances of individual gallantry. Under heavy machine-gun fire, Private J. Nicholson, of the Fusiliers, shot six Germans who were sniping the oncoming waves, and then, although wounded, bombed and knocked out a machine-gun which was holding up the advance.

Private W. T. Taverner, of the same battalion, located a machine gun in Pommiers Trench, and, unable to get at the gunner, who was barricaded in, stood on top of the emplacement, under fire, and shouted to the waves to scatter right and left, thus saving a number of casualties, and well earning his Military Medal.

A D.C.M. went to a Fusilier signaller, Private J. W. Hughes, for a capital piece of work. Having to send a message which he knew was urgent, he chose a white flag, the most visible as it was also the most dangerous, and coolly stood on top of the parapet under a hail of shot and shell. Although wounded, he carried on till a shell dealt him a terrible injury which rendered him unconscious.

At this same stage of the proceedings Private V. C. Taylor, of the Bedfordshire Regiment, showed fine initiative. Sent forward to reconnoitre when his platoon was approaching Pommiers Trench, he saw in the trench one of our men going round a traverse where a German was waiting for him with fixed bayonet, and about twelve more Bosches behind him. Taylor acted promptly, seizing our man by the equipment and dragging him bodily out of the trench. He then crawled up and bombed the party of Germans so effectively that six were killed and the rest taken prisoners.

At this time our left flank was in the air, the neighbouring Brigade being hung up before Dantzig Alley. This was the more uncomfortable since the Germans were holding Fritz Trench (leading into Black Alley, where our left rested) in some force.

The matter was dealt with in a simple way which was a good example of co-operation between Lewis guns and trench mortars. Two Lewis guns of the left company of the Fusiliers were put in Black Alley in such a manner as to command the approach to Fritz Trench. Two 3-inch Stokes mortars were then brought up. They pounded Fritz Trench, the Germans were forced to bolt, and the Lewis guns did the rest.

The most difficult part of the morning work had still to be done, As information from raids had led us to expect, the Germans did not hold their front line in any great strength, except for well-placed machine guns. But the advance from Pommiers Trench to Pommiers Redoubt was a different matter, for the wire had not been sufficiently cut, and the line was held far more strongly and with much more determination.

When the leading waves got out of Pommiers Trench, they were met with heavy machine gun and rifle fire, and the few who reached the wire were shot down. Captain Johnston, of the Fusiliers, attempted to take his men up Black Alley, but the last 60 yards was a straight, and was held by a machine gun. He then attempted to get round the Redoubt, but German snipers in the south-west corner of Beetle Alley proved a nuisance. 2nd-Lieutenant Savage, on his left, rushed them at that spot, and the Fusiliers were able to get close up to the Redoubt without further casualties. Captain Johnston then put his Lewis guns at the end of Black Alley in such a way as to enfilade the front of the Redoubt. This wiped out all the Germans in the trench, and our line was able to dash in and finish the job.

It was, however, 9.30 a.m. before the Redoubt was completely taken, as there were many Germans still in dug-outs, and they put up a very obstinate resistance.

Some good Lewis-gun work by Lance-Corporal H. A. Stebbeds, of the Bedfordshire Regiment, contributed to the capture of the Redoubt. When a part of the attack was held up outside the Redoubt by uncut wire and enemy snipers, he crawled some hundred yards to a flank with his gun, got on to the enemy's parapet, and fired down a straight portion of enemy trench, putting about twenty-five Germans out of action, and enabling our line to get forward.

With officer casualties so high, there was a great call for leadership on the part of N.C.Os., and Sergeant S. Impey, also of the Bedfordshire Regiment, won his M.M. that day. He was in command of his company practically all the way from Emden Trench. When it was held up before the Redoubt, he sprang forward, called on the men to follow, and got them into the objective.

Presently our barrage lifted off Beetle Alley (beyond the Redoubt), and this trench was at once rushed by the Fusiliers and Bedfordshire Regiment, the latter having to push in their reserve company.

By this time the Northamptonshire Regiment had come up in support of the assaulting battalions, and were carrying out the double duty of making strong points and clearing trenches and dug-outs. All the companies had had to pass through a heavy enemy barrage on their way up, and suffered heavy casualties.

In the afternoon parties of the Fusiliers (three platoons) and Bedfordshire Regiment (one platoon) reached White Trench, which lay round nearly 1,000 yards beyond the Redoubt, near Mametz Wood, and after dark the construction of strong points just south of this line was begun. Most of those who took part will remember this digging, after a long and exciting day, as the worst part of the whole show. Everyone was tired out, and if a man ceased digging for a moment he dropped off to sleep where he stood or fell. Perhaps it was worse for the protective screen out in front, for they had not the exercise of digging to keep them awake. Only one little excitement did they have. About 10.30 that night a strong party of Germans was reported in front of Caterpillar Wood, apparently coming over to dispute our right to dig in ground that had so recently been theirs. We opened rapid fire and drove them off, and for the rest of the night there was little to do but dig or try to keep awake and watch the German firework display. This was on a big scale. On our left the enemy was apparently fearing an attack, for our line had been rather held up in the daytime, and Véry lights were being fired into the air by the hundred. To our front, green, white, and red lights were going up, and all the time there was the booming of our guns and the flash of our shells.

At midnight one platoon of the Fusiliers and two platoons of the Bedfordshire Regiment were holding White Trench. The remainder of the Fusiliers held part of Beetle Alley, Maple Trench, and Strong Point No. 5. The remainder of the Bedfordshire Regiment also held part of Beetle Alley, Montauban Alley as far as the junction with Loop Trench, as well as Pommiers Redoubt and Trench. The Northamptonshire Regiment occupied Bund Trench, Black Alley, and five strong points. The Middlesex Regiment was in our original front line.

Three officers of the Bedfordshire Regiment were awarded the M.C. for gallant work in and around Pommiers Redoubt. 2nd-Lieutenant (now Major) W. J. W. Colley was one of the only two officers who survived the attack on the Redoubt. " He was [says the official account of his action] absolutely regardless of any fire, however hot. In fact, he appeared to enjoy it. This example was of the greatest value, for the task of consolidation under heavy fire was carried out most thoroughly. He organized several bombing parties, and helped to clear out both Beetle Alley and Montauban Alley at a critical time, when both flanks of the Brigade were in the air owing to the Brigades on the left and right being held up."

Another M.C. went to Captain (now Lieutenant-Colonel) A. E. Percival, of the same battalion, of whom the official account says : " His coolness under heavy shell and machine-gun fire was an inspiring example to his men. His dispositions to make defensive flanks were quite excellent. It was owing to his initiative that Montauban Alley was eventually cleared of the enemy as far as its junction with Loop Trench, which resulted in assisting the Brigade on our right to make good its final objective. His example went far to maintaining the high morale of his men."

The medical officer of the Bedfordshire Regiment, Captain J. W. Turner, R.A.M.C., who also won the M.C., left the assembly trenches shortly after the first waves had gone over, and did not reach Pommiers Redoubt till three in the afternoon, spending seven hours on the ground in between, tending the wounded both of the 54th and 53rd Brigades, under heavy shelling and continual machine-gun fire from the right. His orderly was killed beside him, and he then carried on unaided. The Bedfordshire Regiment will remember that it was the same gallant doctor who, on the afternoon of July 18th, when the cookhouse was being heavily shelled, remained with the wounded, in spite of the shells continually bursting around.

On the morning of July 2nd the Bedfordshire Regiment was withdrawn to Carnoy, and the Fusiliers took over the defence of the Brigade front. On the 3rd the Fusiliers, in their turn, went back to Carnoy, handing over to the Middlesex Regiment.

That night one of our patrols got in touch with a patrol of the 53rd Brigade in Caterpillar Wood, and on the following day the Middlesex Regiment took over a part of the 53rd Brigade's front, in addition to our own, holding it till relieved on the 6th by the Bedfordshire Regiment.

During the night of 4th-5th the Middlesex Regiment sent forward one company to Caterpillar Wood (half right, about 1,500 yards from the Redoubt), with a detachment at Marlbrough Wood. An officer patrol was sent forward from Caterpillar Wood towards Bazentin-le-Petit to reconnoitre the village, and was cutting the wire in front of the German second line when our artillery started on the same task. " This made the patrol retire," says an official narrative, and it would be difficult to improve on that brief dismissal of a very unpleasant situation.

A patrol sent out towards Mametz Wood on the night of July 2nd-3rd found four German field guns deserted about 300 or 400 yards from White Trench. Accordingly, plans were made to bring them in, and on the night of July 4th-5th the Brigade started the 18th Division's little collection by getting two of them safely inside our lines. Those who remember the remarkable collection of trophies grouped outside Divisional headquarters at Le Cateau in the last days of the war—a group to which the Brigade had very materially contributed—will appreciate how well this habit of appropriating German guns, once formed, was kept up.

On this night of July 4th, 1916, Captain (now Major) S. F. Shepherd, of the 6th Northamptonshire Regiment, was ordered to report with three other officers and 100 men to a R.E. officer at a certain camp. All they knew was they were detailed for a certain fatigue—for fatigues *were* fatigues in those days, before the brilliant notion of making them enjoyable by calling them " working parties " had been thought of—and there was no hint of the exciting task that lay before them.

At the dump they were told about the four German guns, and were given orders to bring them in. It was a cheerful " fatigue." The night was pitch dark, no one knew exactly where the Germans were, except that our patrols were generally fired on, and the party, after going " over the top " for the first time in a big show four days before, 1 ad been under heavy shelling ever since.

The R.E. officer led the way down White Trench. When they had gone as far as they could, he pointed vaguely in the direction where the guns would be found, if luck were good, and then turned back, saying that he would prepare bridges over our trenches for the guns to be dragged across.

Captain Shepherd got out of the trench, and began stumbling among the shell-holes and débris—that is the time when you alternatively curse the darkness for hiding the obstacles and thank it for hiding yourself !—till at last he found the guns.

Two of them had smashed wheels, but the other two were in good condition and could be moved. Falling and blundering back to the trench, he sent out a covering party, and led the rest of the men to the guns. Thirty men and an officer were detailed to one gun, given the general direction of our line, and started on their way back. Then Captain Shepherd began to get the second gun-team ready, but while doing so saw, to his horror, that the first gun was being dragged towards the Bosche lines, direction having been lost at some shell-hole. He rushed out, put this gun on the right way again, and returned to find that the second one had started on its journey and finished up among the wire of a strong point held by the Middlesex Regiment.

Bear in mind that, with all the care in the world, the noise of dragging the guns was—or at any rate seemed to be—terrific, for a gun that is being man-handled across No Man's Land in the darkness seems to acquire all the obstinacy and perversity of a mule. Remember, too, that no one knew where the German wire was, and that on occasions like this the coolest-headed is apt to see a Bosche in every shadow. Once some dark figures were seen dimly at a little distance, and an officer crept out, revolver in hand, to look. Happily it was only a part of our own covering party.

At last the second gun was cut out of the Middlesex Regiment's wire—Middlesex congratulations not yet to hand!—and the uphill journey back to our front line was completed without further mishap. But there another difficulty arose. The R.E. officer appeared and said his men had not turned up, so no bridge could be thrown across the trench.

The men were given a breather in the trench, and then it was decided to knock in the sides and drag the guns across. This was done, the covering party was left behind to rebuild the trench, and it seemed that the task was nearly over, for orders were to haul the guns another 300 or 400 yards, just over the crest of the slope, where gunners with horses would meet them.

The rendezvous was reached, but no men or horses were there. Later it was found that the artillery thought that the job was to be done on the next night. So there was nothing else to be done but to haul the guns another mile farther back—and how the Northamptonshire men began to hate those guns!—till at last men and guns alike were in safety. It was then just dawn, and the "fatigue," which had begun at dusk, was safely accomplished without the loss of a single man.

The next day the guns were seen being taken back by artillery men to Mellecourt, with a board on them which read, "Captured by the 18th Division," and the Northamptonshires never saw their guns again.

On July 8th the Brigade was relieved by the 9th Brigade, and the battalions were marched back to camp in the Bois des

Tailles. Then there were sleep and concerts and baths—and the greatest of these was sleep—and a visit by Sir Ivor Maxse, who told the officers how well the Brigade had done. And thus ended the first phase of the Somme offensive, so far as this Brigade was concerned.

CHAPTER V

TRONES WOOD

THE Brigade was not to have a long rest. Early on July 12th came orders to move up to Maricourt and Trigger Valley, in support of the 55th Brigade, and by twelve noon on the following day the dispositions were as follows :—

Brigade Headquarters 11th Royal Fusiliers 7th Bedfordshire Regiment Trench Mortar Battery Machine Gun Company (less two sections)	Trigger Valley.
6th Northamptonshire Regt. 1 section Machine Gun Company.	Maricourt.
12th Middlesex Regiment One section Machine Gun Company	Original front line British trenches between Maricourt-Briqueterie road and Machine Gun Wood.

That afternoon the Northamptonshire and Middlesex Regiments were placed at the disposal of G.O.C. 55th Brigade, who had been ordered to recapture Trones Wood. The Northamptonshires remained were they were. One company of the Middlesex Regiment was moved to Bernafay Wood, and headquarters and the other three companies were moved to a former German trench known as Dublin Trench. During the night of July 13th-14th the Middlesex Regiment was again moved, a company being sent to Sunken Road and one to Trones Wood. The scattered state of the battalion must be borne in mind in following later events.

In the dark and early hours of July 14th, shortly after midnight, a telephone message was received from Divisional headquarters stating that the 55th Brigade attack on Trones Wood the previous evening had failed, and that the 54th Brigade would attack and capture the wood at all costs in order to protect the right flank of the 3rd and 9th Divisions in their attack on the German second line between Longueval and Bazentin-le-Petit Wood.

The Fusiliers and Bedfordshire Regiment were at once set on the move, the former with orders for Dublin Trench, and the latter for Maricourt. A Fusilier officer's diary has the following note on this stage of the proceedings :—

" Suddenly awakened at 1 a.m., and told we have to move at once. No one knows where we have to go. The battalion falls in, packs are dumped, and in a very short time we are ready for any scrap.

" Just as we reach Maricourt our guns begin to make an unearthly din. Various rumours are going about that Trones Wood has been taken, and that we have to recapture it. The guns get more and more active. Suddenly we get to the forward edge of the village, and see a lovely sight. The whole sky is lit up with gun-flashes and Véry lights.

" Dawn breaks and shows us clouds of smoke. The Germans are putting a barrage on Trones Wood. We get orders to move up to Dublin Trench. Just as we get off, the Huns start a barrage on the Maricourt-Briqueterie Road. We have one casualty, a poor devil who gets his head blown off by a large piece of shrapnel ; but the men keep in their fours and go on as if nothing had happened."

It was decided to attack from the southern extremity of the wood, to drive from south to north, and to establish a defensive flank facing east on the eastern edge of the wood as it was occupied. The Middlesex Regiment was to attack, supported by the Northamptonshire Regiment, who were to " mop up " and establish the defensive flank.

A railway runs through the wood, east and west, at about the centre. As the position of our troops who made the unsuccessful attack was uncertain on the south of this line, it was decided that the barrage should commence on the railway at 4.30 a.m., when the assaulting battalions might be expected to have reached that line, and then step slowly in front of our troops.

Owing to difficulties of communication, all telephone wires being continually cut by shell fire, Lieutenant-Colonel F. A. Maxwell, V.C., D.S.O., commanding the 12th Middlesex Regiment, was given the command of the Northamptonshire Regiment as well during the actual assault.

Colonel Maxwell had come to the Brigade with a big reputation as a fine fighting soldier, and during his command of the Middlesex Regiment (from June to October, 1916) he enhanced that reputation, if it were possible. His old officers and men felt it as a heavy personal loss when he was afterwards killed while commanding a Brigade.

One of his old officers gives the following little picture of his cool behaviour on this occasion :—

" It was in Trones Wood on July 15th," (he writes) "Colonel Maxwell had gathered his company commanders round him to take down some orders. He was at the bottom or broad end of the Wood, and 5·9's were coming down all round us about two a minute. Colonel Maxwell stood in the centre of the group, and his orders, which he was giving out verbally, were drowned every moment by the explosion of a shell within a radius of 25 to 50 yards. He merely blew the earth off his paper each time, rapped out ' Anybody hurt ?' and with a little smile proceeded. This happened at least three times in a few minutes. We were all delighted when the orders were completed."

But to return to the early hours before the attack. The Northamptonshire and Middlesex Regiments were ordered to rendezvous in the sunken road about 1,000 yards south-west of the Wood. On arriving there Colonel Maxwell found the Northamptonshire Regiment (temporarily under the command of Major Clark, Major Charrington being still at Brigade headquarters) ready to move. But only one company of the Middlesex Regiment was here. As already pointed out, they had been scattered over a rather wide area. At that moment a second company was on its way from Dublin Trench, a third was actually in Trones Wood, and the fourth was still in Bernafay Wood out of all touch, and did not rejoin the battalion till the morning of the 15th.

In these circumstances, and owing to the fact that dawn was breaking, Colonel Maxwell decided to use the Northamptonshire Regiment as the assaulting battalion, and the Middlesex Regiment, as it came up, for clearing purposes, and to form the defensive flank.

So at 4 a.m., at about two minutes' notice so far as company officers and the men were concerned, the Northamptonshire Regiment set out, supported by two companies of the Middlesex Regiment. To reach the south-west corner of the Wood, they had to pass over about 1,000 yards of open ground under an exceptionally heavy barrage of 5·9's and larger shells. But, in spite of heavy losses, the advance went forward with great determination. Soon after entering the Wood Major Clark was killed while gallantly reconnoitring ahead of his men.

About 200 yards inside the south-west edge of the Wood the battalion came under heavy rifle and machine-gun fire, and the two leading companies at once attacked on their own initiative. Shortly afterwards Colonel Maxwell and Major Charrington arrived, but by this time the Northamptonshire Regiment had fought their way forward into the blue, and no signs of them could be found. One company of the Middlesex Regiment was found in a trench about 150 yards inside the Wood, where they had been during the previous night, and two other companies of the same battalion now arrived from the sunken road.

No news of the Northamptonshire Regiment was received for some little time, except two verbal messages asking for more bombs, which suggested that the good work was being carried on, and a company of the Middlesex Regiment, under Captain Dennis, was sent to deal with a strong point at the south-east edge of the Wood, on the Guillemont road.

It will now be more convenient to follow the movements of the Northamptonshire Regiment, as far as they can be pieced together from messages received by Major Charrington, who had now taken over command, statements by company officers, and letters from wounded officers.

About 5 a.m. one company was bombing its way up a trench which ran north-east from the south-west corner of the Wood, and ended in a strong point about 350 yards from the edge. This strong point was holding up the advance. Major Clark was by this time killed.

Major Charrington pushed forward, and found two companies pushing through the undergrowth to attack the strong point, which was resisting with heavy rifle and machine-gun fire. Captain Shepherd, though severely wounded in the shoulder, was standing up in the open cheering on his men in a very gallant way, and continued to lead them till exhausted. By this time a fresh supply of bombs came up, the attack was pushed home, and the strong point was captured soon after 6 a.m., the enemy leaving about fifty dead around this fiercely-contested spot. For his gallant leading and fine example at this point Captain Shepherd was awarded the M.C.

Corporal J. Freeman and Lance-Corporal L. T. Roberts won Military Medals in the taking of this strong point, bombing with great courage and accuracy, and always keeping their men pushing forward up the trench in spite of heavy casualties.

Wood-fighting in the summer-time, when the trees and undergrowth are full of foliage, is necessarily blindfold work, and, in spite of the heavy shelling, Trones Wood was still sufficiently thick and entangled to make communication and co-operation somewhat difficult. It is therefore not surprising to find that Colonel Maxwell was for some time ill-informed as to the position, and especially as to how the Northamptonshire Regiment was getting on.

At 9 a.m. Captain Podmore reported all Trones Wood secured, with the exception of the strong point at the south-east edge on the Guillemont road, which Captain Dennis of the Middlesex Regiment was tackling. As a matter of fact, the strong point fell to the Middlesex Regiment, with the assistance of some 7th Buffs and a Stokes mortar, just about the time this message was received. It is clear that by this time 2nd-Lieutenant Redhead (Northamptonshire Regiment), who had been sent by Captain Podmore to work north through the Wood, had done so with great success, moving up the west side and down the east side till he reached the strong point on the Guillemont road. Some enemy were seen running away in disorder from the eastern edge of the Wood towards Guillemont under fire from the machine guns of the Middlesex Regiment, who were now in the strong point, and two Lewis guns which the Northamptonshire Regiment had got into position on the eastern edge.

The next definite news is a message from 2nd-Lieutenant (now Major) T. R. Price of the Northamptonshire Regiment, stating that he had taken over " B " Company, and was holding his position about the middle of the eastern edge of the Wood. After doing much good work with his own platoon this day, 2nd-Lieutenant Price took over " B " Company when no other officers were left, and, although wounded in the leg, carried on till the next day, when officer reinforcements arrived.

About this time " D " Company of the Fusiliers was sent into the Wood to reinforce, and No. 14 platoon was used to garrison the strong point which had been taken by the Middlesex Regiment. The other platoons were withdrawn to prevent unnecessary casualties, as the Germans were now throwing into the Wood everything that came to hand.

To return to the troops under the direct command of Colonel Maxwell.

At about 8 a.m. Colonel Maxwell went to the eastern edge of the Wood to try and clear up the situation, and learned from Captain Dennis that the Middlesex company had not yet taken the strong point. However it was clear that the German garrison of the strong point was being kept thoroughly amused, and too interested in its own troubles to be of any far-reaching danger. He therefore pushed a little way into the Wood, but found only a small party of the Northamptonshire Regiment about 100 yards inside.

As a result of this reconnaissance he came to the conclusion that, with the exception of the parties he had first seen, and the two Middlesex companies he had left at his headquarters at the south-west corner of the Wood, there were no organized units visible, as he had then no news of the rest of the Northamptonshire Regiment. He therefore decided to start afresh, and, collecting every available man, to form a line across the Wood and sweep northwards. For this purpose he got together a number of Middlesex and Northamptonshire men, and began to beat the woods. Little opposition was met, and there were few casualties till he neared the first of the two railway lines that run east and west through the Wood. Here a German machine gun opened on the line from near the western edge, and a hitherto unknown strong point was located.

The line was halted, and Colonel Maxwell, taking seventy men with him, attacked this strong point, and after a rather acrimonious discussion with bomb and bullet, destroyed the whole of the German garrison, and captured the machine gun.

The line was then re-formed, and the sweep through the woods continued. It appears probable that by this time all the men of the Northamptonshire Regiment who had disappeared into the Wood early in the morning were lining a part of the eastern edge of the wood. After crossing the second railway line, hardly a single German was seen in the dense wood to the front, but a number began to break cover to our right, on the eastern edge. Colonel Maxwell ordered every man to fire as he advanced, and this seems to have had a steadying effect on the men's nerves, as well as decreasing the enemy's morale, for no further serious opposition was encountered. As the enemy broke away eastward towards Guillemont, the Northamptonshire's Lewis guns already posted on that edge of the Wood did some pretty work. It must have been these driven Germans to whom the Northamptonshire Regiment's report of about 9 a.m. (from 2nd-Lieutenant Redhead) had referred.

Still moving in line formation, Colonel Maxwell's party swept to the apex of the Wood, and there steps were taken to dispose the various units and their Lewis guns along the eastern edge.

The whole of the Wood was now in our hands, and it was evident that the three strong points already referred to were the chief German defences. After these were captured our troops had chiefly to contend with snipers and detached bodies of the enemy making their way northward and eastward.

Once the whole Wood was in our possession and the eastern edge consolidated as a defensive flank, the enemy made no attempt to counter-attack, but subjected the place to incessant and heavy shelling from guns of large calibre.

Casualties during the attack, apart from the subsequent occupation, were heavy. The Northamptonshire Regiment lost seven officers killed and eight wounded, and had about 300 casualties among other ranks. The Middlesex Regiment had four officers wounded and 150 casualties in other ranks.

During these operations Sergeant William E. Boulter, of the Northamptonshire Regiment, won the V.C. The official account of his action reads :—

" During the capture of Trones Wood one company and a portion of another company was held up by a machine gun which was causing heavy casualties.

" Sergeant Boulter, realizing the situation, with complete disregard of his personal safety, and in spite of being severely wounded in the shoulder, advanced alone across the open in front of the gun under heavy fire, and bombed the team from their position, thereby saving the lives of many of his comrades and materially assisting the advance which eventually cleared Trones Wood."

The Northamptonshire padre, Captain E A. Bennett, had been a prominent figure throughout the day of hard fighting. As on July 1st, he went everywhere, often under the hottest fire, seeking out the wounded and tending them, a work he continued all through the nights following these battles. On

Photo : Buyle] [Brussels

MAJOR-GENERAL W C G HENEKER, C.M.G., D.S.O.,
Who Commanded the 54th Infantry Brigade, March to December, 1915

To face page 48.

Photo : *Swaine*]   [*London, W.*
LIEUT.-COLONEL A. E. SULMAN, M.C.,
Who Commanded the 11th (S.) Batt. Royal Fusiliers from
September, 1917, to July, 1918.

To face page 49.

Photo : *Harrod's Ltd.*]   [*London, S.W.*
LIEUT.-COLONEL C. C. CARR, D.S.O.,
Who Commanded the 11th (S.) Batt. Royal Fusiliers from
September, 1914, to September, 1917.

the evening after the capture of Trones Wood, Lieutenant Newberry, the Northamptonshire medical officer, was killed while gallantly attending the wounded, and Captain Bennett thereupon took charge of the stretcher-bearers, superintending their work till another doctor could be sent up. The stretcher-bearers themselves did splendidly. One of them, Private G. Adams, was awarded the Military Medal. " During July 14th and the two succeeding days [says the official account] he showed the greatest devotion to duty under a heavy fire which killed and wounded many of his comrades." Privates W. Easson, H. Pearn, and J. Goodman were also prominent in gallant work as stretcher-bearers.

The heavy casualties among officers threw a great responsibility on the N.C.Os. of the Northamptonshire Regiment, and they were not found wanting. Sergeants J. Partridge and E. C. Pullen took command of their respective companies, in very trying circumstances, when all their officers had been killed, and led them with great courage and ability. Platoons were led, after their officers had been killed, by Sergeants H. Peek and W. Sullivan and Corporal E. W. Tack.

While Corporal E. Radley was out on a reconnaissance, he ran into a party of four Germans. He at once went for them with his bare fists, knocked one out, returned and reported to his officer, and then took out a party of bombers, who dealt with the rest of the Germans.

Volunteering to go forward and look for snipers who were hiding in shell-holes, Private J. F. Norris came across two with a machine gun. He ordered them out of their shell-hole, shot them when they refused, and brought in their machine gun under heavy fire.

The importance and difficulty of communication in such a task as the capture of Trones Wood are obvious, and the Middlesex Regiment was well served by Corporals A. Jackson and R. Clayton, who were continually under heavy shell fire laying and mending telephone wires.

On the night of July 16th-17th the battalions were relieved in the wood, and by the 19th the whole Brigade was again in camp in the Bois des Tailles. Then came several train journeys, and by August 8th the Brigade was up north and in the line in the Armentieres sector.

On the whole, it was a quiet time, and in at least one part of the line a newspaper boy used to come round each morning. Battalions out of the line were sent by turn in 'busses to the Bois de Nieppe for training in wood-fighting. By the end of the month the Brigade had gone south again, and was training in the St. Pol area ; and on September 23rd all the battalions were at Hedauville and Varennes, a few miles north-west of Albert, ready for the next great show, the capture of Thiepval and the Schwaben Redoubt.

It was during this period of training for Thiepval that the Trench Mortar Battery gave a demonstration of the new Foulis adapter. " Very successful ; cut the top off the cap of a spectator, an officer who had just returned from hospital with shell-shock," is the cheery report on the proceedings by the Tock Emma wallahs themselves.

Chapter VI

THIEPVAL

FOR two years British and French troops had been looking up the slope from the Ancre to the battered village of Thiepval on the crest, where at last, after many bombardments and unsuccessful assaults, nothing could be seen but the ruins of the old Château.

It was known that the Germans attached great importance to the position, for it gave them their last remaining observation posts over the Albert area. Also it was a bastion hindering our further advance in this sector, a nasty salient in our line.

Owing to recent successful fighting it was now possible to attack from the south, the jumping-off point for the 54th Brigade being a trench running east and west, about 500 yards south of Château Redoubt, and at a distance varying from 100 to 250 yards from the German front line. The old British front line, running roughly north and south, enabled the artillery to enfilade the German position from the west.

In considering the dispositions and tasks of the 54th Brigade it is necessary to have a clear picture of the situation in mind. Imagine that Trafalgar Square was Thiepval village. For two years our front line had been where the Thames Embankment stands, and the Germans had naturally an elaborate system of trenches, strong points, and dug-outs facing that front. But we were now able to attack along the Strand towards the Square, and our left-hand battalion must thus fight its way along the whole length of the old German front line trench system. Our whole attack, in fact, was a flank attack along the original German front.

"The 180th Regiment of Wurtemburgers have withstood attacks on Thiepval for two years, but the 18th Division will take it to-morrow." That was the word passed round on the night of September 25th, and everyone was full of confidence. The troops were trained to the minute; attack formations had been practised till it could be expected that the advance would push through to its final objective as a drill movement, whatever the obstacles or casualties. It was known, too, that the artillery preparation had been terrific. As our men took their places in the assembly trenches it was whispered that before "zero" 60,000 rounds of field artillery and 45,000 rounds of heavy stuff would have been fired by the 2nd Corps alone and that a big dose of gas was being put into the village overnight. Clearly the Prussians and Wurtemburgers who held the place were having a thin time.

The 54th Brigade were on the left of the Divisional front, the 53rd Brigade being on our right.

That Thiepval and Schwaben Redoubt—the latter being a little farther north, and dealt with in the next chapter—will ever remain among the proudest memories of the Brigade, and that they were justified in the value they set on the feat is shown by the following words written afterwards by Sir Ivor Maxse :—

> "The capture of Thiepval village and Schwaben Redoubt were distinct and important episodes even in a great European war. They involved in each case a deliberate assault and the capture of a considerable depth of intricate trenches, defended by stubborn regiments who had held their ground against many previous attacks. After visiting the ground in leisure and in peace, I am to this day lost in admiration at the grit shown by the British battalions which fought continuously from September 26th to October 5th, and conquered such strongholds as Thiepval and Schwaben."

To the 12th Middlesex Regiment (Lieutenant-Colonel F. A. Maxwell, V.C., D.S.O.) was given the task of capturing Château Redoubt and the village, while to the 11th Royal Fusiliers (Lieutenant-Colonel C. C. Carr) was given the difficult left flank, where it had to deal with the trenches and dug-outs of the original German front line, which covered Thiepval from the west. As it was known that the Brigade had the toughest job in the Division that day, it was given a front of only 300 yards. The distance to the final objective was 1,800 yards.

It gives some idea of the strength of the position which the Germans had been holding and improving for two years to know that a captured German map showed 144 deep dug-outs in the area allotted to the 54th Brigade, without counting the deep dug-outs around the Château Redoubt, and several strong points on the enemy's original front line, along which the Fusiliers were to fight their way.

Behind the Fusiliers and the Middlesex Regiment was the 6th Battalion Northamptonshire Regiment (Lieutenant-Colonel G. E. Ripley) in close support, and the 7th Battalion Bedfordshire Regiment (Lieutenant-Colonel G. D. Price) was in reserve in dug-outs in Thiepval Wood and the Bluff to the west.

The Fusilier companies were necessarily rather scattered. "D" Company (Captain R. H. V. Thompson), with two machine guns and two trench mortars, was detailed to clear the enemy's front-line trenches. "C" Company (Lieutenant, now Lieutenant-Colonel, A. E. Sulman) was sent over with the Middlesex to "mop up," a job so well done that practically all Germans left behind the leading waves were silenced, and there were no cases of the assaulting battalion being shot in the back as it advanced. The other companies were sent over in support.

Zero hour was 12.35 p.m. on September 26th. A Fusilier officer who went over with " D " Company made the following entry in his diary :—

"We hoped to disturb the Bosche in the middle of his dinner. Our assembly trench was shelled rather heavily at about 12.15, and we thought at first that we had been discovered. However, no one in our company was hurt, and after about ten rounds of 5·9's we had peace. Our shelling had been merely normal, but at 12.35 the biggest barrage ever used was to open out.

"With the first shell we were over the top, and had gone several yards before the barrage had really started. When it did start—my word! It came with a fearful ear-splitting crashing and rending, thousands of shells bursting almost simultaneously. We met Bosches running about, scared out of their wits, like a crowd of rabbits diving for their holes. Men were rushing about unarmed, men were holding up their hands and yelling for mercy, men were scuttling about everywhere, trying to get away from that born fighter, the Cockney, but they had very little chance.

"I had the pleasure of shooting four of them before I was wounded in the wrist. After this everything seems blurred. I found myself in a shell-hole with one of my men who was also wounded. We patched each other up, and then went on. I have visions of excited men tearing after the Bosches, visions of men sitting over dug-out entrances waiting to shoot the first Bosche that appeared."

Both battalions got away well, close up to the barrage. The German barrage came down on our front line five minutes later, but most of the assaulting troops had already been got forward, distances being corrected in No Man's Land, and the left of our line (chiefly " A " and " B " Companies, Fusiliers) was the only part to suffer.

The Fusiliers were the first to get into grips with the enemy, a strong point being encountered where Brawn Trench joined the old German front line. This held up " D " Company, and also the left flank of the Middlesex, but the rest of the attack went on. Captain Thompson sent part of his company over the top to help the Middlesex Regiment in Brawn Trench, and led the rest of his men against the strong point. Unhappily, he was killed just as the strong point was being successfully rushed, and in the hand-to-hand fighting that followed Lieutenant R. A. Mall-Smith was also killed and Lieutenant G. E. Cornaby wounded. A great number of Germans were killed here, and twenty-five were taken prisoners and sent back.

" D " Company Fusiliers now continued along the German front line, fighting every yard of their way. Lewis guns that were pushed up did useful work shooting along the trench, and accounting for great numbers of Germans as they ran from dug-outs.

In the meantime the general line had moved on towards the Château, but was checked there by deadly machine-gun fire. Just at this moment the first of the two tanks allotted to the Brigade came waddling across from Thiepval Wood. This aroused tremendous interest and enthusiasm. Tanks had made their first dramatic appearance on any battlefields only ten days before, but already their fame was on every tongue, and the news that two of them were to help us had been passed round overnight. The first arrival left the Wood at zero and was timed to reach the Château at the same time as the assaulting infantry. This part of the time table worked well. The enemy machine guns were effectively dealt with, and the leading companies of the Middlesex Regiment passed the ruins right and left.

According to programme, this tank, with its fellow, who was now coming up, should have led the infantry into Thiepval, stayed there so long as was necessary to squash any " self-determination " on the part of the German colony, and then moved on to show Schwaben Redoubt how a public nuisance should be checked. But, unhappily, both tanks became " ditched " near the Château, and the infantry had to carry on without them.

At the Château a trench mortar was brought into action in unorthodox style. A section that had started out with two guns and ten shell-carriers arrived there with only one barrel and three rounds of ammunition. These were fired by using a man's shoulder instead of a stand, and a steel helmet as base-plate.

Our left was now badly held up by continuous machine-gun fire from the German front line, and a part of the leading company of the Fusiliers which attempted to get astride the trench was engaged in fighting at this point till next morning.

The position at about 1 p.m. was roughly as follows :—

The right of the Middlesex Regiment was still getting on well, but the left was making only slow progress, as, in addition to holding his old front strongly, the Bosche had a large number of men in the left or west corner of the ruin which had once been Thiepval. The left company of the Fusiliers was still engaged on the old German front line. The dug-out clearing party of that battalion was near the Château, with the Middlesex Regiment, and the other two companies of the Fusiliers were approaching the left of the village. Major Hudson (" A " Company), seeing the Middlesex Regiment in difficulties about the Château, at once pushed forward his men to their assistance. After passing the Château the right of our line had no further landmarks to guide it, and inclined to the right, so that on reaching the first objective it probably overlapped the dividing line between this Brigade and the 53rd. Seeing this, Captain Johnson, of the Fusiliers, fearing a gap in the attack, put in his company and attacked northwards. This resulted in the final capture of the first objective.

The fighting up to this point, as it was seen by a Fusilier officer, is thus described :—

"On the left 'D' Company had very hard fighting along the old Bosche front line. They were eventually held up on that line about level with the Château, having got on well, but with very heavy losses. Captain Thompson was hit in the head, but continued fighting until hit again and killed. Of the three platoon commanders, one was killed, one wounded, and one (Hawkins) stunned by the explosion of a trench-mortar shell, but kept on with the company.

"'C' Company killed a great many Bosches in a trench about 250 yards west of the Château, and running north and south. Along this same trench Major Hudson, of 'A' Company, was hit through the shoulder, but continued until the final line was taken and consolidated. On his way down he got a bullet through the thigh, breaking the bone, and died a few days later.

"Battalion headquarters in the Leipzig Salient had had no news of the fight, so at about 1.15 Colonel Carr took headquarters forward. There was still an intense barrage, and a number of men were hit going up. On getting to the Château ruins, which were merely a heap of broken bricks, we found that Colonel Maxwell, commanding 12th Middlesex, had just arrived there. As there was no doubt as to what was happening on the left ('D' Company's sector), Colonel Carr and Captain Cumberlege, the adjutant, proceeded in that direction. A machine gun immediately opened on us from very short range, and Colonel Carr got three bullets through various parts of him—fortunately none of them serious—and Cumberlege was also hit. Major Hudson had been hit just previously, so Captain Johnson was now in command of the Fusiliers until the evening, when Major Meyricke, the second-in-command, who had been left out, came up and took over. But Colonel Maxwell virtually commanded both battalions, and also two companies of Northamptonshires who had come up, Colonel Ripley, of the Northamptonshires, having also been wounded (he afterwards died).

"The line eventually held was about 300 yards in front of the Château. The Bosche shelled the whole area, and particularly the trench from which the attack had started, until dark, but slacked off during the night.

"For some hours during the night Colonel Maxwell was writing diligently page after page—it was supposed popularly to be a letter to his wife. Shells were passing over and dropping all the time, and one runner who had the wind up gave a groan every time one came. Suddenly Maxwell got up from his writing, saying, ' I can't stand this any longer—send that man here.' He then told everyone round to stand in a line, said, ' I'll give him the first kick—the rest of you pass him along,' and the runner was passed out into the dark.

"The next day I went up to look for Captain Thompson, and found him. We buried him at the cemetery at Black Horse Bridge, Authville. He was probably the best company commander the battalion ever had."

But to return to the events of the day.

The first objective (roughly the road from Mouquet farm running through Thiepval towards the wood) having been taken, progress became slower. Practically every inch of the ground had to be covered, as, in addition to the organized defence, snipers were in every other shell-hole.

It was at this point that Lance-Corporal L. Tovey, of the Fusiliers, distinguished himself. A machine gun suddenly appeared and fired on our line. He dashed straight at it and bayoneted both the gunners. Later, during the confused fighting in the village, he led his comrades when nearly all the officers and senior N.C.Os. had become casualties. Unhappily, he was shot through the head and killed before the day's work was done.

Just about the same time Private L. Platt won the Military Medal. He took back a message from the front line to headquarters asking for reinforcements, after two men had already been killed trying to get the same message through. He then guided the reinforcements up under fire so heavy that less than a third of them reached the line.

The snipers who were such a pest at this stage had a thin time whenever Company Sergeant-Major (afterwards Regimental Sergeant-Major) G. R. Taylor got at them. In the official account of the action for which he was awarded the D.C.M. it states :—

"This Warrant Officer, with the utmost fearlessness, sought out enemy snipers and killed several in personal duels. He coolly assisted his company commander in reorganization, and arranged most ably the despatch to the front line of men, S.A.A., and bombs."

It was about the same time that two Middlesex men, Privates R. Ryder and F. J. Edwards, won V.Cs.

The official account of Private Edwards's action was as follows :—

"His part of the line was held up by a machine gun. The officers had all become casualties. There was confusion and even suggestion of retirement. Private Edwards grasped the situation at once. Alone, and on his own initiative, he dashed towards the gun, which he bombed until he succeeded in knocking it out. By this gallant act, performed with great presence of mind, and with complete disregard for his personal safety, this man made possible the continuance of the advance, and solved a dangerous situation. His was probably one of those decisive actions which determine the success or failure of an operation."

Private Ryder's action was officially recorded as follows :—

"His company was held up by heavy fire from the trench in front of them, and all his officers had become casualties. The attack was flagging for want of leadership. Private Ryder, realizing the situation, without a moment's thought for his own safety, dashed absolutely alone at the enemy's trench, and by skilful manipulation of his Lewis gun succeeded in clearing the trench. By this brilliant act he not only made possible, but also inspired the advance of, his comrades. It seems possible that this single heroic action made all the difference between success and failure in this part of the attacking line."

Up to the time the first objective was reached "D" Company of the Fusiliers had cleared altogether twenty-five dug-outs in the front line. In many of them the Germans showed fight, especially in one large dug-out where numbers of the enemy with two machine guns had established themselves. They were invited to come out, but refused, and there was a rather acrimonious scene. Finally, the place had to be set on fire to put an end to the discussion, as it happened to be one of the Fusiliers' busy days, and they had no time to waste on argument. Many Germans are believed to have perished in the flames, eleven were killed as they came out, and fourteen who were wounded were taken prisoners.

As the advance progressed many Germans bolted northwards, but, owing to the broken nature of the ground, they were (in the graphic phrase of an officer who was present) as difficult to hit as snipe, and a large percentage got away. Farther on, however, two of the Fusilier Lewis guns ("C" Company) enfiladed them as they ran, and Lieutenant Sulman estimated that he bagged at least fifty.

While the left of the Fusilier line was still busy among the trenches and dug-outs, the remainder of "A" Company and two platoons of "C" went through to the second objective (beyond the right corner of the village). They there began bombing to the left, and eventually made a block when their supply of bombs ran out. During this operation they captured two officers and forty-five other ranks, who were sent to the rear. It was while advancing to the second objective that Major Hudson was hit. Captain Johnson now took command of the Fusiliers.

"C" Company, still clearing dug-outs, and capturing prisoners all the time, did a specially good piece of work about this time. Half an hour before zero Lieutenant Sulman had been given a captured German map showing the position of their telephone headquarters. He showed this to his men, and told them to do their best to find the place and to put the exchange and the operators out of action.

Lance-Corporal F. Rudy, with four men, cast about till they found the dug-out, which proved to be quite a palatial place, with a magnificent installation. They attacked and captured it, together with about twenty Germans inside and out, and cut all the wires, which afforded direct communication to the enemy artillery. Lance-Corporal Rudy then held the place without relief or support for twelve hours under the heaviest fire. For this he was awarded the D.C.M.

By this time the Fusilier parties on the left were hung up by cross-fire from German machine guns in strong points in the western side of the village. They also appeared to have their flanks in the air, and asked the Middlesex for reinforcements. All that was left of two platoons—about fifty men—was sent out, but only six men succeeded in getting through.

At the same time one and a half companies of the same battalion were on the northern side of the village, but it was impossible to locate them, owing to the contradictory nature of messages received. Most of these messages came from N.C.Os., the officers being casualties ; and as many of them had no maps, greater accuracy could not be expected.

Bombing down trenches was now going on at several points, and some good individual work was done. Several attempts were made by the Fusiliers to rush the strong points on our left, but each time they were beaten back by bombs and intense cross-fire from machine guns. " It was not unusual " (remarks an officer who was there) " to see from twelve to twenty German stick-bombs in the air at the same time, and the whole area looked like a firework display owing to the number of egg-bombs the enemy showered on us."

A D.C.M. was won at this point by Private H. Bott, of the Fusiliers. When the men around him were held up by a machine gun, he formed and took command of a bombing party, led them up to the trench, bombing as he went, captured the gun, and killed the gunners.

Sergeant P. Adler also did good work here, and later gallantly lead his platoon along the enemy front line. " At night " (says the official account of the action for which he was awarded the M.M.), " though wounded, he repelled intense bombing counter-attacks till his own supply of bombs ran out. He then collected enemy bombs, and used them to stop the enemy rushes."

The same award was won by Private E. Townend. " When his section ran short of bombs " (says the official account), " taking the few bombs he had, he advanced with great boldness up the trench, and held back the enemy bombers, while the men behind him constructed a bomb-stop."

Lance-Corporal E. W. Hope, who was engaged in clearing dug-outs, also did good work. In charge of a bombing section, he entered dug-out after dug-out by himself, and cleared them of the enemy. On two occasions, meeting armed enemies underground, he disposed of them without assistance; in others he sent the occupants up to his party waiting above.

Privates J. J. Mumford and E. J. Butler also did good work as bombers, and both won the M.M. " for conspicuous, daring, and good work in blocking a trench and counter-attacking strong enemy bombing parties " (says the official account). " When their sergeant and two-thirds of their comrades had become casualties, they displayed great courage in assisting their officer to repulse the assaults of the enemy."

The Middlesex men had been displaying equal courage and initiative on the right. There was, for instance, Private F. H. Hatchard, who won the D.C.M. " At a critical moment " (so runs the official account) " the men attached to battalion headquarters were sent up in support when the front ine was held up by a strong point. Private Hatchard, who is no longer young, is one of the regimental pioneers, and therefore but little trained as a fighting man; but, seeing a machine gun which was causing heavy losses, he worked his way alone with a supply of bombs to a shell-hole within easy distance. From there he threw bombs until he had knocked out the gun team. Later, when bombs were running short, he searched the German dug-outs, and discovered a large store. Throughout the night he carried these forward and kept the bombers supplied, thus enabling them to hold a most important position."

Another D.C.M. went to Lance-Corporal A. Woods. " When the left flank was held up, and the advance of the left company checked, this N.C.O., with a private, attacked and cleared a trench which was held by twenty of the enemy with a machine gun. This done, he constructed a block, which took him three or four hours, hindered by continuous enemy bombing."

Corporal T. Kempley was another " sticker," and well deserved his M.M. For four hours he attacked a strong point, and at last bombed his way in. He then proceeded to block the trench, and was three times rushed by the enemy, whom he drove off on each occasion. All this was done under heavy fire from a minenwerfer.

But to return once more to the situation in the afternoon, and the movements of the Northamptonshire Regiment.

At 1 p.m. the leading companies left their forming-up trenches and began to go forward. By this time a very heavy enemy barrage was being put on all communication trenches, and on battalion headquarters at Campbell's Post. One shell burst in the trench 3 yards from battalion headquarters, wrecked a neighbouring dug-out, and blew three men to pieces. A little later the leading company (" C ") had lost Captain Evans and 2nd-Lieutenant Bailey as casualties.

Soon afterwards it was decided to move battalion headquarters forward, and this was done through a heavy barrage, Colonel

Ripley (who died later) and Lieutenant Barkham (Adjutant) being seriously wounded by the same shell. Major Charrington then took over command.

By four o'clock the four companies were together near the new battalion headquarters. The position then, as regards officers, was :—

"A" Company ... One officer left (2nd-Lieutenant Gotch).
"B" Company ... No officers left (Sergeant Partridge in command).
"C" Company ... No officers left (Sergeant Pullen in command).
"D" Company ... One officer left (2nd-Lieutenant Bates). (Two platoons detached as carrying party.)

There were now three battalions in the fight, all pretty well mixed together and used up. The position about 5 p.m. was that we had reached our second objective on the right, but our left was bent back, owing to the resistance put up by the enemy in and around his old front line. Roughly, we held the whole of Thiepval except the north-west corner, and here a strong machine-gun nest among the ruins, protected by a heavy barrage on every side, still held out. With the exhausted troops now in the line, no further progress could be made that night.

The Fusiliers, as the battalion on the left, were the troops chiefly concerned, and shortly before dusk Captain Johnson, then in command, reported the situation to Colonel Maxwell, of the Middlesex Regiment, the senior officer on the spot. The latter instructed him to dig in on the present line, hemming in the enemy strong points as much as possible.

Captain Johnson therefore collected all the Fusiliers, Northamptonshire and Middlesex Regiments in his part of the line, and formed them into front and support lines, with about 50 yards between each line. The front line consisted of groups of six men, each forming a double-sentry post at intervals of from 12 to 15 yards. These men dug towards each other with a view to forming a continuous line. The support line was not continuous, being composed of groups with a sentry over each. A strong point was made round one of the stranded tanks north of the Château, with a garrison of twenty men and the machine guns out of the tank.

On our right and centre the task of organizing the line was allotted to Major Charrington, of the Northamptonshire Regiment, assisted by 2nd-Lieutenant Odgers, of the Middlesex Regiment, and 2nd-Lieutenants Bates and Gotch, of his own battalion.

Not until 11 p.m. was the line finally organized and consolidated. Up to that time there had been continual fighting, especially at the block in the trench where our line on the second objective ran into the corner of the village still held by the enemy. Altogether thirty-six men were sent up to this block, of whom twenty-eight became casualties.

The Germans also made many bombing raids at other points, but each time were successfully repulsed. Later a barrage was put down on the front line they were holding, and this not only stopped further raids, but, judging from their Véry lights, drove them out of a strong point where they were making themselves a nuisance. So ended the attack for that day, and, as the north-west corner of the village must still be taken before we could push forward to our final objective—Schwaben Redoubt —it was decided to bring in the Bedfordshires.

The whole area over which the day's fighting had taken place was of extraordinary difficulty. The ground had probably been more torn up by shells than any other part of France at that time, and the enemy had a very strong and intricate system of defence, machine guns covering and re-covering every yard of the way. In addition, there were great numbers of unknown and unsuspected dug-outs and trenches sheltering men, machine guns, and minenwerfer. Except for the ruins of the Château, there were no landmarks, and it was most difficult to locate and identify points and positions. The numerous craters, a vast number of which held snipers or machine guns, had to be systematically "mopped up," and the early loss of nearly all officers made organization and control a difficult problem. The fight became one of individual initiative and courage, but all ranks rose splendidly to the occasion.

It was now the turn of the 7th Bedfordshire Regiment, who had been in reserve all day. A ticklish problem confronted all concerned—the withdrawal of the three weary and battered battalions who lay before the last stronghold of the Germans in the corner of the village, and their relief by the fresh battalion.

It was about midnight when definite orders reached the Bedfordshire company commanders, and in a pitch-dark night, lighted by the bursting of shells, amid terrific artillery fire, they worked their men up in little bodies, and at last had them all in position. When dawn broke a new and fresh battalion faced the Germans, instead of the three spent battalions who had borne the brunt of the previous day's attack. "Only a well-trained and high-spirited battalion such as the 7th Bedfordshire Regiment can accomplish such a feat, and be ready for a day's fighting the same morning," was General Maxse's comment.

In the meantime Colonel Price, of the Bedfordshire Regiment, had left Brigade headquarters shortly after midnight with plans for the attack that was to complete the task of clearing the village.

On two companies of the Bedfordshire Regiment, under Captain (now Major) L. H. Keep, fell the honour of being selected for this final attack. They were got into position by 5.45 a.m. in the dark, over ground pitted by shell-holes, by Captain Johnston and Lieutenant Sulman, of the Fusiliers. Their orders were to storm the area at 6 a.m. in one rush, and to clear it with the bayonet.

A stiff resistance was encountered. Steady progress was made on the left, in spite of machine guns, snipers, and standing patrols in shell-holes. But the right company was held up soon after the start, and it was here that 2nd-Lieutenant Adlam, commanding the right-hand platoon, won the Victoria Cross.

His platoon was held up by heavy rifle and machine-gun fire from several strong points. Realizing that time was all important to success, he dashed across the open under fire, collecting his men from shell-holes for a combined rush. He also gathered up a number of German bombs, and with them started a whirlwind attack on the enemy. He was slightly wounded in the leg, but continued throwing from a kneeling position, and, in spite of this handicap, outthrew the Germans. Then, seizing an opportunity, he led in his platoon, and killed or captured all who opposed him. He continued at the head of his men that day and the next, until again wounded.

The assault was completely successful. Captain Keep's little force seized and held the last corner of the ruins, and in less than twenty-four hours from zero on the 26th the whole of Thiepval was ours. In this last operation seventy prisoners were taken from dug-outs, and over eighty German dead were counted.

In the capture of Thiepval the Brigade lost 19 officers and 176 men killed, and 28 officers and 563 men wounded. In addition 198 men were reported missing. The 6th Northamptonshire Regiment lost their commanding officer, Colonel G. E. Ripley; but the 12th Middlesex Regiment had the heaviest casualties in the whole Division, with 10 officers (including Majors Scarborough and Whinney) and 60 men killed, and 8 officers and 233 men wounded. The German losses were much higher. Four officers and 606 other ranks surrendered to the Division, and their killed and wounded were believed to exceed 3,000.

"I am convinced," wrote Sir Ivor Maxse, "that if the complete story is ever written of what our men accomplished in the way of hand-to-hand encounters, from the outbreak of the battle until Thiepval and Schwaben were captured, their achievments will bear comparison with any similar feat of arms in this war."

The capture of Schwaben Redoubt must be reserved for another chapter.

Mention has already been made of some of the individual acts of gallantry that marked the capture of Thiepval. In such a day and night of hand-to-hand fighting the full record would be almost a nominal roll of the assaulting battalions, and to make any selection is an ungrateful task. But the following selection from official accounts of deeds for which medals were awarded, though incomplete, is of interest.

The Fusiliers will not forget how their doctor, Captain (now Major) J. C. Sale, R.A.M.C., worked for them that day. He was awarded the M.C. in the following circumstances :—

"When, owing to shortage of stretcher-bearers, it became difficult to convey the wounded to dug-outs, he repeatedly carried them in on his back under very heavy shell, rifle, and machine-gun fire. In the course of his work he was twice flung down and half stunned by the concussion of heavy shells bursting close to him, but he continued his magnificent work undeterred, affording the finest possible example to all concerned, and even remained in Thiepval for some hours after his battalion had been relieved."

Three other M.Cs. were awarded to Fusilier officers, as follows :—

Captain W. H. H. Johnston "led his company with great bravery, and later, when his C.O. was wounded, took command of his battalion. With entire disregard of his own safety, he was indefatigable in organizing the defence of the captured position."

Lieutenant (now Lieutenant-Colonel) A. E. Sulman : "His coolness, resource, and courage were very noticeable throughout the battle, especially during the night of 26th-27th, in the very difficult operation of organizing, consolidating, and defending the line gained."

2nd-Lieutenant J. B. Hunt "led his platoon with the greatest skill, and organized and carried out successful bombing attacks on strong points."

Of good bombing work done by N.C.Os. and men some account has already been given. The Lewis gunners, signallers, and others showed no less initiative and gallantry. The following were among the recipients of the M.M. :—

Private G. Norton : "After his leaders were killed he fought his Lewis gun with exceptional ability and daring. In spite of a worrying fire from a hostile machine gun, he chose his positions so skilfully that he accounted for nearly fifty Germans, firing from the shoulder with his gun resting on the back of another man."

Lance-Corporal F. W. Neal "frequently signalled messages from exposed positions with the greatest courage."

Lance-Corporal R. Lambe "took charge of a section of stretcher-bearers on his own initiative, and showed untiring energy and complete fearlessness in attending the wounded, often under the heaviest fire."

Sergeant J. W. Fryer "displayed the greatest coolness and energy. When sent back to battalion headquarters to report on the situation, he passed boldly through heavy machine-gun and artillery fire, and accomplished his message with great success."

Private G. Morgan: "The supply of pigeons having run short, he hurried back through a heavy barrage, and succeeded in bringing up others. He also distinguished himself during the fighting on July 1st, when he laid cable under heavy fire, and single-handed attacked and captured three Germans."

In the 6th Northamptonshire Regiment a M.C. was awarded to 2nd-Lieutenant F. D. S. Walker. "As Intelligence Officer he displayed the greatest bravery and resource. His services as a guide under heavy fire were beyond praise and of the utmost value."

Sergeants J. W. Partridge and E. C. Pullen both won the D.C.M. for the courage and efficiency with which they led their companies when all officers were casualties.

Among those in the same battalion who received the M.M. were :—

Sergeant W. L. Miles, who "handled his Lewis gun with the greatest skill and bravery. It was greatly due to his untiring efforts that the front line were enabled to consolidate their position."

Sergeant W. T. Scriven, Lance-Corporal F. Shipton, and Private J. Walsh, "formed a bombing party which drove the enemy out of a communication trench which ran into our front line. This post had been preventing consolidation of the line in the vicinity for two hours, and it was not until the enemy had been driven out that a dangerous gap in the line could be filled. These men afterwards formed a block in the trench in this advanced position, which they held during the remainder of the night."

Lance-Corporal A. F. Hill "rendered most valuable assistance in carrying water and ammunition to a forward dump through a heavy barrage almost continuously for thirty hours. He also helped to clear a German dug-out, and assisted in the capture of fifteen prisoners."

Sergeant G. Bury "rendered the greatest assistance to his officer in collecting stragglers, and in getting a complete line consolidated. All through the night he visited covering parties under heavy fire in front of the line, and showed the greatest bravery throughout the entire action."

Private J. F. Norris "worked his Lewis gun with great bravery and coolness on our exposed left flank."

Sergeant J. Evans "as medical orderly displayed exceptional bravery under very heavy shell fire. He worked day and night attending to the wounded in the most dangerous localities."

Sergeant T. W. Jones " as a signal sergeant did excellent work in maintaining communication by lamp for over six hours from the parapet of a trench which was perpetually enfiladed by severe artillery fire."

Company Sergeant-Major A. W. Woolsey was awarded the D.C.M. " By his fearless conduct and total disregard of personal danger, he rallied and inspired confidence in his men in very difficult circumstances, when a large number of officers had become casualties."

Among the awards in the 12th Middlesex Regiment was a D.C.M. to Company Sergeant-Major J. Burrows. " When all but one of his company officers had become casualties, he showed conspicuous power of organization and leadership, and by his coolness and capable handling of difficult situations inspired confidence in all ranks."

Among those in the same battalion awarded the M.M. were :—

Sergeant J. Pilgrim, of whom Colonel Maxwell wrote : " When the three officers on battalion headquarters and the Regimental Sergeant-Major were killed, he acted as my ' staff,' and was invaluable. He is perfectly cool under fire, and I was able to send him first to report on one flank and then on another, knowing that I could rely on his information."

Sergeant S. Insley " was in command of the Lewis guns. Wounded in the face early in the attack, he nevertheless remained with his guns, and by his careful observation placed them in such positions that they kept down the fire of snipers from several points, and also from a bombing post in the vicinity."

Lance-Corporals D. Driscoll and H. Cox and Private T. Fairweather " showed great bravery and resource in attacking and clearing a German bombing and snipers' post, and afterwards in holding it themselves until reinforcements were brought up."

Sergeant A. H. Ready " assisted in the defence of the left of the line, which was in the air, and worked his Lewis gun with great steadiness, frequently leaving cover to search for more ammunition."

Lance-Corporal H. Perry " showed great and persistent gallantry in initiating attacks on an enemy strong point on the left flank. When a block was being made, he held back constant enemy rushes, and as soon as it was blown down he constructed another. He continued his efforts throughout the night."

Private J. Kelly, " finding his party, most of whom were men of a recent draft, without officers and N.C.Os., immediately took charge and led them with conspicuous ability and courage to the objective. There he at once, on his own initiative, set to work to consolidate, and continued throughout the night to inspire his men with his fine example."

Corporal C. Layton "collected bodies of men who were leaderless, and pushed forward. When unable to advance without a fresh supply of bombs, he went back under heavy fire to obtain some. Recrossing the fire-swept zone, he rejoined the men he had collected, and continued to command them until next morning."

Eight stretcher-bearers, Lance-Corporal E. J. Cousins and Privates H. Crawley, J. Hobbs, D. T. Delaney, W. F. Mansell, G. R. A'Court, H. W. Rawlings, and S. A. Clary, also received the M.M. "Owing to the nature of the ground, stretchers were in many cases impossible, and most of the carrying was done by these gallant men on their backs."

A D.C.M. also went to Private A. J. Knight, of the Northamptonshire Regiment, attached to the 54th Machine Gun Company. "When the whole of his gun team had become casualties, he, with one other man whom he got hold of to help, succeeded in keeping his gun in action under very heavy shell fire throughout the night of 26th-27th. Although isolated from his own infantry, he held his position against all attacks until found and relieved next morning."

Another machine gunner, Sergeant J. Templeton, was awarded the M.M. "His officer having become a casualty, he commanded his section most ably. After placing his guns in position in the strong points for which they were detailed, he took charge of a platoon of infantry whose officer had been killed, and arranged the consolidation of the position won."

Corporal A. Butterfield, of the Middlesex Regiment, attached to the 54th Trench Mortar Battery, also won the M.M. "He was in charge of a Stokes gun, which he handled with marked ability and complete disregard of danger under heavy shell fire."

Awards to the Bedfordshire Regiment will be more conveniently dealt with in the next chapter, when the battalion's share in the next stage of the proceedings, the capture of Schwaben Redoubt, is described.

One incident comes to mind in which Bedfordshire men played a part while the battalion was awaiting final orders to take the Redoubt.

Privates Baker and Catling worked round behind a large German dug-out with many entrances, in advance of an outpost line. Finding an unguarded entrance, they went down, and after a sharp fight in the dark compelled the surrender of thirty-two fully-armed Germans. They urged them up the stairs into the open. There the Germans, surprised and disgusted to find that they had surrendered to two men, took up their arms again and resumed the fight. After that one thing led to another, and the result was that of the prisoners, only eighteen reached the cage alive.

Lieutenant-General C. W. Jacobs, as commander of the Second Corps, sent the following message while the Brigade was still struggling for the last corner of the battered ruins :—

"Thiepval has withstood all attacks upon it for exactly two years, and it is a great honour to your Division to have captured the whole of this strongly-fortified village at the first attempt. Hearty congratulations to you all."

Sir Douglas Haig himself called on Sir Ivor Maxse on September 27th to congratulate the Division on its success.

Chapter VII

SCHWABEN REDOUBT AND REGINA TRENCH

ALTHOUGH the heap of ruins and tangle of chalky trenches that had once been Thiepval was now ours, the position could not be regarded as won, and it was very unlikely that it could be held until the final objective, Schwaben Redoubt, was taken.

This was the key to the whole position, overlooking the site of the village from the higher ground some 600 or 700 yards farther north.

The Royal Fusiliers, Northamptonshire and Middlesex Regiments were out of it for the present, their losses in officers having been so heavy that, although nominally in Divisional reserve, ready for an emergency, they could not be used for an organized attack. If the Brigade were to have the honour of helping to complete the task it had so well begun, it was clearly the Bedfordshire Regiment's job.

The plan was to attack with the 53rd Brigade on the right, and the 54th Brigade on the left. The 1/5th West Yorkshire Regiment, of the 49th Division, was placed at the disposal of the 54th Brigade for this operation. The two fresh companies of the Bedfordshire Regiment were to be deployed for the assault, and of the two companies that had already been in action with Captain Keep, one was to be in close support of the assaulting companies, and the other was to " mop-up " dug-outs. Three companies of the West Yorkshire Regiment were to support the Bedfordshire Regiment, leaving the fourth company at the disposal of Colonel Price as his battalion reserve.

Zero hour was 1 p.m. on September 28th, and the forming up by midday was a difficult operation, as the jumping-off trenches, on the north of the village, were in full view of the enemy, and the light was very good. The ground had been so battered about, and every landmark so reduced to mud and ruin, that map references did not count, and all that was clear was our front trench and some uncut wire on the left. The Redoubt was nothing but a heap of mud and shell-holes on the crest.

About two hours before zero a German map, captured the previous day in Thiepval, reached Brigade headquarters. This showed the positions of several German machine guns. This information was at once sent to the artillery and the assaulting battalion, and reached them just in time to be of service.

However, the men were got into position, and as soon as our barrage came down the front wave of the Bedfordshire Regiment was off. The barrage appeared very effective, and little fire was met with until the lifts occurred. The German lines were a hell of bursting shells, and it seemed impossible that men could live there and fight. Keeping closely behind our barrage —though how to distinguish it from the stuff the German guns were putting over was a puzzle—our waves made good progress until a communication trench known as Market Trench, running from the original German front line to the Redoubt, was reached. This was a little less than half-way to the objective. Here the right platoon of the Bedfordshire Regiment came under heavy machine-gun fire, and was completely knocked out.

The rest of the Bedfordshire waves also suffered from machine-gun fire, but succeeded in rushing a number of strong points, and getting farther forward, till they fronted the west side of the Redoubt at a distance of about 250 yards. A machine gun that was giving them much trouble on their left was knocked out by artillery, in response to an urgent telephone message.

The reader must remember that our attack was being pushed along the original German front line, for we were fighting northward along trenches facing west, just as the Fusiliers had to do in the attack on Thiepval. The Redoubt was not immediately to our front—that is to say, we were attacking down a football field in which the goal, instead of being in the centre of the line at the far end, was actually rather towards the right-hand corner.

On the line now reached our front was necessarily rather extended, and the West Yorkshire Regiment was put in with orders to push towards the Redoubt, and so fill the gap that was appearing between the Bedfordshire Regiment and the 53rd Brigade on their right. The latter Brigade was now tackling the southern part of the Redoubt.

By 1.30 p.m. the Bedfordshire Regiment had seized a number of points facing the north-west corner of the Redoubt, and the attackers, led by Sergeant Shepherd, reached a spot on the crest of the hill from which they could see Germans streaming northwards along trenches towards St. Pierre Divion. Our artillery had good observation of this area, and shelled the retreating Germans very effectively. By 2 p.m. Captain L. H. Keep sent back a message by visual that he had reached the final objective.

But it was one thing to be on the objective, and quite another to hold it, and the rest of the day was spent in bombing attacks and hand-to-hand fighting, especially on the right, where our line touched the Redoubt.

Much of this bombing was organized by the late Captain D. S. H. Keep, and some good work was done under his direction. Sergeant A. Wyatt was awarded the D.C.M. in this connection. "Volunteering to carry out a bombing raid [says the official account], he pushed his way along two enemy trenches in face of heavy opposition, and established blocks in both. He then went forward with two men and cleared the trench, bringing back thirty-four prisoners from the dug-outs. Later, after his officer had become a casualty, he organized the defence of the position, and beat off repeated bombing attacks."

Private G. Goldhawk was also awarded the D.C.M. " He volunteered as observer during a bombing attack, and ran along the parapet directing the throws of the bombers. When the attack was held up by a machine gun, with complete disregard of his own safety, he rushed the gun and put the whole team out of action with bombs."

Meanwhile the 49th Division, on the west, behind our old front line, had sent in a small party from the 146th Brigade, who seized Pope's Nose (where the old German front line crosses the Thiepval road), and actually wandered right across our front, with occasional bombing diversions on the way, till they reported to Captain Keep, of the Bedfordshire Regiment, at the north-west corner of the Redoubt, and submitted an application for a few more Germans to kill.

When night fell the position was rather obscure. The 53rd Brigade on our right were in the support line and dug-outs of the south-west corner of the Redoubt, and the Bedfordshire Regiment, with the West Yorkshire Regiment, who had reinforced them, held the more westerly trenches. But everything was so confused that neither Brigade knew exactly what the other was doing on the western face of the stronghold, and night passed in bombing attacks, by which the Germans sought to break what had become our outpost line.

The question of consolidation had to be considered. Only two officers were now left, Major L. H. Keep and his brother, Captain D. S. H. Keep. With two Company Sergeant-Majors who survived, C. Hall and R. M. Brand, they chose a line a little to the rear of the line they had gained, and, with the assistance of some sappers who had come up under Lieutenant Knight, this line was made good and strong posts formed.

Both the Company Sergeant-Majors mentioned above received the D.C.M. I hope there are still many living who remember how Company Sergeant-Major C. Hall's loud voice, heard even above the din of shells and bombs and the clatter of machine guns and rifles, rallied the men at a critical moment. Never was a powerful voice so well used. His action was thus officially described :—

" This warrant officer rallied the supporting troops who were missing their direction, and by his stentorian voice directed them on to their objective. Later he organized bombing and working parties, and was of the greatest assistance to his company commander in the work of consolidating the position gained. Just before the relief of the battalion he took command of the company, all officers having become casualties, and carried out the relief with the greatest skill."

Company Sergeant-Major R. M. Brand also commanded his company on that day, and received the D.C.M. " for conspicuous courage, initiative, and powers of leadership " [to quote again from official sources]. " He took command of his company when all his officers had become casualties, and very ably carried out the consolidation of the position gained."

Mention has already been made of 2nd-Lieutenant Adlam, who was awarded the V.C. at Thiepval. He did equally good work in the second fight, the account of the action for which he received the decoration, after describing his work in Thiepval, already referred to, adding :—

" He again displayed the highest courage in the attack on Schwaben Redoubt. Though again wounded, this time in the right arm, so that he could no longer throw bombs himself, he continued to lead his men with utter contempt of danger till he was ordered to the rear. There is no doubt that this officer, not only by his personal bravery and magnificent example, but also by his prompt and skilful handling of the tactical situation, was largely responsible for the success of the very important minor operation on the morning of the 27th, and materially assisted in the capture of Schwaben Redoubt."

A D.C.M. also went to Lance-Corporal A. W. Harris. " Hearing reinforcements were urgently required, he proceeded on his own initiative to the front line with his Lewis gun, and from an exposed position under heavy fire repulsed repeated counter-attacks. Later he rallied a party of another regiment who were being driven out of a post, and succeeded in holding the post against successive attacks."

On the 29th the 55th Brigade, which had hitherto been in reserve, took over the task which had been so well begun, and the Bedfordshires, badly battered, but with their tails well up, were relieved by the 7th West Kents.

The Bedfordshires had now been fighting since they were brought into the line at midnight 26th-27th at a critical moment.

In their first task, the assault of the last corner of Thiepval, they had lost 1 officer and 43 other ranks killed, and 4 officers and 50 other ranks wounded. Since then they had lost 4 officers and 15 other ranks killed in front of Schwaben Redoubt, and 6 officers and 97 other ranks wounded. Clearly they must be withdrawn for reinforcements.

The taking of the last corner of Thiepval and the defences of Schwaben Redoubt by the Bedfordshire Regiment were essentially " soldiers' battles "—as indeed were so many other actions of a war which made an exceptional call on individual courage and initiative—and all did so well, and so many were selected for special awards, it has been difficult to make a selection, but the foregoing must serve.

From the Field Ambulance point of view, the Thiepval and Schwaben Redoubt operations were the hottest of the whole

Somme fighting, and the clearing of casualties was carried out with the greatest difficulty, alternative routes of evacuation often having to be found to avoid the intense and searching shell fire.

There for the first time a derelict tank was used as a shelter. However, the attention it received from German gunners made it necessary to discontinue its use as a dressing-post in rather quick time, and in future stretcher-bearers generally gave tanks a wide berth.

A story told by a stretcher-bearer well illustrates the ruin and desolation of this area. One of our bearer posts was on the site of Thiepval Château (which was frequently mentioned in the previous chapter). An officer came up and asked a bearer where the Château was. "Sorry, sir, you're standing on it," was the reply.

After the Thiepval and Schwaben Redoubt operations, the Brigade had about three weeks out of the line, chiefly in the Ribeaucourt area, where training was carried on. On October 11th Sir Douglas Haig paid an informal visit, and saw the battalions at work. A move was afterwards made to Albert, and by October 23rd the Brigade was again in the line.

The battalions now found themselves in Regina Trench, near Courcelette, about three miles north-west of Thiepval, with the intention of taking part in an attack on Petit Miraumont, which lay about two miles due north.

"For this attack," writes a Fusilier officer, "the assaulting battalions of the Brigade were to have been the Fusiliers and the Bedfordshire Regiment.

"The weather was awful, and the mud beyond words. Fortunately, the attack did not come off. If it had it must have been a colossal failure. The first objective was, I believe, 1,700 yards away, and in that mud, and after going that distance, the men would have been dead-beat.

"The Brigade was to go on to the Ancre, cross the river, which was in flood and about 300 yards wide, and hold the crossings for the 53rd Brigade to go through. It was seriously suggested that trees might be felled across the Ancre, and the men might cross on them. The only implements for felling trees were bayonets, entrenching tools, and jack-knives !

"We went into the line three or four times with the idea of attacking at dawn on the second morning, but each time it was postponed two or three or four days, and we came out again to Albert. It rained nearly every day ; the trenches had no duck-boards, and were knee-deep in mud. There was one small dug-out which served as two company headquarters, and the trench was continuously enfiladed by shell fire from Loupart Wood. The parapet was always falling in.

"Each time we went in for the attack the men were served out with a haversack ration of potted-meat sandwiches and a hard-boiled egg. Major Meyricke, on the telephone from battalion headquarters, used to inform the company commanders that the attack had been postponed again by the words, ' You *may* eat your sandwiches!'—for if the attack was off, they could eat them whenever they liked, if they had not already done so.

"The men were soaked to the skin with liquid mud for days on end, and after ration-carrying fatigues were dead-beat. It was a long carry, and the mud was appalling. On relief the men sometimes did not get back to Albert till 6 a.m., and had no opportunity of getting properly dry before they went in the line again. The sick rate in the battalions at this time was the worst I have ever known. One morning each battalion in the Brigade had over 150 sick, and one had nearly 250. Eventually the attack was postponed till the New Year, and we were relieved by the Canadians."

It was on November 17th that the Brigade was relieved in the line by the 11th Canadian Brigade, Brigade headquarters moving to billets in Albert, and all battalions to huts south-west of Ovilliers.

The return to the same area in the spring of the following year, and the operations in which Petit Miraumont was at last taken, are dealt with in the next chapter.

The uncomfortable nature of life in Regina Trench is well illustrated by the official accounts of actions for which Military Medals were awarded. I make the following extracts :—

Corporal R. W. Dixon (Fusiliers) : " On one occasion a shell buried two of his platoon, and his prompt action and courage in an exposed position under heavy bombardment resulted in the extrication of both."

Private G. E. Gough (Bedfordshire Regiment) : " During extremely heavy shelling of Regina Trench he remained on duty as signaller in an exposed part of the trench without cover of any kind. Communication with battalion headquarters was repeatedly broken, but on every occasion he went out through the barrage and repaired the wire."

Corporal B. Mulrien (Bedfordshire Regiment) : " Organized a party and dug out four men who had been buried in the trench by a shell. The party was heavily shelled all the time."

Private A. Thompson (Bedfordshire Regiment) : " As stretcher-bearer he showed great devotion to duty, attending to cases under very dangerous and trying circumstances. Having attended to all casualties in his company, he volunteered to go over the open country to another company to assist them, and it was only by direct order of his officer that he did not go."

Corporal W. Dean (Bedfordshire Regiment) : " When not on duty came out of his dug-out during an intense bombardment, and walked from sentry-post to sentry-post, cheering up the men. He was severely wounded, having an arm practically blown off, but after being attended to by a stretcher-bearer continued to encourage the men until sent back to the dressing-station by his officer."

Some good patrol work by the 6th Northamptonshire Regiment attracted notice during this period. 2nd-Lieutenant P. H. Higham of that battalion was awarded the M.C. in the following circumstances':—

" During the night of November 7th, 1916, accompanied by one lance-corporal and one man, he carried out a difficult and dangerous reconnaissance with the greatest bravery and efficiency. After crossing 900 yards of No Man's Land he discovered an enemy strong point. In spite of this he entered the trench, which he reconnoitred for a distance of 400 yards. The information which he brought back was of great value in subsequent operations. During the attack on Thiepval this officer went forward with one lance-corporal and two men to reconnoitre the position for a dump. On arriving there a dug-out containing twenty Germans was found. He shot one, captured the remainder, and formed his dump in their dug-out."

2nd-Lieutenants A. C. Bates and D. I. Gotch, who had done good work at Thiepval, won the M.C. during their tour of duty in Regina Trench. Both were buried several times by shells between October 25th and 29th, but carried on with cheerfulness and courage, which set a fine example to all ranks.

The M.M. was awarded to Sergeant B. Aldham, of the same battalion. " He was in charge of a patrol sent out to reconnoitre an enemy strong point, and brought back valuable information. Before proceeding on his patrol he made a preliminary reconnaissance by himself on his own initiative. On returning he volunteered to take a party out to capture the strong point."

Sergeant J. Corstorphine and Privates G. Rivett and D. Penfold, of the 54th Machine Gun Company, were also awarded the M.M. during this period for digging out buried comrades under fire.

Chapter VIII

BOOM RAVINE

WELCOME days of rest—almost " peace-time soldiering," as we amateurs interpreted the phrase—came to the Brigade at the end of 1916 and in the early days of 1917.

At the end of November the Brigade marched down to the St. Riquier area, near Abbeville, and training was carried on throughout December. On December 14th a move was made to the Canchy area, a few miles farther west, and there Christmas and New Year's Day were spent. In between training there was plenty of recreation, boxing competitions and football matches being got up ; and a Brigade pierrot troop, forerunner of the " Vin Blongs," so well known at a later date, was organized to visit Canchy, Marcheville, and Doinvaast, where the units were billeted. A Brigade cross-country run was brought off on January 6th, and won by Sergeant Bradbury, of the Northamptonshire Regiment.

The Brigade was specially selected to carry out a demonstration attack on the lines of the Somme offensive of July 1st, 1916, on the St. Riquier training area. This took place on December 27th, before the Army Commander and representatives from all Divisions in the Fifth Army, and a good show was put up.

On January 9th a happy association of over two years' standing was broken up, and Sir Ivor Maxse, who trained and brought the Division over to France, coming over to Brigade headquarters to say good-bye on his appointment to command the 18th Corps. There was no formal parade, but each battalion was represented by the officers who had the longest service with the Brigade and Division. At the same time Sir Ivor presented a number of decorations.

On January 11th the Brigade began its march to the forward area, and after halting at Domquer, Fienvillers, and Rubempre, covered the rest of the journey by 'bus. On the 17th we were holding the line south-east of Grandcourt, only about three miles from Thiepval, that place of proud memories for the Brigade.

This was, it will be remembered, the very sector held by the Brigade in October, 1916, and Regina and Desire Trenches, with Miraumont in front, were familiar spots.

Ten days were spent in the line, and though nothing of importance occurred, they were days and nights to remember, for there was a continual hard frost, and one night the temperature fell below zero. Apart from discomfort, this introduced a new problem into trench warfare. If a trench is deep enough to afford cover, the presence even of several feet of water does not affect its safety. But if that water freezes hard and there are only about eighteen inches of cover between the surface of the ice and the top of the parapet, the protection afforded is extremely slight.

This was the sort of thing that happened in certain parts of the line. The Brigade was ever composed of cheerful philosophers, and the discovery that tin hats could be used for the Scottish game of curling in the frozen trenches did much to relieve the monotony. " C " Company of the Bedfordshire Regiment was a very good team, recalls an officer who is accustomed to take a sporting view of life, and was asked how the war stood at that date. But the Germans were poor sportsmen, They would watch the game till they got bored, and then— but hang it all, boredom is no excuse !—they would stop further sport with a few whizzbangs. It will take them a long time to live down that bad sportsmanship, which was fiercely resented by officers and men, who were prepared to accept the ordinary business of " straffing " as all a part of the day's work.

Reliefs were carried out with some difficulty. Duck-boards, which one used to look upon as the only causeway through engulfing seas of mud, now became skating rinks, and climbing the greasy pole is a drawing-room game compared with single-filing down a narrow icy wooden track, near an enemy ready to shoot at sound. Only by wrapping their boots in sandbags could the men keep their feet.

After this short tour in the trenches, the Brigade went back to the St. Martinsart area, indulging in working parties and in rehearsals of the forthcoming attack.

On February 9th they went into the line again for two days, and had a rather lively time, the artillery of both sides being active. On the night of the 10th " A " Company of the Fusiliers (holding the right sector from the west of Miraumont Road to Sixteen Road) rushed and captured a German strong point. The Germans then concentrated machine-gun and trench-mortar fire on the little garrison. Both the officers and nearly all the N.C.Os. became casualties, and in a strong counter-attack the enemy regained the position. Lieutenant Sampson was killed in this affair.

The Brigade had another three days out of the line for rehearsals, and on the night of February 15th-16th took over the battle front for the operations of the 17th. These were part of a big attack on both banks of the Ancre, to seize the high ground giving observation over the upper Ancre Valley.

We were on the south of the Ancre, below Miraumont, and had to attack from in front of Desire Trench due north towards South Miraumont Trench, first across Grandcourt Trench, and then across the deep sunken road known as Boom Ravine, which, so far as this Brigade is concerned, gives its name to the action.

The assaulting battalions were the Northamptonshires (right) and Fusiliers (left). The Middlesex Regiment was in support, and the Bedfordshire Regiment in reserve. The Suffolk Regiment (53rd Brigade) were on our left, and the 2nd Division on our right.

Just why the weather had such frequent pro-German moods during the war is a question to be discussed in a more scientific book than this. But the fact remains that the hard frost, which would have given us almost ideal ground to attack over, broke on the night of the 16th, and most of our troubles were due to the appalling mud which resulted from the untimely thaw.

Our forming-up place was just in front of a depression known as the Gully, and from the Gully a sunken road ran into Boom Ravine. The junction of this sunken road with the Gully was known as "Oxford Circus," and the familiar name may enable me to make the general lie of the land clear to those who know their London.

Assuming that, instead of being in "Oxford Circus" facing Miraumont (a most unhealthy spot in the darkness of the early hours of February 17th), you had the far better luck to be in the real Oxford Circus in London, facing towards Queen's Hall, our forming-up lines would lie to your right and left along Oxford Street. Going towards Queen's Hall and the Langham Hotel, you would first cross the enemy's wire and Grandcourt Trench, and Boom Ravine would be represented by streets running right and left near the church. Beyond, roughly half-right, would be South Miraumont. Now fill Oxford Circus, Oxford Street, and every step that you have to take if you are going to walk to the church, with shell-holes and churned-up ground, knee deep in mud, and call down from heaven deadly hail of shrapnel and high explosive, with rifle and machine-gun fire to sweep every yard of your journey, and you have a fair idea of the conditions.

On the night of the 16th the forming-up lines were taped and our wire cut, in spite of the darkness and some pretty heavy shelling by the enemy. The tapes were from 100 to 200 yards in front of the Gully.

Orders were for all troops to be in position by 4.45 a.m. on the 17th. There were two ways up to the forming-up place, one along the duck-boards (as one might go up Regent Street to Oxford Circus) and one up Cornwall Trench, the only communication trench. Both became very congested, especially the trench, and the scene in the Gully was like a London crowd coming out of a theatre.

Just before 4.30 a.m. the enemy sent up yellow and green lights, and a heavy barrage opened at once on the Gully and the ground immediately to the north. It was discovered afterwards from captured German officers that they had learned full details of the proposed attack, and knew the approximate hour at which it was to be launched.

Both the assaulting battalions suffered heavily in this bombardment, especially the Fusiliers. Crowded together in the Gully and "Oxford Circus," the men had no shelter. It was in the pitchy dark hours before dawn, rain was falling, the ground was deep in slippery mud, and there were no trenches to guide to the forming-up line. One platoon of the Northamptonshire Regiment was almost entirely wiped out as it was led to the forming-up place; and of the total Fusilier casualties in the whole of the operation, one-half were suffered in the Gully and thereabouts. That the battalions were formed up at all, in this dark mouth of hell, was due very largely to their gallant and skilful handling by officers and N.C.Os., and to the courage and discipline of the men themselves, many of whom lay in the mud for hours under heavy shell fire, awaiting the order to go over the top. That, after the terrible ordeal before dawn, they fought their way forward so well as to snatch a very large measure of success out of what might so nearly have been utter disaster speaks volumes for their doggedness and dash.

Some splendid work was done by 2nd-Lieutenants Boulton and Higham and Company Sergeant-Major Cuthbert, of the Northamptonshire Regiment, in getting their men into position. Of the officers of two Fusilier companies in the front line (one on each side of the road leading up to the Ravine), only two—Captain Morton of "A," and Captain Collis Sandes of "B"—were unwounded at zero hour.

At 5.45 a.m. our barrage opened, and the assaulting battalions went forward close up to it towards the first objective. Before he had gone 200 yards, Captain Collis Sandes had a bullet through the neck, and Captain Morton had half his foot taken off by a shell a little farther on. So in the darkness and drizzling rain, over the slippery ground all cut up by constant bombardment, through shell fire and the thresh of machine-gun fire and sniping, the waves went on. The Trench Mortar Battery did good work, getting forward with the assaulting line, though heavily burdened with guns and ammunition, and losing heavily. The section of the 54th Machine Gun Company attached to the assaulting battalions also went forward well. As soon as our barrage opened, the enemy sent up showers of spray lights, and some green, and in answer to this appeal his guns put down a barrage on our front. It was, however, very short-lived, and it seemed that our counter-battery work was very good.

On arriving before Grandcourt Trench it was found that much of the wire was still uncut, and the delay in finding the gaps gave the enemy time to get away and take up fresh positions beyond the trench and on both sides of Boom Ravine. The movement along the front of the wire to find gaps also led to some loss of direction and mixing up of companies. It must be remembered that it was still dark. Not till 6.5 a.m. was there light enough to see more than a few yards. On the whole, the wire was better cut in front of the Fusiliers than in front of the Northamptonshire Regiment. In the case of the latter, the left and centre companies were held up by rifle and machine-gun fire at this point so long as to loose the barrage.

Meanwhile the Fusiliers had been able to get forward, and Boom Ravine was reached at last. Every officer was now a casualty, and the four companies were badly mixed up; but Company Sergeant-Major Fitterer, of " B " Company, although he had a bullet through the thigh, reorganized the men and led them forward. He was well assisted in this by Sergeants Choate (" A " Company), Berry (" C " Company), and Hazell (" D " Company).

At the Ravine the Fusiliers took over 100 prisoners, and these were at once pressed into service by Major J. C. Sale, D.S.O., then regimental medical officer, as stretcher-bearers.

The right company of the Northamptonshire Regiment was also able to get forward from Grandcourt Trench with the barrage, according to time-table, but the left and centre companies were delayed, thus leaving a gap between the left of the Northamptonshire Regiment and the right of the Fusiliers.

The Fusiliers, so splendidly rallied and led by Company Sergeant-Major Fitterer, and the right company of the Northamptonshire Regiment, advanced from the Ravine soon after 6.30 a.m., leaving men of the Middlesex Regiment, who had been sent over as " moppers-up," to carry out their good work among the dug-outs. But there had been so much delay, owing to the mixing up of companies, the heavy casualties among officers, and the great difficulty of crossing this deep sunken road, that the barrage was lost. Accordingly, when they arrived before South Miraumont Trench, they were not only held up by uncut wire, but saw their barrage far ahead and the Germans lining the trench, and could do nothing but drop into shell-holes. A few of the Northamptonshire Regiment, under Lieutenant T. R. Price, D.S.O., the adjutant, who had now come up, and 2nd-Lieutenant Higham, M.C., did actually succeed in entering the trench, but there could be no hope of staying there, with every other part of our line held up.

Soon after this, about 8.30 a.m., a strong German counter-attack was delivered from Petit Miraumont. From captured German orders and statements by prisoners, it appears that these were specially trained counter-attack troops, brought up as soon as news of our intended attack reached them the previous night. They consisted largely of marksmen and machine gunners. Their fire was extremely accurate, while we were in poor plight, most of our rifles and Lewis guns being clogged, owing to the lying in mud in the dark before the attack, and the bad ground that had to be covered in the advance.

Whatever the exact cause, the British line, seeing no appreciable effect produced by their fire on the advancing Germans, began to fall back. Lieutenant Price now handled the Northamptonshire Regiment with the greatest skill and gallantry. He moved to and fro along the line under heavy fire, steadying the retirement, and then, seeing that our right was in the air, swung the little body of survivors to form a defensive flank on the West Miraumont Road. Lieutenant-Colonel R. J. F. Meyricks, of the 11th Fusiliers, who had taken over command of the Northamptonshire Regiment as recently as February 3rd, was killed while going forward from the Ravine with Lieutenant Price.

In the meantime Lieutenant-Colonel C. C. Carr, D.S.O. commanding the Fusiliers, and Captain G. F. J. Cumberlege, D.S.O., his adjutant, had come up and got hold of the Fusiliers, together with remnants of other battalions from the Brigade on our left, and steadied that part of the line. Later this left flank was taken over by Lieutenant C. F. Chute, Brigade Signalling Officer, and Lieutenant Pearcy, Fusiliers Signalling Officer.

The line was now held until the afternoon, when, reinforced by two companies of the Middlesex Regiment, all that was left of the two assaulting battalions again moved forward almost to the crest of the spur overlooking South Miraumont Trench, and occupied a series of rifle and machine-gun posts. This line was handed over to the 8th East Surrey Regiment (55th Brigade) on the evening of the 18th.

Our casualties were heavy, the Brigade losing in all 14 officers killed, 25 wounded, and 2 missing. Of other ranks, 115 were killed, 423 wounded, and 161 missing.

Mention has already been made of the employment of German prisoners as stretcher-bearers. By keeping them constantly at work, all the Brigade casualties were evacuated within a few hours, though it was a very long carry over heavy ground. The difficulties that the medical service had to grapple with that day were indeed very great. Stretcher cases were carried 2,400 yards from regimental aid-posts in Boom Ravine to tramhead at Hessian Trench, then pushed along the tram-line 2,300 yards to the advanced dressing-station. The carry was uphill all the way, under fire, and over ground all churned up by shells and knee-deep in mud. In the opinion of the medical officers of the Brigade it was the heaviest work the bearers have ever had to perform.

LIEUT.-COLONEL A. E. PERCIVAL, D.S.O., M.C.,
Who Commanded the 7th (S.) Batt. Bedfordshire Regiment from January, 1918, to May, 1918; and 2nd Batt. Bedfordshire Regiment from May, 1918, to March, 1919.

The Late LIEUT.-COLONEL G. R. RIPLEY,
Who Commanded the 6th (S.) Batt. Northamptonshire Regt.
from September, 1914, to October, 1916.

LIEUT.-COLONEL R. TURNER, D.S.O.,
Who Commanded the 6th (S.) Batt. Northamptonshire Regt.
from March, 1917, to the Armistice.

In this attack all behaved with such courage in exceptionally trying circumstances that to attempt any complete record of individual gallantry would be to give a nominal roll of those who went over in the darkness and mud of that grim February dawn. In dealing with some outstanding cases one must take the risk of omitting many equally deserving of mention.

It will be remembered that the Middlesex Regiment, as supporting battalion, pushed two companies into the front line at a critical moment when we were getting some pretty bad hammering on the spur before South Miraumont Trench. 2nd-Lieutenant W. B. Godwin, of the Middlesex Regiment, did gallant work at this point. With a few men he got about 200 yards to the north-east of our objective, owing to a fog that had come down. The enemy counter-attacked, and, though greatly outnumbered, 2nd-Lieutenant Godwin and his men stood their ground and fought till all but one were killed. This fine stand was effective in breaking up a threatening counter-attack. Unhappily, the gallant officer himself was killed. Lieutenant V. D. Corbett was another Middlesex officer who did good work in fixing and consolidating our final line of defence under heavy rifle and shell fire. Acting Company Sergeant-Major Kerr of the same battalion will also be remembered. All the officers of his company having become casualties, he reorganized the company, and directed the work of clearing dug-outs in the Ravine until killed.

Mention has already been made of Lieutenant C. F. Chute, R.E., Brigade Signal Officer. He had gone forward to the first objective to establish telephone communication with a visual station. While doing this he saw that the enemy counter-attack on our right was driving back the line in some confusion, owing to the loss of nearly all the officers. He at once went forward, rallied the men under heavy fire, checked the withdrawal, and then got into communication with Brigade headquarters, giving such a timely and accurate report that steps could be taken which resulted in the recapture of most important high ground.

The signalling officer of the Fusiliers, 2nd-Lieutenant G. S. Pearcy, did equally gallant work. During the counter-attack he rallied the men of his battalion, when all company officers were casualties, and by his fine example under fire did much to restore the situation. For a great part of the time he took command of the remnants of his battalion in the front line.

While writing of the signals service one must say a word for the good work done by the men. Pioneer Walter Jones, R.E., attached to Brigade headquarters, worked without rest for forty-eight hours under constant shell fire, laying lines up to our most forward troops and repairing breaks. The runners also did excellent work, delivering messages under heavy fire. Privates F. C. Ross (Fusiliers), A. H. Philby (Bedfordshires), and

R. A. Young (Middlesex Regiment), all attached to Brigade headquarters, attracted attention for devotion to duty. Private S. G. Hazell, of the Fusiliers, also did fine work as a runner, invariably carrying ammunition or Lewis gun drums forward on his own initiative when taking a message, and very greatly helping officers by his accurate observations and reports. Privates E. C. Bailey, H. A. Ashby, and T. H. Bryan, of the Northamptonshire Regiment, did equally good work in keeping up communication in their battalion.

Turning to the officers of the Fusiliers, the work of Captain G. F. J. Cumberlege, then adjutant of the battalion, has already been mentioned, and his action in rallying men of his own and other battalions undoubtedly restored order and enabled us to hold on to an important ridge at a very critical moment. Nor would anyone present regard this record as complete without a word about the work of Captain G. B. Morton, whose courage and coolness did so much to form up his company and get it forward, until he was seriously wounded, and Captain (now Major) J. C. Sale, medical officer of the battalion, whose care for the wounded under heavy fire was an inspiration to all ranks. Lieutenant Bernard Ashmole, in temporary command of his company, was wounded in the knee at an early stage, but hobbled forward almost to the first objective till he collapsed with a second wound.

The fine work of Company Sergeant-Major P. J. Fitterer has already been dealt with. He was ably assisted by a number of N.C.Os. of the battalion. There was Lance-Corporal G. Morgan, who volunteered to take an important message when three runners had already been killed or wounded in trying to get this message through. He succeeded in his task, although blown up on the way. Later he rallied a party of men of another regiment who had started to retire, and kept them in position for the rest of the day under heavy fire.

Lance-Corporal J. W. Butler was another prominent figure. When all his company officers were casualties he took his Lewis gun team forward and kept his gun in action when all the team except one ammunition carrier had fallen, and when the line was compelled to withdraw was the last to come in, bringing back not only his own gun, but another which had been abandoned. Other good work with Lewis guns that attracted attention was that of Corporal C. Franklin, Corporal C. J. Diamond, Lance-Corporal W. G. Oliver, Lance-Corporal P. Salt, Private A. N. Nellor, and Private J. Ball.

With all officers knocked out so early, it was essentially a day for initiative and leadership on the part of N.C.Os. Sergeant F. W. Hazell commanded his company with great coolness and ability throughout the day. Corporal E. A. Hart organized his company under heavy fire when there were no officers left. Later he volunteered to take command of an advanced post, and held it until relieved the following day. Platoons were commanded and led by Sergeants H. Berry and B. Armstrong, Private H. Thorns. Good work in tending and bringing in the wounded under fire was done by Privates W. Whare and E. W. Trott.

Turning to the Northamptonshire Regiment, it has already been seen what an important part the work and example of Lieutenant T. R. Price (then adjutant) played in saving a critical situation. Nor will any who survived that day forget the gallantry of Lieutenant C. G. Kemp, the medical officer, whose cheerful and unceasing work, in spite of many casualties to stretcher-bearers, got the battlefield cleared in such short time.

As in the Fusiliers, so in the Northamptonshire Regiment, the early loss of practically every officer threw a heavy responsibility on the other ranks, and they rose splendidly to the occasion. During the forming up of his company under fire Company Sergeant-Major O. Cuthbert stood on top of a bank the whole time, until the last man was in position, and his coolness did much to steady the men in a very unpleasant situation. All the officers of the company were casualties as soon as the company moved forward, and this warrant officer was shortly afterwards wounded, but refused to go back until he had handed over the company properly to the senior sergeant. Among the N.C.Os. who showed courage and good leadership in carrying on were Sergeants W. D. Toe, G. Quartermain, A. C. Gilbert, S. Flanagan, Corporal W. R. Thompson, and Lance-Corporals A. Lee, W. Wreford, and J. Hall.

At least two other individual efforts attracted notice. Private Charles Chantrell was servant to the officer commanding the leading wave. When this officer and most of the N.C.Os. became casualties, before reaching the Ravine, he at once took charge of the platoon, lead them against a number of the enemy, whom he cleared out, reorganized in the Ravine, and proceeded with the advance.

When Grandcourt Trench was reached, many Germans were found lying out in front, apparently dead. It occurred to Private J. W. Walsh to lift the cap from one of them. The man at once jumped up and held up his hands. The rest of the Germans who were also shamming dead were promptly dealt with. A machine gun and a number of rifles were lying by them, and but for Private Walsh's action the whole company would have been shot in the back.

In the Middlesex battalion a great deal of excellent individual work was also done when Boom Ravine was reached. 2nd-Lieutenant R. Charlesworth was the only officer left in two companies. Taking command, he carried out the work of dug-out clearing with great energy and thoroughness, and organized the consolidation in a very capable manner. In the same work Company Sergeant-Major J. Warner also distinguished himself.

Operations in front of South Miraumont Trench, when two companies of the Middlesex Regiment had been moved up to the front line, was marked by some fine examples of initiative. When an enemy machine gun became a nuisance, Sergeant T. Travers, although suffering from a painful wound, led a bombing attack over the open, blew up the gun and some of the gunners, and took the rest prisoners.

Privates H. S. Elliott and W. Taylor did similar good work. At one time the advance was held up by about fifty of the enemy, and by enfilade fire from a machine gun. Rushing forward with their Lewis gun on their own initiative to a spot where they got a better field of fire, they brought their gun into action with such good effect that the enemy's machine gun was knocked out, and the party of Germans were all killed, wounded, or taken prisoners.

During a counter-attack a certain platoon engaged in consolidating Boom Ravine lost its officer and sergeant. Private A. Humphries at once took command, reorganized the men, and dug in, saving the situation at a critical moment.

In the case of one of the companies, Sergeant G. Rowe took command when all the officers were casualties, took the men forward to the objective, and continued in command till relieved by an officer two days later.

Chapter IX

THE GERMAN RETREAT OF 1917

THE almost immediate result of the operation of which the Boom Ravine action formed a part was a German retirement towards the prepared defensive positions already known as the Hindenburg Line.

The Brigade had a short but welcome spell of rest and training before taking part in the pursuit. Relieved in the line on February 18th, the battalions were first in the Martinsart area, and on March 2nd moved to the Thiepval area. Snow and rain, road-making parties, inspections and practice attacks, were the chief forms of gaiety.

On the 12th the Brigade relieved the 53rd in the line, in the expectation of attacking the Loupart Line at an early date. The units were disposed as follows :—

12th Middlesex Regiment — Right flank assaulting battalion.

6th Northamptonshire Regiment — Right centre assaulting battalion.

7th Bedfordshire Regiment—Left centre assaulting battalion.

11th Royal Fusiliers—Left flank battalion, to form a left defensive flank to the attack of the other three battalions.

Sections of the 54th Machine Gun Company were distributed along the front and in reserve. The 54th Trench Mortar Battery was held in reserve. Brigade headquarters were in a dug-out on the West Miraumont road.

Owing to the darkness of the night, the bad state of the ground after weeks of snow and rain, and the difficulty of taking over a front which consisted of a line of strong points and posts, the relief was not completed till 6 a.m. on the morning of March 13th.

The Fusiliers on the left came in for a good deal of sniping from Achiet-le-petit. Lieutenant Little, battalion sniping officer, was killed by a sniper. He was an artist, and designed two Christmas cards for Christmas, 1916. One in colours, for the Fusiliers, represented a Fusilier taking part in the July attack on the Somme ; the other, for the Brigade, was a pen-and-ink sketch of the square at Albert, showing the church with the leaning figure of the Virgin and the square crammed with troops.

Everything was now ready for an attack which did not come off, owing to the natural law that it takes two to make a quarrel, and the people we had arranged to quarrel with did not wait for the show.

In this connection, and as showing that hardships and hard work are not the inclusive monopoly of the fighting troops, the following account of what an attack means to the clerical staff at Brigade headquarters is of interest. Corporal E. W. A. Campbell describes the affair as he saw it :—

"In those days of trench-to-trench attacks very detailed information and orders were issued for each assault, entailing a great deal of typing and duplicating work. The Brigade clerks worked a whole day and night getting out the orders (luckily rum was issued that night, and kept them going !), and the following day had to pack up, load wagons, and move up to forward headquarters—a dug-out in the West Miraumont road.

"On the way up there we had to pass through Grandcourt, which had previously been obliterated by our heavies, and the state of the roads was almost beyond description. The passable part of the road was naturally very narrow, and a caterpillar had become ditched at a very bad spot. The R.Es. managed to construct a *détour* by bridging shellholes, and all transport had to pass round by an unmetalled track. Owing to the state of the ground, all artillery ammunition was being taken up by pack animals, and long streams of these were continually passing to and fro.

"The *détour* tracks naturally became like a quagmire in a very short time, and, to make things worse, one of the Brigade headquarters' wagons missed one of the small bridges with the off-wheels, and tipped sideways into the water, putting a pair of mules on their backs. It took about three hours to get this out, and then it could only be done by unloading the wagon and man-handling it. All wheeled traffic was held up, but the pack animals managed to get through by splashing through the water. Many of them were so exhausted that they lay down and refused to get up again, and were dragged to one side and left to die in the mud.

"The Brigade headquarters transport, with clerks, servants, and other personnel, finally arrived at the West Miraumont road about midnight, and unloaded at the corner just in Petit Miraumont—on to a dead mule which could not be seen in the mud and darkness ! There was hardly any trace of a road. It was simply a mass of shell-holes, full of water, and one went down knee-deep in mud as one tried to pick a way between the holes. Stationery boxes and office gear had to be carried to the dug-out about 100 yards up the road, and the going was so heavy that the clerks were often brought to their knees with boxes on their shoulders.

"The dug-out was found to be a very poor one. It had either been strained by shell fire or damaged by the Bosche before leaving, and it leaked very badly. It was also very small, and the space allotted for the office was about 4 feet square. There was one small table on which to do typing, duplicating, and all other office work, and the clerks had to sleep either under this table or on the stairs. They had been working continually for over forty hours, so simply went to sleep wherever they happened to fall.

"The crowning joke came between 3 and 4 a.m., about an hour after they had gone to sleep, when a message arrived announcing that 'Jerry' had run away. The Brigade Major came in for somebody to write a message, and was quite upset when he found that all his efforts to wake the clerks were futile. However, one of the signallers finally managed to do so, and one can imagine the thoughts of the clerks when they found that the work which had taken so many hours to do had all been in vain."

What had happened was soon made clear. An Anzac patrol had entered the Loupart line at the south-eastern edge of Loupart Wood at 3 a.m., and found that the Germans had disappeared in the darkness, going through the motions of folding their tents like the Arabs and silently stealing away in the most approved manner.

Patrols had now to be sent forward, a particularly cheering job, as we had only just arrived, the relief was barely complete, and we had not seen our front by daylight. However, by 10 a.m. the Brigade had moved forward, dealt with a belt of uncut wire as well as possible, and occupied the Loupart line from its junction with the Miraumont-Achiet-le-Grand Railway on the left to about the west end of Loupart Wood on our right, where we joined with the 6th Brigade (2nd Division). The Fusiliers again formed a defensive left flank.

Battle patrols pushed forward by the Bedfordshire, Northamptonshire, and Middlesex Regiments gained the Achiet-le-Petit-Grevillers road, with little opposition except for some machine-gun fire. But it soon became evident that the enemy was still in Achiet-le-Petit, and was holding on to the Bihucourt line. Some important high ground was occupied by the Bedfordshire Regiment, after a short skirmish in which two machine guns were captured, but night came down with no alteration in the general position.

The Division on our left having failed so far to take Achiet-le-Petit, the Fusiliers, holding our left flank, had on the whole the busiest time. Captain N. R. Neate, of the Fusiliers, did good work throughout the day in protecting his battalions' left flank, and, though wounded in the leg early in the proceedings, refused to leave his company till evening, when assured that the line was safe against counter-attack.

It was on the same day that Lieutenant D. Fuller, of the Fusiliers, did a gallant piece of work in rescuing one of his platoon. The man had been embedded in the mud for some hours. Although his hands were frostbitten and poisoned, Fuller dug with his hands for three and a half hours, no tools being available. Through a heavy barrage at dawn, and much sniping afterwards in an exposed place where three men had been killed by a sniper the previous day, he toiled on till he had released the man. In this task he was assisted by acting Company Sergeant-Major W. T. Burch, who worked with him till he could hardly move with cold and cramp.

Much good patrolling over a dangerous space, in full view of enemy snipers, was done at this time by 2nd-Lieutenant E. L. Jones, of the same battalion. On one occasion all three men who went out with him were killed, and he had to lie motionless while snipers put bullet after bullet into the dead men. He brought back most valuable information.

Corporal W. Whare, in charge of the Fusilier stretcher-bearers, also showed great gallantry and devotion to duty on this and following days, searching out and dressing the wounded under heavy fire. Another stretcher-bearer, Lance-Corporal T. Watson, who was working with him, volunteered to take a party of stretcher-bearers beyond our lines to a spot swept by snipers and machine gunners to find a wounded officer, and in a gully attended to the wounded for two hours under heavy fire.

Early on the 14th Germans were seen massing near the railway-junction south-west of Achiet-le-Grand, apparently with a view to retaking the high ground which, as already mentioned, had been seized by the Bedfordshires the previous day. The enemy shelled this ground heavily, but a concentration of all our available guns on the German masses put an end to any threat from that direction. Apart from this there was little doing throughout the day, but our patrols were frequently sent forward, and immediately came under heavy machine-gun fire.

Until the morning of the 17th patrols were the chief form of activity, but there was an air of expectancy over the whole Brigade, for everything pointed to a big German withdrawal. Officers and men, sick of trench warfare, with its constant strain and occasional advances of a few yards at terrible cost, were asking themselves whether we were to have open warfare at last. Though the end was still eighteen months away, and the fortune of war was to give us many ups and downs, this was the first welcome sign of the cracking of the German line.

Just before dawn on the 15th a Middlesex Regiment patrol worked its way through the Bihucourt line into Bihucourt village itself, where Germans and transport were seen. As soon as this report came in, the officer commanding the Middlesex Regiment sent forward a strong battle patrol to occupy the

Bihucourt line, and the Bedfordshires endeavoured to advance in the direction of Achiet-le-Grand. But, probably owing to the fact that the first patrol had been seen, these battle patrols came under very heavy machine-gun fire from Bihucourt and Achiet-le-Grand villages, and they were unable to advance. They at once took cover in folds in the ground, and casualties were few.

During the day the enemy heavily shelled our forward positions, but this was easier to put up with in view of the hopeful outlook, for Division had ordered that, in view of a probable enemy withdrawal, we were to have an advance-guard of all arms ready to go through. The war seemed to be rapidly improving, and we were well on our toes for the word " go."

Early on the 17th our patrols reported the Bihucourt line unoccupied, and the Middlesex Regiment occupied the village of that name with little opposition and few casualties, but were unable to advance beyond owing to heavy machine-gun fire. Shortly afterwards the Bedfordshire Regiment also got forward, and occupied the village of Achiet-le-Grand with little loss, and at the same time Achiet-le-Petit was occupied by the Division on our left.

During these operations Private Christopher August Cox, of the Bedfordshire Regiment, was awarded the V.C. for his fine work as a stretcher-bearer. The official account of his action reads as follows :—

" For conspicuous gallantry and devotion to duty as a stretcher-bearer during operations in front of Achiet-le-Grand on March 15th, 1917, and subsequent days.

" During the attacks on the 15th, under heavy rifle, machine-gun, and shell fire on an exposed crest, Private Cox worked continuously, carrying back wounded men on his shoulders. On the 16th and 17th he continued this work without rest, and with a complete disregard of his own safety.

" This man has been in every engagement in which his battalion has taken part since July, 1916, and has always displayed the highest example of unselfishness, devotion, and personal courage."

Much good work was done during the patrolling activities of these few days.

On one occasion Sergeant H. A. Clarke, of the Bedfordshire Regiment, with one man, carried out a daring reconnaissance for 300 yards along a trench leading to the enemy's position, and later led his platoon with great skill. When some of his men were buried, he worked for half an hour under heavy shell fire digging them out.

During the same period Sergeant Walter Fritz, of the Northamptonshire Regiment, also distinguished himself on patrol, on one occasion exploring some 400 yards of enemy trench, and bringing back very useful information. It was he who, on the morning of March 13th, reported to his battalion that the enemy had evacuated the Loupart line on their front.

In the case of the Middlesex Regiment much good work was also done, notably by Sergeants A. Hampson, J. Kenney, and S. V. Whale, not only in carrying out valuable patrol work, but in leading their platoons in difficult circumstances. Lance-Corporal H. J. Langley and Private John Dunlop were also noted for good work on patrol.

No one who was there will be likely to forget the fine work of the machine guns and the gallantry of the gunners. Corporal J. Goodall, a Yorkshire Territorial attached to the 54th Machine Gun Company, took command of two guns when his officer and sergeant were casualties, and fought them with great courage and skill. Three Gordons, also attached to the Brigade's Machine Gun Company, displayed the same fine spirit. They were Lance-Corporal J. Douglas, who, when all the rest of his team were casualties, remained on sentry at his gun position for eight hours under heavy shell fire, and Privates D. Lees and A. Bradley, who kept their gun in action in a very exposed place, and so helped the infantry forward, when the rest of their team were killed. Later they dug out three men who had been buried under heavy shelling.

Before dawn on the 18th Bedfordshire and Middlesex patrols found that the enemy had made a further withdrawal from his line of posts north-east of Achiet-le-Grand and Bihucourt. These two battalions were then ordered to push patrols forward and make good the ground 800 yards beyond the aforementioned villages, to allow of an advanced guard passing through our outpost line at Bihucourt. It seemed too good to be true, after knowing nothing and hearing nothing of anything but trench warfare since arriving in France, to be setting out into open country with an advance guard. Were the weary days of trench warfare giving place to open warfare at last? The very words " advanced guard " were cheerful and inspiring. This was " Infantry Training " and " Field Service Regulations " come true, and we asked for nothing better than to tear up all the latter-day manuals on trench warfare and get on with the war.

The advanced guard was commanded by Lieutenant-Colonel R. Turner, D.S.O., commanding the 6th Northamptonshire Regiment, and composed as follows :—

> 6th Northamptonshire Regiment.
> 1 Squadron Yorkshire Dragoons.
> 1 Section 54th M.G. Company.
> 1 Company 80th Field Company R.E.
> 1 Section 82nd Battery R.F.A.

At 8 a.m. on March 18th it passed through our outpost line, with the village of Ervilliers, three miles almost due north of

Bihucourt, as its objective. It was the first fine day of spring, the ground was drying up, there was sunshine over the countryside, and we were moving over unshelled, unshattered country, with officers mounted and a march of no less than three miles into " enemy country " before us. A good war indeed !

Cavalry patrols were on ahead, followed by a line of infantry scouts, then the two leading companies of the Northamptonshire Regiment in artillery formation, with the rest of the advance guard following in column of route. That progress in fours into land so recently held by the Bosche was the crowning joy, and as the ground was drying up, we were able to go straight across country, independent of roads, to where the little village of Ervilliers stood on its hilltop.

Brigade headquarters were moved to just south of Bihucourt. The other units of the group remained in their present positions.

The advance guard reached Ervilliers after an eventful march, the cavalry failing to get into touch with the enemy till they reached the high ground beyond the village, on the way to St. Leger. An outpost line on the line of the Ervilliers-Behagnies road was occupied that night, and on the following morning the march was continued a further two and a half miles north-east to St. Leger, which was occupied with little opposition. During this day's march some Indian Cavalry (Lucknow Cavalry Brigade) co-operated.

After the occupation of St. Leger, Croisilles, a small town about two miles farther on, was found to be strongly held. The advance guard therefore took up an outpost line roughly on the line of the St. Leger-Vaulx-Vrancourt road, the latter place having been occupied by the 1st Anzacs. In the afternoon the Fusiliers were brought up on the right of the Northamptonshire Regiment, with headquarters and two reserve companies at Mory. Brigade headquarters and the Bedfordshire Regiment moved forward to Ervilliers, and the Middlesex Regiment to Behagnies and Sapignies. Indian cavalry patrols protected our left flank. Up to the present we had seen nothing of the Bosche, with the exception of one found asleep in his billet, and sent back a prisoner on a cable cart to Bihucourt.

Things were going very well, but that the Germans were not exactly in full flight, and that it was unwise to push forward " into the blue," was shown by an incident which some of the Fusiliers' officers will remember. Colonel Carr, commanding that battalion, was told by the commanding officer of the battalion he relieved at Mory that Ecoust (about four miles farther east) was unoccupied, that his second-in-command had ridden up to it, and could have ridden right through it if he had had time. He urged Colonel Carr to report that he was in possession, and was quite hurt at a refusal. Next morning the Anzacs on our right attacked Ecoust, but were met by heavy machine-gun fire and suffered heavy casualties, and as a matter of fact the place was not taken until a week or two later.

Orders were issued that night (March 19th) for the advance guard to push forward next morning, with a view to occupying Croisilles if it were not too strongly held by the enemy.

During the night one section of the 82nd Battery R.F.A. was moved into action to support the proposed assault, and at dawn on March 20th the advance guard moved off. The attack was supported by the " Chestnut " Battery R.H.A., as well as the field guns already mentioned, and by overhead machine-gun fire by the 54th Machine Gun Company, posted south of St. Leger. Cavalry protected the flanks, the Corps Cavalry on the right, and the Indian Cavalry on the left.

The four companies of the Northamptonshire Regiment advanced in line—" A," " B," " C," " D," from right to left. Their attack followed roughly the line of a valley running from St. Leger to Croisilles, " A " Company being on the south of the valley, " B " seeking to work up the valley itself, and " C " and " D " advancing on the northerly slope.

Things did not go well, and it was soon evident that the place was too strongly held for a one-battalion attack with so little artillery support. " A " Company were unable to leave the wood in which they had deployed for the attack, owing to heavy shelling and machine-gun fire, and suffered rather heavy casualties.

" B " Company had better luck, managing to work up the valley and dislodge a German advanced post, and making good progress in spite of heavy shelling.

" C " and " D " Companies, on the northern slope of the valley, got ahead at first, but after going 400 or 500 yards came under heavy machine-gun and shell fire, and were held up.

By 10.30 a.m. it became evident that the attack could not succeed, and the rather difficult job of extricating the assaulting companies had to be carried out. This was done in perfect order, and by 12.30 all were back in the outpost line they had been holding, except about forty men of " D " Company, who were collected by Sergeant F. D. Lawrence in a fold of ground where they were hidden from the enemy, but from which it was not wise to move by daylight. There they decided to lie till dark. But about 4 p.m. a party of Germans came up on their right, threatening to outflank them. They therefore came back in small parties without casualty. They left behind one or two wounded men, who were recovered the same evening by the 8th Devonshire Regiment, who relieved the Northamptonshire Regiment.

Sergeant J. C. Tite, already wearing the Military Medal for gallantry, led his platoon forward under fire, in the absence of an officer, and when the order came to withdraw brought them out of the firing line in the same cool and skilful manner.

The cavalry on either flank were also unable to get forward, owing to machine-gun fire. Two companies of the Bedfordshire Regiment were moved up to St. Leger to support the Northamptonshires' attack, but in the circumstances were not put into the line.

Arrangements were then made for more artillery to be brought up for a further attack on the following day. However, that afternoon news came that the Brigade was to be relieved by the 20th Brigade (7th Division), and by 7 p.m. this relief had been carried out, the Northamptonshires handing over to the 8th Devonshires, and the Fusiliers to the 1st Gordons.

On the following day the 54th Brigade was concentrated in the Bihucourt area, and the first little experience of open warfare was over, to be renewed exactly a year later, with the Germans doing the pushing, and ourselves doing the rearguard work and the withdrawing. But that is a later story.

The Brigade was now sent on a little tour of France, to end up eventually in the spot where they started. On March 22nd they marched to the Contay area (west of Albert). The next day's march (due west) brought them to the Villers-Bocage area.

Here the Army tried an experiment in concentrating a Division in lorries. It was a weird and wonderful performance. The units of the Brigade were scattered over an area roughly six miles north of Amiens, and the problem, as seen by higher authority, to get them to an area a mile or two south-west of the city—say, a three-hour route march. As the experiment was seen by at least one battalion, it meant a two-mile march to where the lorries were to be met, a four-hour wait for the lorries, a four-hour journey by lorry, and then a six-mile route march to billets. No rations were available, as transport had been sent on ahead. It was encouraging to hear a fortnight later that " the experiment was most successful."

This had brought the Brigade to the south-west of Amiens. Headquarters, with the Machine Gun Company and the Trench Mortar Battery, were at Revelles; the Fusiliers, Northamptonshire Regiment, 54th Field Ambulance, and 80th Field Company , R.E., were at Dury; the Bedfordshire Regiment at Bovelles; and the Middlesex Regiment at Vers.

On March 26th the Brigade entrained for the north, and on the following day detrained in the Aire area, being billeted at Thiennes, Steenbeck, and Guarbeck, about half-way between Bethune and St. Omer.

While here news was received that General T. H. Shoubridge, commanding the Brigade, who had proceeded on leave when we came out of the line at St. Leger, had been recalled to command the 7th Division, and on April 6th Brigadier-General G. Cunliffe-Owen took over command of the Brigade.

Training, with football and boxing tournaments and cross-country runs, now occupied our days.

On April 21st the Brigade moved a few miles south to the Busnes area, and continued training till the 26th, when a move was made yet a little farther south to the Pernes area. The following day's march was to Bryas, a little north of St. Pol, where the Brigade entrained for Arras.

Arras was not reached till nearly 11 p.m., and then followed a march of some miles south-east to Neuville Vitasse. It was after 1 a.m. on April 28th when at last the weary battalions found themselves among the ruins of the village and the trenches and shell-holes in front, where they bivouacked. The word went round that we were close up to the Hindenburg line, and everyone wondered what next would happen. The sector in front of Heninel was taken over, and all was in trim for the next attack.

On the night of May 1st Captain H. M. Eldridge, of the Northamptonshire Regiment, commanding the 54th Trench Mortar Battery, did a gallant piece of work. A shell burst on a dump of 18-pounder ammunition, setting fire to the camouflage covering. Although knowing that it might explode at any minute, he rushed to the dump and, no water being available, put out the fire by throwing earth and stamping on it, thus saving the ammunition and the lives of many men who were near at hand.

One hopes that there are many Fusiliers still left who remember an amusing incident—at least, it seemed amusing at the time, and served to brighten a tired and " fed up " moment—when the battalion was marching into this sector from Arras.

Late at night a company came to a railway level-crossing, the gates of which were shut. The Major in command walked to the gate-keeper's cottage, and after much knocking at the door, an old Frenchman appeared in what he may have called his *robes de nuit*.

The Major was not fluent in French, but having faith that pigeon-English would take a man anywhere, solemnly said : " Plentee English soldier come ! Open gates, quick, quick !" The old Frenchman did not grasp this at all, and the Major repeated it louder, but still with no result. Thereupon the Major became furious, and shouted at the top of his voice : " Plentee English soldier come ! Open gates, quick, quick !"

The Frenchman again shook his head. Thereupon the humour of the situation dawned upon the Major, who burst into laughter, saying : " Hang these Frenchmen ! They're so ———— dense !" A man of the company who knew a little French then intervened, the gates were opened, and the march was resumed. But the men no longer dragged their legs wearily along. They now stepped out cheerily, singing to all the popular tunes of the day : " Plentee English soldier come ! Open gates, quick, quick !"

I suppose the whole point of the story is that it has no real point at all, but it serves at least to show how slight are the humours on which men will seize to cheer themselves up in weary moments, and perhaps that is an excuse for so many stories of this war that look a little thin when set down in cold blood.

Chapter X

CHERISY

THE attack on May 3rd was to be against the Cherisy position, about four miles north-west of the point the Brigade had reached in its pursuit of the retreating Germans in March.

The Brigade front was from Cherisy on the left nearly to Fontaine-les-Croisilles on the right. Fontaine Trench, which was heavily wired, and about 500 yards from our forming-up line, covered Cherisy. Our task was to force the line of the Sensee River, which here runs roughly north and south, between the above mentioned villages, then to push forward to the high ground east of Cherisy, and dig in there. The operation was part of a big attack from Bullecourt in the south almost to Lens in the north. Our jumping-off line consisted of trenches and shell-holes about 150 yards west of the crest between Heninel and Cherisy, and from this point there was no observation over Cherisy or the Sensee Valley.

The assaulting battalions were the Bedfordshire Regiment on the right and the Middlesex Regiment on the left. "B" Company of the Fusiliers (Captain Neate) was attached to the Middlesex Regiment to "mop-up" Cherisy village, and two platoons of "D" Company of the same battalion were attached to the Bedfordshire Regiment for "mopping-up." "C" Company and the rest of "D" were in support, and "A" Company was used to move up dumps. The Northamptonshire Regiment was in reserve. The Bedfordshire Regiment attacked with "A" Company (Lieutenant Tremeer) on the right, "D" (2nd-Lieutenant Driver) on the left, "B" (Captain Bull) in support, and "C" (Captain L. H. Keep) in reserve.

It was evident that the Germans had a great number of heavy guns opposite us, but his field artillery had apparently been withdrawn. We had a big concentration of field guns behind us, 18-pounders being wheel to wheel along the ridge in front of Heninel.

A Bedfordshire officer who took part in the attack afterwards jotted down the following narrative :—

" The forming up took place without incident, and zero hour was to be at 3.30 a.m. About 3 a.m. each man was visited in his shell-hole, and all seemed in good fettle. Unfortunately for us, when our barrage opened at precisely 3.30 it was still pitch dark, and in point of fact it was not light enough to see until after 4 a.m. This was a serious handicap, as we had to go [with men extended to nearly 10 yards apart] about 500 yards

[Photo: Swaine, London, W.]
CAPTAIN G. F. J. CUMBERLEGE, D.S.O., M.C.

LIEUT.-COLONEL THE HON. C. M. HORE-RUTHVEN, D.S.O.

[Photo: Langfier.
MAJOR E. G. MILES, D.S.O., M.C.

Three former Brigade-Majors.

To face page 96.

Photo: *Elwin Neame*] [*London, S.W.*
LIEUT.-COLONEL G. PRITCHARD-TAYLOR,
D.S.O., M.C.

Photo: *Lafayette*] [*Belfast.*
MAJOR CAMPBELL, D.S.O., M.C.

Two well-known Officers of the 54th Field Ambulance.

To face page 97.

up a slope, over a crest, and down the other side, before we came to the first Bosche trench.

"With no landmarks to guide us in the dark, it was almost impossible to maintain direction. The Bosche was very smart [about twenty to thirty seconds] in getting his heavy barrage down on and in front of our forming-up line, and the rear companies suffered severe casualties in passing over our front lines.

"On reaching the crest of the slope the Bedfordshires found themselves enfiladed from Cherisy on the left and from Fontaine Wood on the right by very deadly 'grazing' machine-gun fire. However, the officers, led gallantly by Major [then Captain] Keep, rallied the men and pushed on through this withering fire until, seriously reduced in numbers, they were confronted by a deep belt of uncut wire in front of Fontaine Trench.

"It was now broad daylight, and the remnant of the Bedfordshire Regiment was reorganized amidst this hail of machine-gun fire, to which had now been added the fire of snipers posted in Fontaine Wood and in the ruins of Cherisy. The Bedfordshire Regiment then consolidated a line immediately in front of Fontaine Trench, having made good, but at a terrible price, an advance of over 400 yards. Many feats of gallantry were performed that day, and many that have never and can never be reported. It has, however, since been established that small parties of the Bedfordshire Regiment fought their way right through Fontaine Trench and beyond until they were all killed.

"Of the company officers who started, two only came out of the action unwounded. Captain Bull, of 'B' Company, who had just returned from England after being wounded on July 1st, 1916, was killed. His was a very great loss, as he was one of the very finest officers we ever had.

"Lieutenant P. J. Reiss won the M.C. that day. With his platoon he set a fine example to the regiment in holding on and fighting the Bosche all day, and, though wounded early in the proceedings, and in spite of the great heat, he remained in command of his men until exhausted in the evening.

"Sergeant 'Alec' Lancaster, who won the M.M. in a raid early in 1916, got a bar. Seeing the situation, he, in spite of machine-gun and snipers' fire, in broad daylight walked down the whole of the battalion front, giving a word of cheer here and there, and organizing posts. He then recrossed No Man's Land, reported the situation to the Colonel, and returned to his post.

"A D.C.M. was more than earned by Private Gladwish, servant to 2nd Lieutenant Kydd, of 'B' Company, who was killed near Fontaine Trench. Gladwish tried to carry him back, but lost his way, and in the evening found himself on the wrong side of Fontaine Trench. For three days and three nights he tried to find his way back, though he could easily have given himself up to the Bosche. In spite of terrible thirst and hunger, he hid by day in shell-holes and reconnoitred by night. Finally, after three nights out, he found himself challenged by a British sentry, and was safe, though exhausted and looking like a hunted creature. His great devotion for his officer had led to his being cut off from his pals.

"In the dusk of the evening of May 3rd the Northamptonshire Regiment was ordered to take Fontaine Trench, starting from our old front line. Many of the Bedfordshire Regiment voluntarily joined in as the Northamptonshires came up to their positions. It was impossible, however, to hold Fontaine Trench with the few men who succeeded in getting into it."

A Fusilier officer who was with the Middlesex Regiment also jotted down his recollections of the fight, as follows :—

"When the Brigade got up to Fontaine Trench they found the thick wire uncut. In consequence the whole of the Bedfordshire Regiment and half the Middlesex Regiment were held up and lost heavily. The troops remained in front of the line in shell-holes, sniping until dark, when they were withdrawn.

"Lieutenant Knight, 12th Middlesex Regiment, attached 54th Trench Mortar Battery, came back to report on the situation, and, though sniped at all the time, got through without being hit by dodging from shell-hole to shell-hole. He then returned with orders from the Brigade in the same way, and withdrew the parties in his neighbourhood after dark.

"Meanwhile the left part of the Middlesex attack, with Captain Neate and 'B' Company Fusiliers, had got right on, as they were to the left of Fontaine Trench, and cleared the Bosche out of Cherisy. They were soon afterwards strongly counter-attacked from the right, and the Germans regained possession of the village. Very few men and no officer of 'B' Company got back to tell the story, and I think no officer of the Middlesex Regiment. Neate was last heard of firing his revolver at the Bosche coming on, and his death has since been confirmed.

"Company Sergeant-Major Fitterer, who had done so well at Boom Ravine, had his jaw and face badly smashed by a bullet in Cherisy, and came back through the 55th Brigade area on our left. He was hit at the beginning of the Bosche counter-attack.

"Neate was as gallant a boy as ever breathed. He was badly wounded in the head by a trench mortar early in 1916, and was never really fit afterwards. His sight was permanently damaged, but he managed to persuade a Medical Board to send him out again somehow or other. He was wounded and awarded the M.C. at Achiet-le-Petit. Whilst in a casualty clearing station he heard that the battalion was marching through the village, so broke out of hospital and rejoined. He was nearly left out of the Cherisy fight, but in the end Colonel Carr allowed him to go. He was a lad of very high ideals, a most efficient officer, and as brave as a lion. He was loved by the whole battalion, and was certainly one of the very best officers we have ever had.

"In the middle of the morning 'C' Company of the Fusiliers were ordered to attack Fontaine Trench. There was no preliminary bombardment or barrage, as the survivors of the dawn attack were still lying out in front of the line of Fontaine Trench and in No Man's Land. It was not a very hopeful project. As soon as they got over the ridge 150 yards in front of our front line they met a hot fire from machine guns and field guns and lost heavily, without being able to get near the trench."

The position was necessarily obscure. All that was clear in the afternoon was that the Brigades on our right and left had been forced back to their jumping-off places, and that the remnants of the Middlesex and Bedfordshire Regiments were somewhere out in front, holding on among the shell-holes as best they could, and unable either to go forward or to withdraw.

At any rate, another attack was ordered for the evening, with the object of taking Fontaine Trench, or at least extricating what was left of the two assaulting battalions which had gone over before dawn.

Two companies of the Northamptonshire Regiment, "B" (Captain Mobbs) and "C" (Captain Shepherd), were deployed for the attack, with orders to take Fontaine Trench at all costs. An artillery preparation began at 6.30 p.m., paused for fifteen minutes at 7.0, and at 7.15 down came the barrage, and over went the assaulting companies close behind it.

As Fontaine Trench was approached a party of Germans with a captured Lewis gun popped up and began a dispute that was ended in fine style by Lieutenant G. P. Harding, who rushed to a flank and bombed the gun out of action, killing two of the team, a feat for which he was awarded the M.C.

The wire in front of Fontaine Trench proved too formidable an obstacle, and most of the line had to drop into shell-holes, where they were pinned down by heavy machine-gun fire for the rest of the proceedings. But on the left a sunken road running into Cherisy enabled Captain Shepherd, with Lieutenant H. C. Osborne and about thirty men, to work round and enter the trench.

Lieutenant Osborne was the first to get in, and shot several of the enemy with his revolver. Though severely wounded in the head, he got together a team and led them bombing along the trench, which was cleared for about 150 yards. He was wounded a second time, but carried on with great courage and devotion to duty, winning a M.C. for this good piece of work.

He was well backed up by Company Sergeant-Major E. W. Tack, who had won the M.M. at Trones Wood, and now won a bar to it. Under heavy machine-gun fire he organized his men, carried on the bombing operations with good effect, and when all our bombs were exhausted used German bombs.

At this stage eight Lewis guns which had been lost earlier in the day were recaptured, and eventually four of them were got back to our lines, the other four only being lost because the men who tried to bring them in became casualties.

Bombing operations in the trench became all too lively, for a tunnel gave the Germans a way of escape to a support trench about forty yards farther back, from which they bombed our men with plenty of spirit. Our supplies were running out, Captain Shepherd attempted to send for more, but five runners, all volunteers, were shot dead one after the other as they left the trench to try and get back.

By this time darkness had fallen, but machine-gun fire was sweeping the top of the trench so that not a finger could be shown above ground, and the place was alive with bombs.

It became apparent that the trenches could not be held, for only ten men now remained of the thirty, who had entered it, and orders were given for the survivors to make their way back the best they could. Diving from shell-hole to shell-hole, the old German cable trench that ran back into our line was at last reached, and here a bomb block was constructed, and a message sent back for more bombs.

Later that night Captain Shepherd and Company Sergeant-Major Tack went out in the darkness and guided in the men who had been lying out before the German wire. This was no easy job in the darkness, and at least one party, seeing the guides advancing, took them for Germans, and made off in the other direction, and were not seen again.

So ended a bad day. What went wrong, and why the attempt failed, are questions that need not be thrashed out here. But at least officers and men of the Brigade had done all that could be done in very adverse circumstances, and the awards made revealed a number of cases of splendid individual heroism.

Lieutenant R. Knight, a Middlesex officer attached to the Trench Mortar Battery, was awarded the M.C. in circumstances already referred to. According to the official account, he " went forward with an assaulting company of the 12th Middlesex Regiment. When the retirement took place, he and two or three men maintained their position in a shell-hole and sniped the enemy during the day. When darkness came on, realizing that the counter-attack had not succeeded, he made his way back to our lines, and in doing so came across a party of the 7th Bedfordshire Regiment, about fifty strong, who had consolidated a series of shell-holes about 500 yards in front of our line. On his return he reported this fact, and when it had been decided that this party should withdraw, he volunteered to go out again and bring them in. In this he was successful; and, notwithstanding heavy rifle and machine-gun fire, he brought the whole party back without casualty."

Corporal S. H. Martin was one of five Fusiliers awarded the M.M. for that day's work. " He displayed great courage and tenacity in holding for several hours ground which had been gained in the advance. With a small party, in spite of casualties caused by heavy artillery and machine-gun fire, he kept the enemy in a strong post under continual fire, thus enabling the troops on his left to withdraw with comparative safety."

Captain K. H. Nelson, R.A.M.C., the Bedfordshire Regiment's medical officer, won the M.C. that day. According to the official account, his " unselfish devotion to duty throughout the action was the direct cause of many lives being saved. He worked throughout the day in No Man's Land under heavy machine-gun fire, and at times intense artillery fire. It was through his careful search of the battlefield that most of the more serious cases were found and brought back. Time after time he went practically as far out as our most advanced positions in the endeavour to attend to the wounded."

For similar work a D.C.M. went to Corporal H. Swannell, of the Bedfordshire Regiment, who worked continuously for over twelve hours tending the wounded under fire.

Among the Northamptonshires, Captain (now Major) Shepherd was awarded a bar to the M.C. he had won at Trones Wood, and the awards to Lieutenant Osborne and Harding and Company Sergeant-Major Tack have already been mentioned.

A D.C.M. went to Sergeant S. V. Whale, of the Middlesex Regiment, who already wore the M.M. " After all the officers of his company had been killed [says the official account], he took command of a mixed body of troops from several battalions, organized them, formed strong points and posts, and controlled their fire with good effect. Upon the party being reduced from fifty to a mere handful, he collected other men as reinforcements, and sent back progress reports."

For good work with this sergeant, Private Alfred Fox, of the same battalion, also received the D.C.M. When the party was forced to retire, he, with Sergeant Whale, covered the retirement for half an hour with a Lewis gun, and afterwards volunteered to take a report back under very heavy fire.

Among other Middlesex men whose good work that day won recognition were the following :—

Sergeant E. Isherwood, D.C.M. : " Besides leading and keeping his platoon together under very trying circumstances, he volunteered to form a strong point on the outskirts of the village (Cherisy), leaving a remnant of his platoon under another sergeant. Taking ten men under very heavy rifle and machine-gun fire, he formed the strong point, from which he was able to inflict severe loss on the enemy, and hold it throughout the day."

Sergeant T. T. Lucas, D.C.M. : " After his platoon commander was wounded very early in the fight, he rallied his men and took them as far as the German trench. When the company sergeant-major became a casualty, he took over the duties, and was instrumental, with other N.C.Os. and certain officers, in rallying the men of his own and the Bedfordshire Regiments, when they started to retire, getting them, in spite of heavy enemy shelling and machine-gun fire, to go forward to the attack once more. They advanced in spite of heavy losses, as far as the wire in front of the enemy trench, but were unable to get through owing to the intensity of the enemy fire and the fact of the wire being intact. The party were subsequently ordered to retire, and Sergeant Lucas displayed great initiative and resource in organizing the retirement, and when the retirement had been successfully carried out, and not till then, did he himself retire."

Private F. List, M.M.: " Was No. 2 on a Lewis gun. For two hours he kept his gun in action from a position quite close to the enemy's lines. No. 1 was then killed, and List remained with the gun for a further sixteen hours, then returning under cover of darkness to our lines, bringing the gun with him."

Corporal H. Lucas, M.M.: " On reaching the outskirts of the village (Cherisy), he found men of various units disorganized and without a leader. He got about forty together, led them forward to the river beyond the village, where they made a vigorous but unsuccessful attack on a hostile machine-gun emplacement."

Sergeant J. G. Holmes, M.M.: " Succeeded in rallying and leading forward to a fresh attack men of his own and another regiment who had started to retire. The party dug themselves in close to the enemy's lines, and maintained the position for several hours until, when darkness came on, they were ordered back. He organized the retirement, bringing up the rear. He afterwards went out again with 2nd-Lieutenant Knight, and brought in all men who could be found, about fifty, and later personally conducted stretcher-bearers to where wounded were lying out."

Lance-Corporal D. H. Hughes, M.M.: " On being unable to ascertain from whom the order to retire originated, he refused to return, collected a few men, and formed a strong point close to the enemy's wire."

Captain H. Perks, of the Middlesex Regiment, who was at first reported killed, but was afterwards found to be a prisoner, did some fine work in the village of Cherisy. He was in command of the support company. Seeing that the attack on the right had failed, and that German reinforcements were pouring in from Fontaine-les-Croisilles, he got together some fifty or sixty men, and attempted to form a defensive flank near the cross-roads at the southern end of the village. In doing this he exposed himself freely, and was wounded several times, but carried on till he was hit in the head and fell apparently dead. The little garrison continued to hold up the enemy till a general retirement took place later in the day, when all that were left, only eight men, made their way back.

On the night of May 4th the Brigade was relieved and went back to Neuville Vitasse, and afterwards to the Henu area. There they remained in support till the beginning of June, carrying on with training and working parties.

The Brigade took over the Divisional front on June 2nd, in front of Cherisy, the Northamptonshire Regiment holding the left sector, the Fusiliers the right, with the Bedfordshire Regiment in support and the Middlesex Regiment in reserve.

While the relief was in progress, the enemy put over a heavy bombardment on the sector where the Northamptonshire Regiment was taking over from the 7th Royal West Kent Regiment, and rushed and captured certain advanced posts which had been held by the latter battalion. The West Kent Regiment, aided by two platoons of the Northamptonshire Regiment, at once counter-attacked, and retook the captured posts, with the exception of one known as Horseshoe Post.

This particular post figured largely in events of the next few days. It was, as its name suggests, a small horseshoe-shaped trench which the Germans had dug out around a shell-hole in front of Fontaine Trench, about half-way across to the trenches and shell-holes which we were now holding. As it could be enfiladed by the Germans from Cherisy village, it was by no means a health resort, but at the same time its position made it of interest to both sides. Thus it often changed hands—one night we would hold it, and the next the Germans would shell us out and take over, only to be ejected in turn when our trench mortars got busy.

As it was lost to our side during the relief, it was up to the Northamptonshire Regiment, according to the rules of the game, to get it back the next night. Accordingly our trench mortars and 4·5's gave it some spell of discomfort on the afternoon of June 3rd, and at 11 p.m. that night two platoons of the Northamptonshire Regiment, led by Lieutenant Beckenham, rushed across under shrapnel and recaptured the post. Twelve dead Germans and twenty-five rifles were found in and around the spot. On the following day the Germans heavily shelled the post at intervals, but we managed to hold on, and on the 5th the post was wired in.

At best the Horseshoe was only a shell-hole that had been consolidated and improved, and it never changed hands before it had been battered out of recognition. But size is relative, and the capture of many square miles of territory later in the war did not attract so much attention as the fortunes of this little post. When the London newspapers reached the Northamptonshires a few days later they found in *The Times* a heading in big type : " Lost British Post Regained."

On June 18th the Brigade was relieved and marched back to the Henu area, whence on July 3rd they marched to Doullens and entrained for the north.

Chapter XI

THE YPRES SALIENT AND GLENCORSE WOOD

THE Brigade now entered on a tour of duty in the Ypres salient, that place of so much heroism and hard fighting.

Detraining at Godewaersvelde, the battalion proceeded to camps in the Dickebusch area (about three miles south-west of Ypres).

All thoughts and efforts were now turned towards the next offensive, which was expected about the end of the month. It was not altogether a comfortable period. The Germans shelled our camps with a good deal of regularity, and the working parties that went up to the line each night had a rather bad time with high explosive and gas shells.

" The Bosche seemed to have an inkling of the approaching battle," writes a Bedfordshire officer, " for he massed a greater amount of artillery than ever against the salient, and many of us remember those nightly crossings of the Ypres-Camines Canal, and the subsequent enforced loitering about the neighbourhood of that hell on earth, Zillebeke Lake and village. There were many casualties at this time, among them being Captain D. S. H. Keep, M.C., who insisted on accompanying his company on these nightly working parties, till one night, probably the worst we experienced, he was killed on the banks of Zillebeke Lake, amidst a combined shower of rain, high explosive and gas shells, lasting the whole of the night. So bad was it that the companies could not return till dawn."

Major Sale, who was then the Fusiliers' medical officer, also has vivid memories of those days, and has jotted down the following notes :—

" The area to which our working parties had to go, particularly round Zillebeke, was very unhealthy. It was just at this time that the Bosche started making use of mustard-gas shells, and our men were among the first to get some near Zillebeke.

" The whole area was waterlogged, and stank of putrefaction ; it was a most depressing spot, and the men hated these working parties more than anything. They had a fair march by cross-country tracks to get there, the route running by Café Belge, Bedford House, Transport Farm, Zillebeke, and a trench named Vint Street.

" A parody was made up in the battalions of a well-known popular song, as follows :—

> " I'm going back to dear old Zillebeke,
> That's the hottest place I know.
> Can't you hear the busmen calling,
> ' Café Belge, Bedford House, Zillebeke and Vint Street ?'
> I won't hesitate to duck my head
> When a shell is coming near.
> Oh, find me a shelter anywhere—
> Dug-out, shell-hole, I don't care.
> There's a Red Cross car awaiting there,
> In dear old Zillebeke."

As it happened, the expected offensive did not materialize on July 31st, and eventually came off on August 10th.

On our part of the front (according to the plans for the earlier date) the 30th Division were to advance south of the Menin Road, take Stirling Castle (a bit of high ground east of Sanctuary Wood), cross the Menin Road, and go up to the edge of Glencorse Wood. They were then to be leapfrogged by the 53rd Brigade, to which the 11th Battalion Royal Fusiliers were attached. Later, if all had gone well, the remainder of the 54th Brigade were to leapfrog the 53rd Brigade and advance into Polygon Wood. In anticipation of success, it was said that one battalion had arranged a race meeting for the near future on the racecourse in Polygon Wood.

A very elaborate model of all this area had been made by the corps in a field between Ouderdom and Poperinghe, and was visited by every officer and N.C.O.

After days and nights of intense artillery duels by both sides, August 10th and the attack came at last.

The assaulting battalions were the Fusiliers on the right and the Bedfordshire Regiment on the left, and were formed up on a front of about 750 yards, with the right near the Hooge-Menin Road.

The Northamptonshire Regiment sent a company to each of the assaulting battalions to " mop up," had another company as carrying party, and a fourth to garrison strong points. The Middlesex Regiment was held in reserve, two companies at Dickebusch, one in Ritz Trenches, and one in Château Wood, in front of Hooge.

The objectives of the Brigade included Glencorse Wood and the high ground which, in an area where a few feet formed a prominent hill, would give observation over a good stretch of country.

The assaulting battalions formed up on the tape without being observed by the enemy, and at zero—4.35 a.m.—went over, the enemy only indulging in desultory shelling as our troops moved off.

It will now be more convenient to follow the fortunes of each of the assaulting battalions in turn.

On the right the Fusiliers (having the 55th Brigade on their right) pushed ahead with little difficulty until the right company came under heavy machine-gun fire from Inverness Copse and Dumbarton Lakes (in the 55th Brigade's area), and eased off to the left. The effect of this was that when the line of the final objective was reached, the right of our attack only reached Fitzclarence Farm, and was out of touch with the 55th Brigade. There was also a gap between the Fusiliers and the Bedfordshire Regiment on the north.

A company of Northamptonshires attached to the Fusiliers (under Captain Grace, who was killed) followed the attacking waves, bombed all dug-outs, and took about forty prisoners, mostly from the south edge of Glencorse Wood.

By 6 a.m. all the officers of the Fusilier attacking companies were casualties, and a heavy counter-attack was launched by the enemy from Inverness Copse on our right. This attack was preceded by hostile bombing along Jargon Trench and other trenches which crossed our front from the Copse to Glencorse Wood. As a result the Fusiliers were driven back, and, under orders from Brigade headquarters, took up a line about 200 yards in front of Clapham Junction, where they were able to join up with the 55th Brigade. This line was held till the battalion was relieved by the 8th Norfolk Regiment, about 4 a.m. on August 11th.

In the meantime the Bedfordshire Regiment had got well forward behind the barrage, and at 5.13 a.m. a message reached Brigade headquarters saying that they were on the final objective. Three companies then attempted to consolidate, but, owing to marshy ground and deep mud, only isolated posts could be established.

At 9.17 a.m. a message was received from Captain Driver, commanding the left company, to the effect that they still held the final objective, but the companies on their right flank were badly bent back (this would refer to the difficulties the Fusiliers were experiencing).

Repeated enemy counter-attacks were made from Nonne Bosschen Wood (to the Bedfordshire Regiment's left front), but our artillery dealt effectively with these. More serious was the position in Glencorse Wood, where, owing to the Fusiliers having been pushed back, the enemy were able to push through in good numbers. As a result, the Bedfordshire Regiment by midday was holding Jargon Trench, about half-way to their final objective, as their main line. At dusk the enemy put a smoke barrage across Glencorse Wood and again counter-attacked, but this was beaten off by our artillery barrage and by rifle and machine-gun fire, and the line was handed over at 2 a.m. on August 11th to the 6th Royal Berkshire Regiment.

After the attack had been launched at zero, the Northamptonshires' strong point company (" C," under Captain Shepherd) pushed forward and occupied the allotted positions on the left. Several parties for other strong points, however, had to be pushed up to deal with counter-attacks on the Fusiliers' front.

The 54th Machine Gun Company had two guns with each assaulting battalion, four to go forward to the strong points, and four in reserve. These guns did splendid work, especially those garrisoning the strong points, and there is no doubt that more of the enemy were killed this day by rifle and machine-gun fire than in any previous attack by the Brigade. The lessons preached during the past few months on the importance of the rifle seemed to have borne fruit, and the majority of men who started out with 170 rounds of small arms ammunition returned with less than 20 rounds.

The 54th Trench Mortar Battery had two guns with sixty rounds each in action in the strong points, and did excellent work. More ammunition was afterwards brought up, but the bad state of the ground prevented a big supply being carried forward, and the two guns were the utmost that could be kept in action.

So much for a general survey of the attack. Such an operation is necessarily best seen from many points of view, and the following accounts of officers who took part are well worth quoting.

The first is from an officer of the Fusiliers, who writes :—

"On August 7th we moved up to take over the line from the 12th Middlesex Regiment just north of Menin Road. The 18th Division were not allowed to use the Menin Road, but a track had been constructed from near 'Shrapnel Corner,' running north of Zillebeke and through Sanctuary Wood, joining the Menin Road at the commencement of the Menin Road tunnel.

"Owing to the heavy rain and the passage of guns and limbers, this 'A.T.N. track,' as it was called, was in a most appalling state. Rations and ammunition had to be brought up from Canal Camp, Dickebusch, by pack train. The transport probably had their worst experience here ; it was pitch dark and raining most nights, the country was full of big shell-holes half full of water, and if a mule once got into one, it was with the greatest difficulty that he could be got out again. It was not uncommon for the pack train to leave between 4 and 5 p.m., and not get back till between 7 and 8 a.m. next morning.

"The Fusilier dispositions were : 'B' Company (Captain Fuller) on the left, 'D' (Captain Gray) on the right, 'C' (Lieutenant Watt) in support, and 'A' (Captain Horne) in reserve. The forming-up tape was laid by Captain Gray and Lieutenant Horton on the night of the 8th, only 150 yards from the Bosche line. They had just returned from laying them out when an order came in postponing the attack for twenty-four hours. So, in case the tapes should be seen in daylight, they had to go out and take them in, and put them down again on the night of the 9th.

"On the ridge about 200 yards from the south-west corner of Glencorse Wood was a group of about ten concrete pill-boxes. These stood up clear on the sky-line. For the whole of the afternoon of the 9th our 9-inch guns attempted to knock this strong point to bits, but the damage done to the pill-boxes was practically nil. There were about a dozen derelict tanks laying about our front, the result of a previous unsuccessful attack, and corpses everywhere.

"The barrage opened at dawn, and the men got away very well. They got well on into Glencorse Wood, and on the open ground some of 'D' Company, including Captain Gray, got right up to Fitzclarence Farm. Unfortunately, the battalion on our right did not get on at all. Our men were caught by a very heavy enfilade machine-gun fire in consequence, and soon afterwards the Bosche came out from Inverness Copse in strong force and got almost in rear of 'C' Company, our support company.

"Casualties had been very heavy, particularly amongst officers. In 'B' Company, Fuller was shot through the head trying, with only his Lewis gun sergeant, Sergeant Franklin, to rush a machine gun in a concrete emplacement. Horton, his second-in-command, was hit by a bullet through the chest shortly after leaving the strong point. Calthrop had been killed. In 'D' Company, Gray was last seen lying in a shell-hole close to Fitzclarence Farm, shot through both knees and using his revolver over the top of the shell-hole. Watt, commanding 'C' Company, was twice wounded, but continued fighting until again wounded, this time mortally. In 'A' Company, Stovell, another plucky lad, was killed by a bomb. Sergeant Bott, who had got the D.C.M. at Thiepval, and was on this occasion commanding a platoon, was killed at the edge of Glencorse Wood. Captain Hoare, of 'A' Company, was the last surviving officer, and he was shortly afterwards sniped through the head from the direction of Glencorse Wood.

"By this time the Fusiliers were withdrawing from their advanced posts, and a line was established 200 yards east of Clapham Junction.

"At this stage things were critical, as we had very few men left to man all this line, and there were no troops in reserve behind us nearer than Sanctuary Wood. The Fusiliers had no company officer left, and only one company sergeant-major—Burch of 'C' Company. However, Lewis guns, and later machine guns, were placed to cover the gap on our right. Pearcy, the signalling officer, came up from headquarters, which was in the Menin tunnel, with all available men—servants, runners, and pioneers—and a company of the Middlesex Regiment came up from Sanctuary Wood and went into the line just north of the Menin Road. Two platoons of the Northamptonshire Regiment who were there to garrison certain strong points which were to have been established forward were also on the ridge, and Captain (now Lieutenant-Colonel) Minet, of the 54th Machine Gun Company, and Captain Shepherd, of the 6th Northamptonshire Regiment, took charge of and organized the line.

"Twice the enemy formed up for counter-attacks on the strong point during the day, but each time they were stopped. During the early hours of the day, when things were critical, the remaining N.C.Os. of the battalion had done splendid work by driving out the Bosche who had come in from Inverness Copse, and in taking up the new line."

The Bedfordshire Regiment's side of the show is thus described by Captain Driver :—

"Just before 4 a.m. we were ready, the companies being in position as follows : ' B ' Company (Captain Driver) on the left, ' C ' Company (Captain Kingdon) on the right, ' A ' Company (Captain Clarke) in support, and ' D ' Company (Captain Fergusson) in reserve. Dawn broke quietly, and so well concealed were our men that the Bosche evidently decided that no attack would take place. We even watched him taking off some of his night forward posts, and our spirits went up.

"The ' going ' was very bad, owing to the number of shell-craters, all full of water, and more or less linked up by little canals. The Bedfordshire Regiment had furthermore to capture a trench with wire defences this side of Glencorse Wood, and then fight its way through the Wood and out the other side, and take up a position on the edge of Nonne Bosschen Wood. Never have the Bedfordshire Regiment been in better form. Held up by the wire of the first trench, it was an inspiring sight to see the leading wave firing at the Bosche in the ' standing ' position, while others cleared gaps in the wire, and then to see them rush the trench with a cheer, although machine-gun bullets were flying all round. The Bedfordshire Regiment literally surged through the morass inside the wood, the trees of which had been rendered naked and mutilated by shell fire ; but at the highest part of the wood, and in other suitable spots, the Bosche was holding fortified pill-boxes.

"It must be remembered that this was the British Army's first experience of pill-boxes. Without a halt the Bedfordshires fought their way through, using bomb and bayonet, to their final objective and beyond it, until they were held up by our own barrage, which had become stationary.

"But it was not very long before the Bedfordshires found themselves in a very exposed position. The Cheshire Regiment on the left were not quite up in line, and on the right the Fusiliers had encountered a withering fire from machine guns, with the consequence that, having lost practically all their officers, they had to be content with small progress.

"The Bosche still held Inverness Copse and the country between it and Glencorse Wood. However, in spite of this, the Bedfordshires dug in where they were, and sent some men to link up with the Fusiliers, with the result that, while touch was maintained, the Bedfordshires holding Glencorse Wood were forming a very nasty salient, and were subject all day to fire from their right flank from pill-boxes manned by determined machine gunners and snipers. Consequently during the day many casualties were suffered in this way.

"In the late afternoon it was apparent that the Bosche was preparing a determined counter-attack from the direction of Polygon Wood. But the Bedfordshires had not been idle, and had thoroughly consolidated their position, and received supplies of ammunition and machine guns. Also our artillery was warned, and when the Bosche started to deliver his counter-attack, he was met by a deluge of fire from both infantry and artillery, causing shocking casualties. Needless to say, our line was intact at the end. That night the Bedfordshires were relieved."

Captain Driver, who already wore the D.S.O., was awarded the M.C. for this day's work. To quote the official account: "After gallantly leading his company in the attack, he skilfully and at great personal risk consolidated his advanced posts. He continually visited his posts, although under constant enemy sniping, and directed the fire, thus harassing the enemy while they were endeavouring to form up for a counter-attack. Through his daring reconnaissances, movements of the enemy were noticed and severely dealt with by our artillery on his information. Although fired at by snipers and machine guns, he showed not the slightest hesitation in continuing his rounds from post to post, and when hit by a sniper, although his jaw was broken and his tongue shot through, he endeavoured to carry on, and only gave up when suffering from loss of blood. Even then he wrote a full account of the situation."

Of splendid work by individuals that day one might go on telling stories to the end of this book, and again comes the difficult task of attempting a selection.

Among the Fusiliers, Lieutenant G. S. Pearcy, the signalling officer, won a bar to the M.C. that had been awarded for his work at Boom Ravine. "When all company officers were casualties [says the official account], he took command of the scattered companies, and details of other battalions, and showed marked ability and gallantry in resisting a heavy counter-attack successfully."

The following awards to other ranks of the Fusiliers are also quoted from official accounts :—

Private Thomas Adams, D.C.M.: "From early morning this stretcher-bearer carried men from the thickest part of the enemy barrage to the aid post. Later, at a very critical moment, when the attacking troops had lost all their leaders, and were wavering before an enemy counter-attack, by his excellent example and contempt for danger he succeeded in encouraging them to go back to the ridge they were vacating. He also collected various stragglers of different units, and posted them in groups in the line. Throughout the day, and again that night, he worked indefatigably in dressing and carrying back the wounded on his back under fire."

Sergeant Ernest Wilson, D.C.M.: "When all the company officers had become casualties, he collected his men together and assisted to garrison a very important strong point, and succeeded in beating off repeated German counter-attacks. Later, when surrounded and overwhelmed by great numbers, he and his garrison were driven from their positions, whereupon he rallied his men, attached them to another unit, and helped to recapture the position."

Sergeant Henry Berry, D.C.M.: "When all his officers had become casualties, he took charge of his company. Although wounded, he organized the defence of the line, and successfully destroyed repeated enemy counter-attacks. When the troops on his left were dislodged temporarily from their position during the night, he organized and led part of the counter-attack which regained the position."

Sergeant (Acting Company Sergeant-Major) W. T. Burch, D.C.M.: "When all company officers had become casualties, he rallied the men at a critical moment, and then reorganized the line, garrisoning a strong point of vital importance. By careful judgment in placing Lewis guns, he destroyed German infantry who were trying to form for an attack. During the night he and his garrison beat off a very determined counter-attack."

Corporal H. Hallett and Lance-Corporal T. Wright were also awarded the D.C.M. for skilful handling of their men when officers had become casualties, and for similar good work the M.M. was awarded to Sergeant G. H. Whittington and Lance-Corporal W. Rickards.

Private Arthur Jakes, M.M., had an exciting time. Cut off and surrounded by the enemy, he remained in a shell-hole a long way in front of our position, and continued to snipe the enemy throughout the day. After dark he made his way back across trenches full of Germans, and safely rejoined his battalion.

Among officers of the Bedfordshire Regiment, Captain A. J. Colley was awarded a bar to his M.C. "When the troops on the right began to retire, the effect of which would probably have passed along the whole front line, he rushed forward, assisted to collect the retiring men, moved them forward again, re-established them in a fire position, and so prevented what might have been a great disaster."

The M.C. was also awarded to Captain J. A. Vlasto, medical officer to the same battalion, and Lieutenant F. Corner, the quartermaster.

Captain Vlasto " attended to over 300 cases under extremely heavy shell and rifle fire. During a gas- and smoke cloud he worked ceaselessly in the firing line."

The award to Lieutenant-Corner was for work during the days and nights preceding the actual attack. " On August 6th the enemy suddenly opened a very heavy shell fire on ten horsemen and wagons, with two days' rations for the battalion. When the whole was in danger of being destroyed, he went through the heavy shelling, and by his cool courage saved men, horses, and rations. He was very badly shaken by shell fire. On the night of August 8th-9th the enemy barraged the front, support, and rear lines for some hours. He made a personal reconnaissance of the route, and was able to guide the rations through to the battalion."

Good work was done by Corporal Ernest Jones (orderly to Captain Vlasto), who was awarded the M.M. in the following circumstances : " He collected during the day 250 cases of wounded, and four times in succession went through an extremely heavy artillery barrage to bring them in. When he was clearing a derelict tank of wounded who were sheltering there, the enemy opened heavy artillery fire, killing and wounding several, and almost severing one man's arm. Corporal Jones held the artery under heavy fire until the wound was dressed, thus saving the man's life. When Captain Vlasto was exhausted, Corporal Jones carried on, and, although suffering from gas, repeatedly journeyed through Glencorse Wood to the front line till all the wounded had been cleared."

Among other awards made to the Bedfordshire Regiment were the following :—

Sergeant W. Peck, D.C.M. : " An enemy machine gun was seriously holding up a platoon. He rushed the gun alone, killed the gunner, and then, jumping on the emplacement, bombed the rest of the team. This act of gallantry enabled the attack to be carried to a successful conclusion."

Lance-Corporal G. H. Fitzgerald, M.M. : " Rushed forward and bombed out of action a machine gun which was causing us casualties. The gun was afterwards turned upon the enemy by the Machine Gun Company."

Lance-Corporal F. C. Spring, M.M. : " The wires being frequently broken by the enemy's barrage, he asked permission to try to establish visual signalling. This entailed his going to the enemy's side of the ridge. He went there through the heavy barrage and machine-gun fire, and established communication. He was soon spotted by snipers, and continually shot at, but stuck to his post."

The Northamptonshire's medical officer, Captain W. B. Postlethwaite, was awarded the M.C. for gallant work under fire, and other awards in the same battalion included :—

Lance-Corporal J. F. Norris (already wearing the M.M. and bar, and now awarded the D.C.M.) : " This N.C.O., with his Lewis-gun team, formed part of a ' mopping-up ' company to the Fusiliers. After clearing dug-outs he joined the attacking force. He located and put out of action two enemy machine guns which were holding up the advance. Later a third machine gun was located by one of our aeroplanes, which fired tracer bullets at it. The position was then picked up by this N.C.O., and the gun team was put out of action."

The D.C.M. was also awarded to Privates F. L. Smith and F. Farrar. " These two Lewis gunners noticed a German machine gun, and with no other assistance made a daring attack. Private Farrar rushed the position and killed the two gunners, while Private Smith engaged the gun with his Lewis gun, and then rushed forward, killed one of the enemy, wounded another, and took five others prisoners."

Three Middlesex officers were awarded the M.C. :—

2nd-Lieutenant E. D. Alcock " was in command of a carrying company. With great courage and skill he led his men through a heavy barrage, carrying 80,000 rounds of small arms ammunition from the dump at Zillebeke to the vicinity of the front line. During the latter part of the journey the company was subjected to hostile machine-gun fire, in addition to being shelled. Although 30 per cent. of his men became casualties, he delivered the whole of the ammunition."

2nd-Lieutenant G. A. Bond " brought rations to the front line each night on pack animals, over very difficult country which was shelled almost continually. In addition, he brought up in the same way all the material for the forward Brigade dump for the attack on August 10th. In spite of casualties to animals, and several stampedes caused by shells dropping amongst the train, he never failed to deliver the whole of the goods."

The third M.C. and some awards for other ranks were won during a minor operation on August 15th and 16th, when this battalion (together with the Bedfordshire Regiment) was temporarily attached to the 53rd Infantry Brigade.

2nd-Lieutenant K. G. Calvert " was in charge of headquarters' company on August 16th in the attack against Westhoek Ridge, and was ordered to bring his men across from Stirling Castle to the Menin Road tunnel. There was very heavy shelling going on, and a certain amount of panic and confusion resulted. 2nd-Lieutenant Calvert at once grasped the situation, and by able handling of his men brought them quickly and successfully through to their destination, by getting them down into shell-holes and then choosing with great coolness the right moments to push forward again."

Captain (now Lieutenant-Colonel) E. C. T. Minet, of the 54th Machine Gun Company, was awarded the D.S.O. for his work on August 10th. "When it became apparent that the right of the Brigade was outflanked and driven back, he took charge of all troops in the vicinity, and established a defensive flank at a most critical moment. Throughout the day he was in the front line, passing from gun to gun, controlling the fire and encouraging all ranks."

A D.C.M. went to Sergeant J. Goodall, of the Machine Gun Company. "He assisted in capturing a concrete machine-gun emplacement, with ten prisoners and a machine gun. He immediately manned this gun and used it against the enemy."

A similar award went to Private L. Lewis, of the Machine Gun Company. "His gun was destroyed by shell fire, and he immediately returned through the barrage and obtained another. He then went forward again alone, found his team, brought his gun into action, and maintained his position until seriously wounded."

On leaving the Glencorse Wood sector the Brigade was for a time in the Buysscheure and Wormhoudt areas (north of St. Omer), engaged in training, and afterwards moved up to the St. Janter Biezen area and Tunnelling Camp (near Poperinghe), with a view to taking part in operations in front of Poelcapelle.

"Here, on September 15th and 16th [writes a Middlesex officer], Thiepval and Schwaben Redoubt were celebrated by inter-battalion raids at midnight across ploughed fields.

"About the first or second week in October the officers were interviewed by Sir Ivor Maxse, who told us about the forthcoming attack for the Westroosebeke Ridge. I believe it was on this occasion that he said : ' Gentlemen, I've arranged a very nice battle for you, with lots of Huns to kill !'

"On October 15th we crossed No. 4 bridge over the canal [just north of Ypres], and went on by duck-boards to Cane Trench, near Pilkem, where we spent the night in bivouacs. We were shelled occasionally through the night, and suffered a few casualties. We left next day and went forward. Battalion headquarters was about 800 yards west of the church in Poelcapelle, and the line ran north and south through the church.

"This was the first occasion on which an American doctor went into the line with us. This was Lieutenant Anderson, and he was kept busy with the 96 casualties we had by the time we reached the front line.

"The Hun was very nervous about being attacked, and from 4 a.m. on the 17th until daybreak put a barrage down every hour, each lasting fifteen minutes. At 6 a.m. he blew up a pill-box about fifty yards in front of us, and we sent a patrol out to see what was there. Subsequent information showed that there was a garrison of one officer and seven men with two machine guns.

"On hearing this, Brigade inquired how we came by this information, and that is rather a humorous story in itself. A very new gunner officer had been sent up to find our headquarters, and when about 500 yards in front of the same thought it time to inquire his way. He asked someone where headquarters was, and received the usual intelligent answer, 'Over there!' accompanied by a nod of the head.

"He went on, followed by his batman, who was armed with a stick, passed beyond the front line, and approached the pill-box indicated. The occupants, thinking he had come to surrender, came out to welcome him in, and proved to be the aforementioned garrison. The German officer advanced to meet him, and each, thinking the other wanted to surrender, placed a hand on the other one's shoulder, and signalled in which direction to go.

"Meanwhile the batman, taking in the situation, slipped into a pill-box and found an old Mauser rifle, with which he covered the Huns. Neither side could fire because both officers were in the line of fire. Both then backed away from each other and turned and ran to their own lines."

The 531d Brigade was due to attack on the 22nd, and the 54th had orders to stand by in support, two companies of the Middlesex Regiment, under Major Warr, being sent up to Cane Trench as counter-attack companies.

However, the whole battalion was pushed into the line again that night, and took over a line east of Poelcapelle and astride of the Spriet Road. Many S.O.Ss. were sent up during the night, and were followed by barrage and counter-barrage, and a few prisoners of the German 76th Regiment were captured.

The expected attack did not take place, and after being withdrawn to "Dirty Bucket Camp" (a very appropriate name for a very uncomfortable place), the Brigade afterwards went on to "P" area (Woesten), where conditions were even worse.

It was about this time (on October 22nd, to be exact) that Brigadier-General L. de V. Sadleir-Jackson took over the command of the Brigade, and, as events proved, he was to lead us through the rest of the war, except for an unlucky absence through a wound in the closing months.

Now we moved into the Houthulst Forest sector, and that health resort deserves a chapter to itself.

Chapter XII

HOUTHULST FOREST

WHENEVER two or three officers of the Brigade were gathered together, and we discussed this book, someone was sure to say, " Put in a bad word for Houthulst Forest."

And so many bad words were volunteered that if they were printed here the book would be suppressed in the interests of our national morals.

As a matter of fact, anyone can make a Houthulst Forest of his own. It would make a nice war souvenir. Take a low-lying swamp, crossed by streams which wander wherever they like and never follow the same course two days running, and dot a few trees over the area. Everything must be so flat that the 20 contour, which is the highest ground, seems almost like a mountain range.

That is the raw material. Then you shell the place for three years, till land and water are thoroughly mixed up, and the few trees left standing are splintered skeletons. Everything is now ready. You must walk some 8,000 yards across this area in pitch darkness, with enemy shells constantly bursting around, and shell-holes full of water or deep mud awaiting you if you step off a wooden track which is constantly being blown to pieces or floating away. Now go ahead and enjoy yourself, and have a real good time.

I forgot to mention that when you make your little pleasure trip across the area you must first load yourself with all the kit and stores that you can possibly carry, and then get a fellow pleasure seeker to pile a few pounds more on top.

The forest lies north of Ypres, and the Brigade had to hold a line on the far side of the area of which I have just given an all too rosy picture. Just why we wanted to get out in front of it, and deny the Germans access to it, was the sort of thing weary officers and men, trudging up to the front line, could never understand. It all seemed an unnecessary piece of good nature on our part to warn him so carefully away from a spot where he would certainly get his feet quite wet.

The front line was a particularly comfortable place, and those on duty there used to crouch in mud and water and wonder whether it was influence or merit, or just downright hard luck, that got them the job. It consisted of shell-holes, with breastworks that used to slide back into the holes, for no trenches could be dug in the waterlogged ground. Behind the line were a few captured pill-boxes, which served as company and battalion headquarters; but as the Germans had the position of these to an inch, they came in for a good deal of artillery attention.

The Germans occupied a mountain range at least ten feet high in front of us, and naturally elected to keep out of the wet, only sending down an outpost line at night. And we sat in our puddles and wondered whether it would be against the Hague Convention and all the other rules for mitigating the horrors of war if, one dark night, we slipped quietly away, and left the Germans our puddles to sit in for a change.

Even the pill-boxes, to which men out in front looked back as resorts of almost sinful luxury, were not the first class hotels an Englishman visiting the Continent might desire or expect, for they were at least four or six inches deep in a nasty smelling essence of distilled German. Pump and drain as you might, the low level and the cracked foundations allowed the water to have the better of you.

Brigade headquarters were situated in a luxurious and comfortable pill-box some 7,500 yards from the front line. The way up was along a track of duck-boards which wound among the shell-holes, and often ended abruptly in a new shell-hole if enemy artillery had been busy. Smashing up our duck-board track was the chief German industry at this part of the line. This introduced fresh complications in the ever-engrossing game of finding your way up in the dark. When the track suddenly came to an end, and you stepped off into deep mud to search for the next piece, it was highly probable that, after splashing round in the dark, you would at last find another bit of duck-board, begin to tramp wearily and warily along it, only to discover that you had got back to the old track and were retracing your steps. That counted several points to the German, for it was his laugh, and you began again.

As there are women and children present, I can't tell you half the pet names we had for those miles of duck-boards.

Since the front line could not be visited by day, the little garrisons in outlying shell-holes were booked for a long spell in the wet when they had once reached their positions. It was about this time that the real value of the steel helmet was discovered, for it was found to make an excellent seat in the mud.

Except during frost, the state of the ground made any really serious attack with numbers an impossibility for either side at this time of year. The Germans established this fact by careful experiment. On a night of November they made an attack on a Lewis-gun post and a part of the French line on our left. The Germans came on well until their two lines were held up by mud and water. Then Private M. Bristowe, of the Bedfordshire Regiment, managed to get his gun team out into the open, and enfiladed the lines while they were stuck in the mud. And so that attack ended.

General Sadleir-Jackson has supplied the following notes relating to these days, which will interest fellow-sufferers :—

"The number of guns at the disposal of the Brigade was very considerable on paper, but a personal visit disillusioned one as to the weight of metal that could be thrown to meet any emergency. Many were found sitting on their tails, like plaintive and patient sea-lions, in the beds of the Broombeck and Steenbeck, having been washed away during the night.

"Though we were told that we had just gained a most important victory [Passchendaele Ridge], and that we were masters of the air, the sea, and the land, one could not help being a little sceptical when being pursued down the duck-boards by a specially attentive German plane, which had no difficulty in thoroughly terrifying one with its machine gun, and then quickly disappearing.

"One grey cold winter morning I staggered up the duck-boards with Colonel [then Major] Percival, who was acting Brigade-Major at the moment, and on arriving near a certain well-known spot called ' Faldherbe cross-road ' [known to the men as ' Fed-up cross-road '], the early morning German plane came out to spy out the nakedness of the land. Out of sheer *joie de vivre* he sailed over battalion and company headquarters in turn, giving each a nice cheerful burst. I remember crouching under an extremely prickly and very thin hedge, watching the pilot amusing himself, and cursing inwardly that no one snugly sheltered in pill-boxes condescended even to notice his presence. This sector was stiff with Vickers and Lewis guns, and the plane was only 500 feet up, but the attractions of early morning tea far outweighed those of early morning fighting.

"The bad weather conditions and the discomforts of the front line involved heavy casualties from trench feet, as many as 100 per battalion occurring after a tour of duty in the shell-holes.

"This brought about the institution of the famous ' Pedicuria ' establishments. I fear my Staff Captain, who was indefatigable in his efforts to make the organization a success, will go down to his grave with ' Pedicuria ' inscribed on his heart. Scientifically, I believe there is a considerable difference of opinion as to the actual value of this treatment. Be this as it may, imagination plays the strongest part in our lives, and ' Pedicuria ' became not only popular, but the rage, and trench feet gradually disappeared.

"The system arranged that the man should march up in his boots, change into dry socks and waders, then after a tour of twenty-four hours undergo ' Pedicuria ' treatment at platoon headquarters, change into dry socks and waders in support, and finally march down in his boots. But this was not always a success. Barbed wire cut the waders, and men's feet began to swell so that they could not get their boots on, and consequently had to walk out five miles in waders.

"One of the dangers of walking out in waders was that if you fell off the duck-boards into a shell-hole, you stood a good chance of being drowned, as all equipment had to be pulled off before you could be dragged out. Even if not drowned, you rapidly assumed the colour of a boiled lobster, as all the water in the shell-holes was strongly impregnated with Yellow Cross gas.

"I recollect passing Cinq Chemins, where there was a very large shell-hole, and noticed a crowd of about ten people howling with laughter. A wretched platoon commander had fallen into the shell-hole, and was just keeping his head above water with difficulty by hanging on to the sides. Every few minutes he went under, and a spout like that from a whale shot up as he came to the top spluttering. No one was interested in saving the wretched officer; all were enormously amused. It was, as a matter of fact, an exceptionally dangerous spot to loiter in, but this was completely forgotten in the amusement afforded by the unfortunate officer. Such is the British soldier, and his phlegm makes the world marvel.

"'Pedicuria' now being established, the next thing to do was to wire the front, approximately a distance of about 2,500 yards, with practically no landmarks, the enemy posts being about 50 to 100 yards distant. With the assistance of the whole of the 55th Brigade and every available man of the 54th, carrying parties 2,500 strong were organized. I would like here to bear tribute to the good work of Captain Davies, 79th Company R.E. [though I know he will curse me to his dying day for my insistence upon the most minute attention to detail], who successfully organized all the dumps. The carrying parties, without exception, arrived at their destinations, and wiring parties, composed of two specially trained battalions, the Middlesex and the Bedfordshires, practically completed the task on one of the dirtiest and blackest winter nights one can imagine. The work was finally completed by the Northamptonshire Regiment and the Fusiliers on the following night.

"Having got our 'Pedicuria' establishments working, improved the conditions of existence, and strengthened our defences, we now turned our minds towards offensive patrols against the enemy, as we were not satisfied that we had attained the necessary moral superiority over his snipers and machine gunners to make life comfortable. A great controversy had arisen over the loss of a place called Turenne Crossing, and the concensus of opinion was strongly in favour of its recapture, the chief arguments advanced being that many of the pillboxes in the piquet and support lines were being rendered uninhabitable owing to machine-gun fire from the place. One specially referred to was Egypt House.

"The long walk up the duck-boards, the fact that the front line, and to a smaller degree battalion headquarters, could only be visited at night, which was frequently dark and nearly always wet, prevented frequent visits from the staffs of higher formations. This probably led to false impressions regarding the value of Turenne Crossing. To prove that it was of no great value to the enemy, battalions and afterwards advanced Brigade headquarters were established in Egypt House, which was impregnable even to 8-inchers, and the Crossing itself was in a hollow.

"There was some difference of opinion as to the actual distance between the Crossing and Egypt House, and accordingly Major Shepherd personally measured it one night with a tape. It was not a job to be taken up with enthusiasm—rather a 'windy' affair, in fact—for there was always the chance that the Germans would resent a British officer wandering around with a tape in an area to which they laid claim. At last Major Shepherd arrived safely back at Egypt House with a very muddy tangle of tape, representing the actual distance, which he proceeded to measure off on a yard stick. His story that he had to elbow out of the way the Germans who crowded round out of curiosity while he was measuring in their area is not believed in the best circles."

It was now considered that the night positions of German machine guns could be very well tackled by our Stokes mortars; but as retaliation was always possible, the gunners used to retire as soon as they had fired a burst.

The only drawback was the sodden state of the ground, which made it very difficult to get a solid base for the bedplate of the mortars. The tops of the pill-boxes in which companies had their headquarters had an irresistible attraction for the trench mortar officers, but as this brought down a prompt "hate" from German artillery, the idea caused constant friction between the Tock Emma people and the company officers. One's sympathy was rather divided. The trench mortars had to silence the machine guns, and company headquarters alone afforded a satisfactory site for the mortars. On the other hand, the company officers had to live, or attempt to live, through the "hate" that would come down after the trench mortars had done their little stunt and cleared off. But no one doubted the enthusiasm of the trench mortar people, and they were always most optimistic after they had done a shoot. According to their reports, all the machine guns and gunners in the German Army must have been seen flying through the air at one time and another during this period, and shouts and screams were always reported by observers after each burst.

"To show how extremely difficult it was in reality to mark down German machine guns [says General Sadleir-Jackson], the following account of preparation for a raid bears on the point :—

"The intelligence officer of the 12th Middlesex Regiment was wounded on patrol, and it was decided that the offending machine gun should be dealt with next night. The position was absolutely certain. A preliminary reconnaissance to guard against wire or advanced snipers was arranged. I arrived at 11 p.m. at Egypt House to meet O.C. raid, and all details were duly gone over. When I finally inquired whether all was clear and understood, O.C. raid remarked : ' Oh yes, the arrangements are excellent, but we have only just come from where the gun is supposed to be, and there is no gun !' In point of fact the gun was a full 400 yards farther away.

"A few nights previously I had occasion to visit the front line with Captain Knight, my Stokes mortar officer. Unfortunately, the night was inky dark, and raining like a deluge. Captain Knight, though an excellent cricketer, was very short-sighted, and I fear that on this occasion his Chinese Mandarin spectacles became like wet window-panes, and of scanty use. This was very unfortunate, as it entailed his missing the kinks in the duck-boards every hundred yards, with a consequent toss into a shell-hole. Not unnaturally our progress was slow, but a complete stop had to be made when I missed the thing and went clean into a shell-hole up to my middle, thus filling my waders and rendering myself quite immobile. In fact, I was stuck so fast that Captain Knight had to lift me out of the waders, which we scraped out afterwards. Our walk, normally of two hours, took us four and a half hours."

While the Fusiliers were going into line for one of their tours of duty, Captain O. C. Whiteman, who had taken over the duties of adjutant on Captain Cumberlege being appointed Brigade Major, was killed. He was going up Hunter Street, about ten minutes in advance of the battalion, with Major Ford, second-in-command, and a runner. The Bosches were shelling our particular spot in the track, sending over about one shell a minute from a 4·2 howitzer. When Major Ford and Captain Whiteman got within thirty yards of this spot, they reached a concrete pill-box, and decided to remain behind it until the next shell came, and then to double across the shelled area. Unfortunately, the next shell landed just over the pill-box almost on top of them, killing Whiteman and wounding the runner, Fletcher.

"Whiteman [writes a fellow-officer] was one of the officers who originally came to France with the 11th Royal Fusiliers. He was a very smart adjutant, and another of the cheery ones—a very witty fellow, and an asset to any mess."

The Brigade commander's habit of wandering about the line, especially in unhealthy spots, led to some amusing encounters.

He had visited a headquarters near the front line, and induced a rather reluctant officer to accompany him on a somewhat dangerous tour. The tour was safely completed, and it was thought that he had gone back, but suddenly his unmistakable voice was heard again outside the headquarters, and a voice from inside, in a loud whisper that he could not possibly miss, asked anxiously : " Is that the old —— back again ? "

That is a story the General likes to tell against himself. Another of his favourites concerns a certain company sergeant-major, who, when he visited Panama House during a rather lively "strafe," said, " We don't want no dead Brigadiers around our pill-box," and threw him inside.

There was, as a matter of fact, a good deal of excitement at Panama House that day, for the Germans, who had been turned out of the place once, were showing signs of wanting it back again. What happened is best told by the General himself :—

" Major Percival and I, on reaching Faldherbe cross-road, *en route* for Ajax House, battalion headquarters, thought good to visit the company headquarters first, as a certain amount of artillery activity was making itself apparent. I would remark that this residence boasted about six square feet of standing-room. A few minutes after our arrival it was perfectly obvious that great things were afoot. Ominous orders were being issued by the company commander, and his servant actually ceased making tea and commenced to load his revolver. There was great activity amongst the Vickers gunners, who formed part of the defence, and much firing, mostly in the opposite direction from that from which the attack was expected.

" An exhausted runner arrived and stated that the Germans were coming down the road eight deep, hundreds had been slaughtered, the platoon was still holding its ground, but six more Lewis guns were required to deal adequately with the situation.

" About this moment, from the entrance to the pill-box, exclamations of great excitement began to arise. These were eventually traced to the Vickers gunners, who discovered they had no water in their casing, and no more belts of ammunition. The company sergeant-major apparently considered that the moment had arrived when some decisive action was necessary, and proceeded to emerge from the bunk at the back of the pill-box. Six other human beings had previously emerged. He expressed himself somewhat trenchantly and to the point, and I regret to say that I fell under the ban of his displeasure. ' We don't want no dead Brigadiers round our pill-box !' was the admonition I received, and with this I found myself hurled back into the struggling mass of humanity.

" In about twenty minutes' time, having collected Major Colley, the battalion commander, we visited the scene of the contest. The platoon commander, revolver in hand, first pull-off already gone, embraced me and inquired whether he was to be court-martialled for sending up an S.O.S. The total pick-up was one dead German!"

As already mentioned, our front line consisted of a line of outposts in shell-holes and the ground had been so battered and pulped by artillery and water that it was sometimes rather difficult to say where our area left off and the Germans' began. This led to some awkward moments, as it was always possible to wander into the German lines by mistake. One of our wiring parties, put out to do a night job, found next morning that they had carefully wired in a German post instead of our own. The Germans appear to have sat quiet through the whole proceedings, probably only too glad to have the work done for them.

But that wiring party was not half so disgusted as a certain German sergeant-major who came striding into our lines one night, and was very surprised at being taken prisoner. He was off on leave, and had taken the wrong turning.

These geographical difficulties lent a quite unnecessary excitement to front-line work. It would, for instance, be difficult to improve on the official account of the brisk few minutes in which Private T. Wright, of the Fusiliers, won the M.M. :—

" In the Houthulst Forest sector, on the night of November 24th-25th, 1917, he was accompanying his platoon officer, who was visiting his front line posts, when an enemy patrol was seen approaching. The officer and Private Wright, who were in No Man's Land at the time, allowed the patrol to get close to the post, and then placed themselves between the patrol and the enemy's lines, and called upon the patrol to surrender.

" The patrol, consisting of an officer and a corporal, attempted to get away, but were prevented from doing so by Private Wright, who shot the German officer in the thigh, and then knocked down the corporal, who offered considerable resistance, and moreover was a strong opponent, standing at least six feet one inch in height, and strongly built. The two were made prisoners, and valuable documents and other information was obtained from them."

And there is a certain battalion transport officer who nearly delivered the rations and rum to the Germans one night. In his more cheery moments he looks back on the episode with some pride, and calls it " The great cavalry break-through." But he'd better tell the story himself :—

" It was in November, 1917, and the Brigade was amusing itself imitating submarines opposite Houthulst Forest. It was decided that rations should be taken up as close to the line as possible, owing to the awful state of the ground, and Egypt House was decided upon as the spot where I should dump the bully and other luxuries.

" By the time we had reached the charming old-world village of Koekuit [ex-mud-wallowers of the Brigade will remember it] it was as black as —well, as black as a dirty night in the Salient—and on that account I missed the turning to the right.

"I strode cheerfully on, with my mules all marching strictly to attention behind me, till at last I remarked to my sergeant that we seemed to be getting rather close to the Véry lights. He agreed heartily, and we called a halt. Spotting a pill-box a little to my right-rear, I decided to drop in for a drink and information.

"I got off the track and struck across country for the pill-box, and had got about half-way when suddenly four heads popped up out of the ground, and someone wanted to know all about it. I tried to explain, and asked who they were, and what they were doing. They said that they were 'B' Company, holding the line, and their officer was in the pill-box. I crawled in there, and found that the war had taken a nasty turn, for my mules with the rations and rum were some 150 yards out in No Man's Land. A little farther and we should have handed them over to Jerry.

"I ran out, and with a very quiet ' About turn !' made those mules come back on tip-toes, and so the British cavalry didn't break through after all."

The Brigade had the good fortune to be out of the line at Christmas-time, resting and training in the comparative peace and goodwill of the Haringhe area.

Here it was that the Brigade cinema, which had been bought out of canteen funds, gave its first show on the night of December 18th. Two nights later the "Vin Blongs," the Brigade concert party, also gave its first show. Unfortunately, this was followed by disaster. Soon after it was finished a fire broke out in the hut, and within half an hour piano, stage, costumes, etc., were a heap of ashes. However, the show was set going again three days later, with borrowed costumes and scenery composed of blankets, and for over a year the "Vin Blongs" remained a welcome feature of leisure moments out of the line.

The year ended on a note of tragedy. On December 31st a trench-mortar demonstration was being held when a shell went off prematurely, causing all the remaining ammunition by the gun to explode. About seven were killed and six wounded, including Major Podmore, commanding the 12th Middlesex Regiment, killed, and Major Harrison, his second-in-command, wounded.

On January 10th the Brigade was again in the line, but was out again by the end of the month, and on February 9th began its move to the south, where it was destined to take part in the hard fighting of the last German offensive.

CHAPTER XIII

THE MARCH RETREAT

THE move in February, 1918, was from Farthest North to Farthest South, orders being for the Brigade, together with the rest of the Division, to join the Fifth Army on the extreme right of the British line. This was a part of the plan for reinforcing our front on the sector in which, as Sir Douglas Haig rightly anticipated, the Germans were to make their last great effort of the war.

No one was sorry to leave the north. Whatever atmosphere of heroism or romance may cling to the Ypres salient, those whose daily task it was to build up its traditions were too close to the picture to appreciate its beauty, and for sheer discomfort and unhealthiness they will give full marks to the Houthulst Forest sector.

The move was completed on February 10th, when the Brigade found itself south of St. Quentin, in the Noyon area. Brigade headquarters were in the Château at Morlincourt, and the battalions were billeted around—the Fusiliers at Behericourt, the Bedfordshire Regiment in Salency, and the Northamptonshire Regiment in Morlincourt. The Middlesex Regiment was in Noyon for one night, and on the 11th moved to Muirancourt.

A glance at the map will show that, as in the British offensive on the Somme in 1916, the 54th Brigade was nearly on the extreme right of the British line. The Fifth Army joined up with the French just south of Barisis, in the Forest of St. Gobain, less than twenty miles from where the Brigade had now arrived, and from where it was thrown into the line a few weeks later to play its part in stemming the German onrush. As it was fully realized, at any rate in the higher commands, that the Germans would make their great offensive at this point, with a view to breaking through between the French and the British Armies, and rolling up our line in a great sweep on Amiens, the Brigade could congratulate itself on being at the post of honour and danger.

The enemy promptly greeted its arrival. An air raid was made over its billeting area on the evening of February 11th, the Bedfordshire Regiment losing ten killed and eight wounded, a bomb falling on a barn in which a platoon was sheltered, and another falling within 150 yards of the Château where Brigade headquarters were situated.

On the following day, February 12th, happy associations of over three years' standing were broken up by the departure of the 12th Middlesex Regiment. The reorganization of Brigades on a three-battalion basis meant that in each Brigade the junior battalion (reckoned by its old regimental number) must be struck off. Service battalions were necessarily temporary units —for the duration of the war or less, as required—but they had built up for themselves traditions and an *esprit de corps* of which every officer and man was rightly proud, and it was a sad moment for the 12th " Die-hards " and for their comrades in the Brigade when they ceased to exist. A number of officers and other ranks remained with the Brigade to reinforce the remaining battalions, drafts were sent to other units, and the rest of the battalion went to form the 18th Entrenching Battalion.

The scheme of defence in this sector involved the distribution of troops in depth, and three defensive belts were constructed, the three remaining battalions of the Brigade taking their part in the necessary digging, during the latter days of February. Finally, on February 27th, the Brigade moved up to Caillouel as Corps Reserve, or counter-attack Brigade, less the Bedfordshires, who were sent forward to Rouez, just west of the Canal Junction at Tergnier, to carry on further work in the battle zone.

There was little more to be done now but to wait for the German onset. Training, with special attention to counter-attack formation, was carried on almost daily, working parties were still frequent, and there was constant reconnaissance of the battle zone. Of all these activities the Germans took little notice, and there was an almost uncanny silence over the whole front. Caillouel itself was a pleasant village, and everyone had pleasant billets—the last little bit of comfort the Brigade was to have for many a long day of hard fighting. Competitions of every kind were organized to make the training more interesting, and there was much spectacular night firing by Lewis guns with the aid of Véry lights.

In such spare time as there was battalions organized entertainments for the men and dinners for the officers, and by the 19th all had fully recovered from their hard times in the salient, and were ready for anything.

So the eventful day drew near. There were many " windy " rumours on and around March 18th, and on March 20th came orders to stand to, ready to move.

It was still dark on the morning of March 21st when a terrific German bombardment began—" the most terrific roar of guns we have ever heard," is the verdict of surviving members of the Brigade, all connoisseurs of bombardments by this time. The great push had started, and along the whole of our front gas and high-explosive shells from every variety of gun and trench mortars were being hurled over.

Everyone realized that the great ordeal for which they had been training and planning for weeks was upon them.

It had been the custom during the past week for a lorry to report at 9.30 every morning at Rouez to take officers of the Bedfordshire Regiment to reconnoitre the line. Punctually at 9.30 that morning the lorry driver reported to Colonel Percival for orders. The lorry came in very useful, as it was put at the disposal of Captain Fergusson, the Brigade amusements officer, who had been " showing " at Rouez Camp the previous night, and had all his pierrot kit and cinema there, with no means of getting it away. But for this lorry the kit and cinema would probably have been lost.

The " Vin Blongs " got back safely to Caillouel, and there began their grand trek to Noyon. One of the party found a perambulator, another a wheelbarrow, and so they journeyed along the Noyon road, clinging like grim death to their costumes and rations. They wandered all over the place for two weeks, and finally rejoined the Brigade at Boutillerie. All their costumes and properties were lost on the Brigade dump at Noyon, so for the second time in their career they had to start afresh.

To return to the events of March 21st. Shortly before 10 a.m. the Germans launched an attack on a front of fifty-four miles, from the River Oise (near the spot where the Brigade now stood ready) to the Sensee.

To appreciate what followed one must understand the odds our troops were facing. Sir Douglas Haig's comparison of the forces engaged, in his despatch on these operations (published in the *London Gazette* of October 21st, 1918), is as follows :—

" In all, at least sixty-four German Divisions took part in the operations of the first day of the battle, a number considerably exceeding the total forces composing the entire British Army in France.

" To meet this assault the Third Army disposed of eight Divisions in line in front of the enemy's initial attack, with seven Divisions available in reserve. The Fifth Army disposed of fourteen Divisions and three Cavalry Divisions, of which three Infantry Divisions and three Cavalry Divisions were in reserve. The total British force on the original battle-front, therefore, on the morning of March 21st was twenty-nine Infantry Divisions and three Cavalry Divisions, of which nineteen Infantry Divisions were in the line."

The day had been well chosen for the attack. To quote again from Sir Douglas Haig's despatch :—

" Favoured by a thick white fog, which hid from our artillery and machine guns the S.O.S. signals sent up by our outpost line, and in numbers which made loss of direction impossible, the attacking German infantry forced their way into our foremost defensive zone. Until 1.0 p.m. the fog made it impossible to see more than fifty yards in any direction, and the machine guns and forward field guns, which had been disposed so as to cover this zone with their fire, were robbed almost entirely of

Photo: *Walter Scott*] [*Bradford.*

MAJOR G. LEDGARD, M.C.   THE LATE MAJOR G. BREMNER, D.S.O., M.C.

Two of the Officers who commanded the 80th Field Company R.E.

To face page 128.

Photo: *Swaine*] [*London, W.*
THE LATE CAPTAIN C. F. PAVITT, M.C.

Photo: *Robinson*] [*Redhill & Guildford*
CAPTAIN E. M. WEST, M.C.

Two well-known Officers of the 152nd Company R.A.S.C.

To face page 129.

their effect. The detachments holding the outpost positions were consequently overwhelmed or surrounded, in many cases before they were able to pass back information concerning the enemy's attack."

When the bombardment opened, the Brigade was still at Caillouel, less the Bedfordshire Regiment at Rouez. Shortly after 8 a.m. orders were received to proceed to a position of readiness in the Bois de Tombelle, with Brigade headquarters at the little village of Faillouel, just west of the Crozat Canal, that was to play such an important part in the operations of the next few days. The journey up was made in lorries, and was completed by midday.

By this time the enemy, assisted by a long spell of dry weather, had crossed the Oise River and Canal north of La Fere and south of St. Quentin, between Essigny and Benay. This situation had to be dealt with, if only to gain time, and shortly after 1 p.m. orders came by telephone for the Brigade to counter-attack at once to regain the " Camisole Switch " (a part of the defensive system dug by our battalions) between Montescourt and Ly Fontaine, on the farther side of the Crozat Canal. The Germans were reported to be in Gibercourt, about half-way between these two villages.

With advanced and flank guards, the three battalions were moved across the canal to the south edge of the Montescourt—Ly Fontaine Ridge, moving through wooded valleys till the Fusiliers on the left were at Montescourt and the Northamptonshire Regiment on the right at Remigny. The Bedfordshire Regiment was in reserve, sending one company to hold the high ground east of Ly Fontaine.

The attack was launched at dusk, and met with very slight opposition, the whole of the " Camisole Switch " being occupied as ordered soon after 7 p.m.

By this time the situation, obscure as it necessarily was at the time to those on the spot, had developed rapidly. Fargnier and Quessy, on the Crozat Canal, about five miles south of the Brigade, had been captured by the Germans towards the end of the afternoon, and it was obvious that all British troops east of the canal must be withdrawn. Thus the Brigade had no sooner occupied the " Camisole Switch," and settled down to consolidate, than orders came to form a rearguard covering the retirement of the 14th Division over the canal, and, that job accomplished, to withdraw themselves behind the canal and hold the line at that point.

To follow properly the adventures and misadventures of each battalion during the next few days would fill a volume of individual reminiscences, if they were forthcoming. It was a time when every company and platoon—indeed, every section—made its own history and had its own point of view, though by good leadership and splendid co-operation by all concerned

K

the Brigade always remained a united and (to coin a word) " handleable " formation.

Of the withdrawal to the canal an officer of the Fusiliers writes :—

" Orders were given for the battalion to assemble at a certain map reference and march back to Jussy. Alas for maps and map-reading ! ' A ' Company and battalion headquarters formed up in one field, and the other companies could not be found. I spent an anxious hour looking for them, and found them eventually through running accidentally into Major Deakin, who was commanding ' C ' Company. They had been within 400 yards of us all the time. Then followed the march back to Jussy. By this time everyone was very hungry and thoroughly tired out, and I shall never forget the welcome sight of the cookers, in charge of Captain Minchin—than whom there was never a better quartermaster or more dearly-loved comrade."

It was after midnight when the withdrawal was completed, and the Brigade held the line Jussy-Mennessis, between the railway embankment and the canal. Orders had been given to destroy the canal bridges. It is, happily, not necessary in this book to discuss why the job was not properly carried out. General Sadleir-Jackson himself made every effort to see that the work was done, and at one time the Bedfordshires were making vain attempts to destroy the Montagne bridges with trench-mortar shells. But the fact remains that the bridges had not been prepared for demolition, adequate supplies of explosives were not on the spot, and the bridges were not properly destroyed.

Soon after daylight on March 22nd the enemy, helped again by fog, massed for a great attack on the canal crossings on the Brigade front. The canal makes a sharp bend north of Jussy, and machine guns were able to enfilade the village, so that the Fusiliers holding the left of our line had an extremely uncomfortable time and movement became difficult. Field guns and trench mortars opened heavily on the whole of the Brigade front, and 5·9's were paying unhealthy attention to Faillouel to our rear.

The early evening saw some bitter fighting. Strong assaults were delivered on the Jussy and Montagne bridges, and at both points the enemy secured a footing on our side of the canal. A counter-attack by " B " Company of the Northamptonshire Regiment, hurried up from support, restored the situation on our left, and the Germans were thrown back across the canal. By this time cavalry had been sent to reinforce the hard-pressed infantry, and the Brigade had twenty-seven of the 20th Hussars and thirty Royal Scots Greys, with four cavalry machine guns, in the line with them.

The situation at the Montagne bridge, where the enemy had crossed, was dealt with in the afternoon by three companies of the Northamptonshire Regiment (" A," " C," and " D ") and one company of the Bedfordshire Regiment, who counter-attacked in great style and drove the Germans to the other side of the canal, taking three machine guns and several prisoners, and re-establishing a bridge-head with a Lewis gun. In this counter-attack the Northamptonshire Regiment lost 2nd-Lieutenant Pointer (attached from the Middlesex Regiment) killed, and Captain Fawkes, 2nd-Lieutenant Jones, and 2nd-Lieutenant Woodland wounded.

It was at this time that 2nd-Lieutenant A. C. Herring, of the Northamptonshire Regiment, did the magnificent work for which he was afterwards awarded the V.C. The official account reads as follows :—

"On March 23rd the Germans crossed the Montagne bridge, after severe fighting, and gained a position on the south bank of the canal. 2nd-Lieutenant Herring's post was cut off from the troops on both flanks and surrounded. He at once counter-attacked with his post and recaptured the position, taking over twenty prisoners and six machine guns. The post was attacked continuously throughout the night for eleven hours, and all attacks were beaten off. This was entirely due to the splendid heroism displayed by 2nd-Lieutenant Herring, who continually visited his men personally throughout the night and cheered them up. The initiative and individual bravery of this officer were entirely responsible for holding up the German advance for eleven hours at an exceedingly critical period. The magnificent heroism and personal bravery of this officer, coupled with his initiative and skill in handling his troops, were most important factors in holding up the German advance over the Crozat Canal."

Darkness closed in on that day of hard and bitter fighting, and still the line of the canal was held. During the night the enemy contented himself with sniping and bursts of machine-gun fire.

Captain H. C. Browning, then adjutant of the Bedfordshire Regiment, whom many will remember as Acting-Staff-Captain at a later stage, won his M.C. that day. "The enemy [according to the official account] attacked with large forces, crossed a bridge which had not been demolished, and succeeded in pushing back the left flank of the battalion. He was immediately counter-attacked and thrown back across the canal. This was largely due to Captain Browning, who displayed the greatest coolness and magnificent leadership in collecting and organizing the men and launching the counter-attack at a critical moment under intense artillery and machine-gun fire."

Things had looked so bad for the Bedfordshire Regiment at one time on the afternoon of the 22nd that, with the enemy within about 200 yards of the battalion headquarters, Colonel

Percival and Captain Browning destroyed all maps and secret documents to prevent their falling into German hands.

When day broke on the 23rd the weather still favoured the Germans. Fog was thick over the rivers and canals and in the little valleys, so that he could bring up fresh masses of troops unseen. Then, when he had made his preparations, the fog suddenly lifted as though rolled up by the German staff, and low-flying enemy aeroplanes came over, coolly examining the dispositions of our thin line of defence.

Our own patrols, pushed out into the fog, soon found that the enemy had forced a passage over the canal at Jussy, and was coming on our left flank (Royal Fusiliers) in some force. A little handful of a mixed force was thrown at him in counter-attack—a weak platoon of Fusiliers and thirty Royal Scots Greys—and he was pushed back into the village.

A patrol was sent into Jussy, and found the place strongly held by the enemy. A detachment of Northumberland Hussars, with Hotchkiss guns, who had just reported to the Brigade as reinforcements, were pushed out to strengthen this weak left flank. A little later the Canadian Mounted Brigade sent up four machine guns, and these were put out on the same flank, where they did some magnificent work.

At about 11 a.m. the Bedfordshire Regiment reported the enemy across the canal in strength in the cemetery at Mennessis. Later came news of the enemy marching down the Jussy-Faillouel road, and shortly after midday they were reported in the Bois de Frieres in our rear.

The Fusiliers had been having a very bad time of it. " The fog was thicker than the London pea-soup variety," says the Fusilier officer whom I have already quoted, " and parties of Bosches began to trickle in on both flanks and to cut off parties of our men in the advanced positions. In this way we suffered a considerable number of casualties, including Major Deakin and Captain Pearcy, who were taken prisoners, Lieutenant Simmons and Lieutenant Knott, who were killed, and several other officers who were wounded. Lieutenant Knott, having killed four Bosches with his revolver, and having exhausted his ammunition, was killed while clubbing a fifth.

" A fresh line of defence was now formed about 200 yards behind the canal, but matters were in a very confused state, to which the fog greatly contributed, and when the Brigade staff found that the enemy were well through on both flanks, orders were given to withdraw towards Frieres Faillouel. These orders reached the other battalions of the Brigade while the fog was still intense, and they were able to withdraw with comparatively slight losses. The company of the Fusiliers to which the writer was attached never received these orders, and as far as can be ascertained they were never received by anyone in the front line.

" About midday the fog suddenly lifted. We then found that the Bosche was in front, and that parties were working round in rear on both flanks, and we were subjected to terrible machine-gun fire. At about 2 p.m. the position became untenable, and an attempt was made to withdraw by those in a position to get away, while the remainder were forced to surrender.

" The few who escaped withdrew behind the railway line, about 600 yards farther west, where another stand was made with the help of headquarters' details; but again we were out-flanked and compelled to withdraw with the utmost haste and more or less in disorder. The Colonel held out here with a few men until the Bosches were within 100 yards of him, and then managed to escape unhurt, thanks to their bad marksmanship."

Many officers and other ranks of the Fusiliers distinguished themselves by good work during these desperate hours. Among other officers who won the M.C. were Captains H. W. Brookling and H. L. Smedley.

Captain Brookling " for fourteen hours defended the position held by his company on the canal line against repeated attempts by the enemy in large numbers to cross. The thick mist made this extremely difficult, and it was by his personal example and skilful handling that the enemy were frustrated, with considerable losses. Eventually he was badly wounded, but continued to encourage his men with the utmost disregard of danger. His untiring work prevented the piercing of the Brigade front at the junction of the battalions."

Captain (then 2nd-Lieutenant) Smedley's action is thus officially described:—

" At dawn on March 23rd the enemy forced the canal and occupied the village on the left of the battalion, leaving the flank of the Royal Fusiliers in the air. The situation was obscure, and 2nd-Lieutenant Smedley scouted right out to the flank and up to the village under heavy machine-gun fire. This highly valuable work was carried out with the greatest pluck and determination. During the subsequent withdrawal 2nd-Lieutenant Smedley, although wounded, carried his task to completion by covering the left flank."

A D.C.M. was well won by Private H. Jordan, a company signaller. When the Fusiliers were being withdrawn, he was called upon to surrender with some others by the enemy. " He immediately, on his own initiative, organized a number of men for an attack, and led them, with the result that the enemy were driven back at the point of the bayonet, and the remainder of the company was able to withdraw in safety. He was wounded in the attack, but continued until the withdrawal was complete, and then rejoined his company."

Sergeant W. Brisby, M.M., also won the D.C.M. at this time. " He did very useful work by sniping at the enemy, and caused the withdrawal of an enemy machine-gun team. Later, when his company was at last forced to surrender, he assisted in rallying the men who were prepared to attempt to rush back over ground swept by machine-gun fire. On reaching battalion headquarters he was instructed to accompany an officer to Brigade to report on the position. He begged to be excused, and rejoined the remnant of his battalion, who were making their last stand under heavy fire, and was wounded, but escaped capture."

It was shortly after midday on the 23rd when the Brigade commander decided, in view of the enveloping nature of the German movement on our front, to withdraw to the ridge south of Faillouel. Soon after this line had been taken up, early in the afternoon, came further welcome reinforcements in the shape of 200 of the Canadian Mounted Brigade (Fort Garry Horse and Lord Strathcona's Horse), who were pushed out to our front.

By 4 p.m. it was seen that a further withdrawal would be necessary. The enemy shelled and seized a hill north-west of Faillouel, and, bringing up machine guns and trench mortars, made the position of our troops north of the village impossible. They accordingly fell back fighting through Faillouel, where Germans had already arrived in lorries. Heavy hostile shelling and machine-gun fire continued ; machine guns had us in enfilade from the north edge of Genlis Wood, and eventually the Brigade had to be withdrawn and concentrated at Caillouel.

During the day a gallant piece of work was done by Lieutenant C. E. J. Richardson, with Nos. 3 and 4 sections of the 80th Field Company R.E. They were at Rouez, and carried out a little counter-attack on their own initiative, driving the enemy from some high ground to the east of the village. Indeed, they drove the enemy so far that they were themselves eventually almost surrounded, and had to fight their way back.

Thus ended an eventful and costly day. The Fusiliers, having held the most exposed flank of our line on the canal, and suffered heavily in the fighting and withdrawal in the fog, were now only two officers and twenty-five other ranks strong. The Bedfordshire and the Northamptonshire Regiments had each about six officers and 200 other ranks.

Splendid work had been done by the cavalry reinforcements attached to the Brigade—the Canadians, the Scots Greys, the 20th Hussars, and the Northumberland Hussars. The latter had all their Hotchkiss guns knocked out by shell fire, but brought them out of action.

It was obvious that a lot of trouble was still in store, but the Brigade still had their tails well up, and remained " full o' heart," to use a phrase which was becoming a sort of Brigade motto. Though badly battered, they had done their job, and remained an organized body, and everything possible was done to keep them fit and fresh for further ordeals. Therefore, after a good meal, everyone who could be spared was sent to bed, and thus had the last good night's sleep they were to enjoy for some time.

On the following morning (March 24th) battalions were paraded and reorganized. " Battle surplus " had been picked up at Caillouel, and was used as reinforcements, and a few stragglers had come in. Thus the Fusiliers now became a battalion of eight officers and about 180 other ranks, including transport and other details. Three companies were formed— " X," " Y," and " Z "—the latter consisting of the orderly-room sergeant and clerks, drums, police, pioneers, tailors, shoemakers, etc., under command of the adjutant, Captain Wattenbach.

As soon as this was done the Brigade was ordered to hold the high ground east of Caillouel, gaining touch with the French (9th Cuirassiers) on the left about Beaugies, and the 55th Infantry Brigade on the north edge of Caillouel. The Bedfordshire Regiment was put in the line on the left, and the Northamptonshire Regiment on the right, with the Fusiliers in reserve behind the Crepigny Ridge.

There were slight patrol encounters during the day, and the 5th Royal Horse Artillery Brigade, supporting our line, engaged some targets effectively. But on the whole things were fairly quiet, though it was realized that the situation was developing rapidly on our left, where a strong German attack, after stiff fighting, drove the French out of Guivry.

With the object of finding out the exact position on our left officer patrols were sent out after dark towards Beaugies, then understood to be still held by the French. Soon after 9 p.m. it was learned that the Germans were over the east edge of Beaugies and on the road to Maucourt, towards which village the French were retiring.

Some patrols achieve information, others have it thrust upon them. In the latter class comes a patrol sent out that night under Captain Wattenbach, of the Fusiliers. He started out to have a look along the road which runs north from Crepigny and through a thick wood to Beaugies. Five of his own men and a Frenchman went with him. The following is his account of what happened :—

" We strolled out, just armed with rifles and revolvers, putting points out in the usual way. We went on and on, taking care to make no noise, and came across nobody, but got thoroughly tired, having walked about two and a half miles under very nervy conditions after a very hard day. Very shortly we saw the end of the wood, and, approaching very slowly and cautiously, we found a group of about twenty-five or thirty men in the centre of the road, evidently, we thought, a British or French standing patrol. I looked very carefully, and it entered my head that it might not be one of ours; then I noticed one or two people creeping up under cover on both sides of the road, with the obvious intention of enveloping us. I looked again at the crowd in the road, and Field Service Regulations at once came to my mind. I had learned that bayonets should never be fixed on a moonlight night on patrol duty; these people had their bayonets fixed, and they were short, broad bayonets. Then I heard gruff voices [they were not very far away then], and I knew at once they were Bosches.

"I had one Frenchman and five of our own men with me—not much match for thirty odd Bosches. I remembered, also, that we were about two and a half miles from what I believed to be the nearest British troops. We did not go hot-headed for them and fire all the rounds we had, because we should have been overwhelmed, and discretion, at such a period, I take to be the better part of valour. We did not waste much time in getting back to our battalion and reporting that nobody was in touch on the left, and that the line was very much disconnected.

"On the following day we found that the enemy was well round the other side of the spur, so that on the previous night we must have penetrated to a considerable depth in his lines."

At midnight (March 24th—25th) the withdrawal began, and by 2 a.m. on the 25th the Brigade was roughly on the Crepigny line. Except that heavy firing could be heard from our left, the situation in that direction was still obscure, and at daylight General Sadleir-Jackson, with his liaison officer—Lieutenant Lee, of the Fusiliers—and two mounted men, rode off to see how things looked at Maucourt.

That cleared up the obscurity in no uncertain way, for from Cave Woods, overlooking Maucourt, German columns, with bugles blowing, could be seen marching along the road to Quesny. At the same time heavy firing could be heard from the Guiscard direction, a little farther north.

A little later Captain Cumberlege, then the Brigade-Major, saw from the Grandru spur (or Montagne de Grandru) a column of German troops and transport in column of route in the valley to the north, all marching along in great spirits, with a band leading. A couple of machine guns were got up and opened unexpectedly on the column, putting the transport to flight and inflicting several casualties. It was all very cheerful, but, like all the hard fighting of that morning, it could only delay the inevitable retreat.

As an illustration of the inevitable confusion when mixed bodies of troops under different commands are withdrawing before an enemy who is trying to hustle them, an experience of the Northamptonshires is interesting. The battalion was being withdrawn in artillery formation, and the leading platoon had just got over a crest when they suddenly came under lively machine-gun fire from the opposite ridge. Though the general situation was known to be obscure, it appeared impossible that the Germans had got so far round to our rear. After a while the fire died down, and the battalion got forward. Later on the ridge from which the fire had been opened was reached, and French troops were found in position with machine guns. Some mild remonstrance was made at their action in firing at us, and they were disinclined to admit any responsibility until a tin of bully beef was produced from an officer's haversack with one of their bullets sticking in it. It is only fair to say that they apologized very handsomely then over this rather awkward case of mistaken identity.

Things now began to move rapidly. It was evident that the Germans were moving in force to turn the woods to our north, and possibly to cut off our retreat over the Oise River and Canal bridges to the south of us. The position is best explained to those who do not know the ground by imagining that we were on the Thames Embankment between Northumberland Avenue and Westminster. The enemy are in Whitehall. If they move down Whitehall and round by Big Ben towards the river, they will obviously prevent us from retreating by way of Westminster Bridge. All the buildings between us and Whitehall represent the woods round which the Germans were working, with Beaugies and Quesny somewhere on the Horse Guards Parade. Of course, this represents the actual scene of the fighting on a very small scale.

To make sure that the enemy did not get on the Maucourt-Grandru road before the retirement was completed, the Fusiliers were sent to occupy the Montagne de Grandru, facing north, and the retirement, in conjunction with the French (9th Cuirassiers) and the 55th Infantry Brigade, began at 8.30 on the 25th.

At about 11 a.m. machine-gun fire was heard from the direction of Behericourt, and heavy artillery fire from the direction of the little village of Babœuf. Following the illustration just given, this practically meant that some of the enemy had got on the Thames Embankment near the lower end of Northumberland Avenue. Shells and bullets began to fall among the Fusiliers, and there were all the makings of a very ticklish and unpleasant situation. A little later the Maucourt-Grandru road was receiving a great deal too much attention from artillery and machine guns near the point where it ran round the spur on which the Fusiliers were perched.

To extricate the Fusiliers and cover the retreat, the Bedfordshire Regiment was withdrawn by platoons to the Montagne de Behericourt, a further stage on the westward road to the bridge by which we must cross. (Call it Westminster Bridge, if you have followed the little illustration already referred to.)

This manœuvre was carried out, the Fusiliers were got back by platoons, under artillery and machine-gun fire, and finally the line at Behericourt was held on the left by some French troops who had come up (1st Dismounted Cavalry Division), and the Northamptonshire Regiment, and the Fusiliers and Bedfordshire Regiment were withdrawn into reserve.

All seemed now ready to make the crossing to the south side of the Oise River and Canal, and the Fusiliers and Bedfordshire Regiment were ordered to march on the Babœuf bridge. But before the crossing could be reached, Captain Wattenbach, of the Fusiliers, and Lieutenant Lee, Brigade liaison officer, who had ridden ahead to make sure that the bridges were intact, found Babœuf held by the Germans.

There was nothing to be done now but to divert the crossing to the Varesnes bridge, over two miles farther west, and the whole Brigade was being withdrawn in that direction when it was suddenly faced about to make an amazing counter-attack that, in the minds of those who took part, will live as the most memorable incident of the retreat.

Remember that the Brigade had now had five days of hard fighting and hard marching, taking endless punishment in that always difficult operation, a rearguard action, and that by all the text-books it should have no fight left in it. Indeed, it was sheer unconquerable impertinence that it existed at all after the handling it had received. As for counter-attacking and taking a village—well, it has happened very often in the history of the British Army that the text-books have been neglected in the hour of need, with glorious results. Corunna was one such instance, and the 54th Brigade may be allowed to think that Babœuf was another.

Let us get the situation as clear as possible. The whole Brigade was now making westward for the crossing at Varesnes with—let it be admitted—as much speed as the ordinary precautions of rearguard warfare and due thought for the dignity of the British Army would allow. It was badly out-voted in the little debate that had now been going on for some days, and the weight of the argument had been entirely with the Germans. In short, the Brigade was very tired and very badly punished, and had been fought so nearly to a standstill that it ought not to count. And so it surprised its friends and foes alike by showing that it was still to be reckoned with.

As the Brigade retired, a gap of some 2,000 yards had been left between the French on the high ground north of Behericourt and the 53rd Brigade on the railway-line to the south of Babœuf. Several French batteries of 75's were in this gap, firing towards Babœuf, with no infantry in front of them. It was to save these guns and to delay the Germans, who were thus cutting in between the French and the 53rd Brigade, that General Sadleir-Jackson decided to counter-attack and seize the high ground north of Babœuf and the village itself.

So the tired battalions, now cut down to less than half-strength, were faced about, and shortly after 5 p.m. were deployed for the attack. The front extended from the Babœuf-Compeigne main road, inclusive, on our right, to the south edge of the woods above Babœuf. The Fusiliers were on the right, and the Bedfordshire Regiment on the left, with the Northamptonshire Regiment in reserve.

Within half an hour from the first decision to make this move the attack had been launched, without any artillery preparation. In the excitement of this unexpected move, all fatigue and hardship were forgotten, and everything went forward with a swing. The village was held with machine guns, but the attack pressed on with surprisingly few casualties. One can only assume that the Germans thought something more lay in the move than an assault by a tired, hard-fought Brigade, now barely as strong as a single battalion. At any rate, he gave way, the village was captured, ten machine guns were taken and destroyed, and 230 Germans killed or taken prisoner.

Few will forget the fight up the little main street of the village, where a calf calmly wandered at the head of our line, although a hot interchange of shots was taking place with the Germans. The Fusiliers, who had gone into the attack very weak, met with some little resistance in "mopping-up" the south side of the village, and two companies of the Northamptonshire Regiment were moved up to their assistance. Finally the place was cleared, and by 6.30 p.m. the position was being consolidated in the meadows on the Germans' side of the village. Tools were collected from houses in Salency and sent up in a limber, together with rations from the ever-welcome cooker. There was some shelling of the village, but nothing very serious. As the light failed, the enemy had been seen digging in about 800 yards farther east. So the night came on, a signal-lamp flickered between the village and Brigade headquarters at Salency, and the men settled down wearily, but full of heart, for what seemed the inevitable German counter-attack at dawn.

But the object of the operation had been attained, and there was no intention of holding the position. Orders came to hold the line until 2 a.m. on the 26th, and then to retire over the river and canal. So one by one the tired and battered battalions—first the Fusiliers, then the Bedfordshires, and last of all the Northamptonshires—made their way through the darkness to Salency and across the bridge at Varesnes.

An exhausted motor despatch-rider reported to the Bedfordshires that the bridge was just on the point of being blown up, and Colonel Percival had to send an urgent message to prevent its being blown up before they arrived. On arrival at the bridge they were warned to break step in crossing, as the supports were already half demolished, and might give way before they got over. Everybody was glad to get safely on the other side.

The speed with which our allies destroyed the Oise bridges proved most inconvenient to the Brigadier's liaison officer, who had remained behind to direct the rearguards. This officer was mounted, and found to his dismay, on reaching the Oise, that the river bridge had been demolished, and the sappers were just on the point of blowing up the land bridge. He had a wet journey the rest of the night, as there was nothing for it but to abandon his horse and swim across.

By 6 a.m. they were at Caisnes. The village was already full of French heavy artillery, but the Bedfordshire and Northamptonshire Regiments were squeezed into shelter, and Brigade headquarters were established at Caisnes Château. The Fusiliers were sent a little farther on to L'Aigle. Soon after daybreak all had had hot tea and were settled down for a little rest.

Then followed much moving about, but on the whole a few days of quiet, while the Brigade was pulled together and thrown into another part of the line.

Caisnes had been reached soon after 6 a.m. on the 26th. By 4 p.m. on the same day the Brigade was marching out for Audignicourt, where by 10 p.m. all the battalions settled down for a night in some caves on the north of the village. The caves were filthy, and full of broken bottles, but it was something to have a corner in which to fling a weary body, and to have some sort of certainty that one would not be dragged out in the hours of darkness to march and fight.

On the following day the Brigade was marched to St. Aubin. Here the Royal Sussex Pioneers and the 80th Field Company R.E. were attached. Some French baths were got working, and everyone settled down to the well-earned delights of food, rest, and baths.

The next move was at 4 p.m. on March 30th, when the Brigade marched to Nampcel, whence lorries took them a long, slow journey of twelve hours to Boves, a little south-east of Amiens, where the next phase of the fighting, the defence of Amiens, took place.

In difficult operations, where all did so well and so many were awarded well-won decorations, it is difficult to deal as fully as one would like with individual actions. Those already quoted have been selected merely as illustrating the desperate character of the fighting.

Chapter XIV

THE DEFENCE OF AMIENS

EVENTS of the next few weeks fall under the general heading, "The Defence of Amiens." It was realized that this important centre of communications was the enemy's objective, and the Brigade had a front seat for the show.

The move from St. Aubin was made in French 'busses, and took the whole of March 30th, as a big détour had to be made. The trip was not without its bright moments, as the French drivers had been on the move for about a week, and several of them dropped off to sleep at the wheel and ran the 'busses into trees. It was after dark when Boves (a village about five miles south of Amiens) was reached. The Brigade was all beautifully mixed up. A battalion commander who could find as much as a company of his men was looked upon as almost too lucky for such a war, and the Brigade commander and his officers spent hours wandering up and down a long string of 'busses, sorting out the men, and putting them for the night into streets where nobody knew us or expected us or loved us.

On the following day (March 31st) the Brigade was ordered forward to Gentelles (about four miles due east). The first task was to hold the high ground between Hangard village (held by the French) and Hangard Wood (held by the 53rd Brigade), and accordingly the 6th Northamptonshire Regiment was put into this part of the line. They were relieved by three companies of the 7th Bedfordshire Regiment on the next evening, but again took over the line twenty-four hours later, and continued to hold it for about a week. And not a pleasant week by any means. The troops were accommodated in slits, out of which Jerry shelled them at his pleasure; the weather was very wet, so that everyone was always wet through, and hot food and drink could only be got up to the line after dark.

The enemy were seen digging in on the high ground north of Aubercourt, and on April 2nd it was thought well to attack this ridge and advance our line. The plan was to form up among the trees of the river valley (which here runs practically east and west), and attack north-east.

The attack was to be delivered by one company of Fusiliers on the right, and one company of the Bedfordshire Regiment on the left. Each battalion held a company in close support. It was timed to take place at 6.45 p.m., but was afterwards put off to 7 p.m. on account of the unusual brightness of the evening.

Early in the afternoon the assaulting companies moved out of Gentelles by half-platoons. Unfortunately, as they endeavoured to " trickle " into the forming-up place, enemy observers on the ridge anticipated the attack, and heavy shelling was begun, together with machine-gun fire. The Fusiliers were fired on from front, rear, and right flank, enemy machine guns south of the River Luce doing specially heavy damage, and knocking out all the Lewis guns.

Soon after 7 p.m. rockets and Véry lights went up from the enemy behind the ridge which was the objective of the attack, the barrage and machine-gun fire increased in intensity, and it became clear that the task was beyond the powers of the assaulting troops. The Fusiliers had by this time lost two officers and forty other ranks, and the Bedfordshire Regiment four officers and sixty other ranks.

Accordingly the assaulting battalions were withdrawn to Gentelles, and the Northamptonshire Regiment continued to hold the line.

Now followed heavier shelling by the enemy, and constant attempts to break through. On the misty morning of the 3rd small bodies of his troops were seen trickling into the valley between his line on the Aubercourt Ridge and the line held by the Northamptonshire Regiment. Our Stokes guns put down a hurricane barrage into this valley till knocked out by a minenwerfer. In the meantime hostile shelling continued, and at 4 p.m. a heavy barrage was put down on the line to our left. This began to bend back, the movement spread to a part of our line, but any rot that was setting in was stopped at this stage by General Sadleir-Jackson, who galloped to and fro under fire, rallying the men.

" The men [writes an officer who was present] were met by an infuriated figure galloping up and down the front line. Aghast at the awful language, they stopped. It was the General. It was safer in the line, and they returned."

Our men were rallied on the sunken road which runs north from Hangard to Hangard Wood. Captain Mobbs, of the Northamptonshire Regiment, did good work on the difficult left flank, where the troops we should have been in touch with had fallen back. From here they were taken forward to the original line, which was still in our hands that night.

The retirement of the troops on our left having made the position on that flank rather obscure, a mounted patrol was sent out, and found that the enemy were in the east of Hangard Wood, and our line through the wood and to the north was weak and disorganized. The Fusiliers, who had been detached as divisional reserve, were ordered up to the north of the wood to improve matters. The adventures of that battalion are best dealt with by Major Wattenbach, who was then the adjutant :—

"On the night of April 3rd, just as dusk was creeping on, the battalion received a wire direct from the Division to say that we were to counter-attack through certain squares, whatever they were—anyhow, we were to attack over a distance of three miles—and were eventually to take up a given line. It was raining very hard, and the ground was extremely heavy. The battalion formed up just north of Gentelles, and all officers in possession of compasses took careful bearings. We launched out into artillery formation over very thick plough. The men were wet through, and sank well over the ankle in mud ; it was getting darker every moment, and it was very cold. In short, everybody was properly miserable, and the thought of a long night and all that might happen before daybreak was not exactly a stimulant. However, the battalion plodded along over what seemed to be an endless tract of country. There were no stars to guide the way, and maintaining touch with companies, platoons, and sections under such conditions was no easy matter.

"We carefully counted the roads we crossed, and on nearing the wood, which was on our right, several Bosche Véry lights went up no very great distance from battalion headquarters. Runners were constantly coming in from the front [goodness only knows how they found their way, when we were continually on the move], and it was reported that the Bosches were seen in front digging in on the road, which was part of our ultimate position. Scouts on the left reported one on two Frenchmen, on the right there was no touch, and we came to the conclusion that we had to fill a gap in the line. For all we knew there were no British troops for miles. With great difficulty, and after consultation over soaked maps with an electric torch under a waterproof sheet, we eventually constructed a line on paper, and endeavoured to conform to it on the ground, with a fair amount of success.

"Lieutenant-Colonel [then Major] Gwynn was then sent back by Colonel Sulman to explain the situation, and point out the necessity for another battalion at least to help fill the gap with us. The Essex Regiment eventually arrived just as we were consolidating our new line, and thank goodness things were more or less straightened out. We were then informed that we should have to side-slip past one battalion, and take up the line of the road with our left resting on the Monument [on the Aubercourt-Villers-Bretonneux road]. It was then purely a question of time, as dawn gradually broke with its usual mist, and the battalion began to trudge wearily towards Villers Bretonneux to take up the new line. This we did, and the battalion got into its new position and the Essex Regiment came up on the right just as dawn had broken. One can imagine the feelings of the Bosche on discovering a fairly well-formed line not very far away. We held this line until relieved by the Australians, when we went back to billets in Gentelles."

Leaving the Fusiliers to carry on with their separate entertainment, let us now return to the rest of the Brigade.

April 4th was a day of intermittent shelling of our front and support lines, but there was no hostile infantry action. But the following day was to relieve any boredom that might be creeping over us.

April 5th broke wet and misty, and as visibility improved Germans were seen creeping up the valley and into the dead ground within a hundred yards of our front line. Throughout the morning heavy artillery and trench-mortar fire was directed on our line, and the Northamptonshire Regiment was enfiladed by machine-gun fire from Hangard Wood. As things appeared about to happen, the Bedfordshire Regiment was now brought up from Brigade reserve. Two companies were dug in in a series of small slits, each containing two men, along the ridge between the Domart and Hangard valleys, and two companies were held as counter-attack troops in the Domart valley. Strong points, garrisoned by the Bedfordshire and Northamptonshire Regiments, were also formed, and a section of the Trench Mortar Battery was put on our left flank.

Heavy shelling and machine-gun fire continued throughout the morning and early afternoon, with a good deal of gas. About three o'clock a haystack where a signal-station had been established, about a hundred yards west of a line of poplars that the Northamptonshires will remember, was set on fire by an incendiary shell, and blazed merrily. The Brigade commander had just been making a personal reconnaissance of the front line from this stack, but luckily had left in time.

" Meanwhile [writes a Northamptonshire officer] our front line was being literally battered in by shell fire and trench mortars, inflicting tremendous casualties on the few remaining troops. No tribute can be too high for those gallant officers, N.C.Os. and men who stood firm that day until they were killed, wounded, or taken prisoner. Two officers, Lieutenant Law and 2nd-Lieutenant Hall, were killed, and 2nd-Lieutenant Caswell was taken prisoner.

" By five o'clock the line was pierced in many places, and the remnants of the battalion were collected and took up a position on the ridge midway between Gentelles and Domart. Just as arrangements were being made for our relief an urgent message was received from the officer commanding the French troops on our right, stating that they had been driven out of Hangard, and were about to make a counter-attack to retake the village, asking if our battalion would assist by co-operating, and attack simultaneously on their left flank. To this Colonel Turner at once consented, sending confirmation to Brigade. At the moment fixed for the French troops to commence their advance, 7.20 p.m., the runner returned with the Brigadier's order to assist.

THE 54TH INFANTRY BRIGADE BATTLE FLAGS.

The Pennant (on left) was generally flown at Brigade Headquarters.

To face page 144.

BATTLE FLAG OF THE 11TH (S.) BATT. ROYAL FUSILIERS

"The objective of the battalion was the sunken road running north from the village to Hangard Wood, 1,500 yards distant. Colonel Turner led the attack, assisted by Major Stewart. We met with considerable artillery opposition, and sustained several casualties early in the advance from shell fire. Midway to our objective were the glowing embers of a straw stack which had been set on fire a few hours previously, and silhouetted against this light our line became a ready target for the enemy machine guns now brought up into the copse adjoining our objective. Nevertheless, we had succeeded in getting to within fifty yards of the sunken road, when a large volume of machine-gun and rifle fire held up the advance. At this point a heavy shell fell a few yards in front, wounded Colonel Turner and killed Major Stewart and 2nd-Lieutenant Cuzens. The road itself being strongly enfiladed by machine guns, a line was taken up just short of it, where we dug in and held on till relieved some hours later by the Australian Corps.

"Throughout the period from March 23rd Colonel Turner was continuously with the battalion. His personal bravery had long been a byword with us, but never before did his valour show so conspicuously as during this week. No one who took part in this final counter-attack will forget the manner in which he led the few remnants of his battalion forward, himself at the head, cheering and urging them on, and finally, when wounded, sitting up and encouraging the men to dig in."

That night our front was handed over to the Australians, and the Brigade was withdrawn to Gentelles, where it was held for counter-attack purposes till the 13th, when it was sent a little farther back to Cagny and Boutillerie.

The M.C. was well earned by Captain B. C. Gillott, of the Northamptonshire Regiment, on the night of the counter-attack just described. He had done good work throughout the day under heavy fire, and after the commanding officer had been wounded and the second-in-command killed, he, as adjutant, was chiefly responsible for organizing the new position and keeping touch with the French.

The remaining work of the Brigade, which was now held in readiness to counter-attack anywhere on the Corps front, was chiefly in connection with the enemy's last great effort before Amiens. At dawn on April 24th a particularly heavy bombardment awoke any who happened to be asleep in Amiens and the surrounding villages, and the word went round that the Germans were attacking again.

The Brigade was soon under arms, and by 7 a.m. was crossing the river bridges at Fort Manoir Farm, on its way up to the line once more. A position was then taken up roughly on the St. Nicholas-Blagny-Tronville track (west of Bois de l'Abbe), ·nd the battalions dug in. But orders soon came to get farther ·ward, and by 1 p.m. the Brigade was dug in on the high ground between Gentelles and the south-west corner of the Bois de l'Abbe, across the enemy's main line of approach to Amiens.

The situation to our front was somewhat obscure, but it was gathered that, following closely on the heavy bombardment at dawn, the enemy had launched a determined assault on Villers Bretonneux, and was now holding the eastern edge of Bois de l'Abbe. He was also disputing the possession of Cachy.

Cachy was at this time covered by a composite body known as "Shepherd's Force," taking its name from an officer of the 6th Northamptonshire Regiment who had been put in command.

The battalion had reached Cagny, and Major Shepherd, after a good dinner, had taken his clothes off for the first time for a week, and gone to bed in a real bed. He might have known that such luxury was too good to last, and the events that followed are worth quoting as typical of a quiet night in rest billets.

At 1 a.m. a German aeroplane came over and dropped bombs on the village, badly smashing up a company of the London Regiment who were marching through, and partially wrecking Major Shepherd's billet, bringing his bed in ruins to the ground. He spent some hours in slippers and pyjamas collecting the wounded of the London Regiment, and had just refixed his bed with a view to getting asleep again, when a runner dashed in with a message. It was an order to report to the 175th Brigade at 10 a.m.

On reporting there he was told to take over command of a scratch team, to be known as "Shepherd's Force," and to hold the line in front of Cachy, with headquarters at Gentelles. He accordingly proceeded, with Captain Gillott as adjutant, to the latter place, where a long queue of officers with small parties under their command reported for duty. Eventually the force was sorted out, and found to consist of :—

    2 companies 6th Northamptonshires (" A " and " C ").
    1 company 1-4th Suffolks.
    1 company London Regiment.
    70 R.Es., under Major Byewater.
    Part of 175th T.M.B. under Captain Peabody.
    7 tunnellers.
    8 machine guns.

The days that followed were full of excitement, the German gunners and gas merchants doing all in their power to keep "Shepherd's Force" from getting bored with the proceedings.

An attack was expected any day. Captured Germans stated that at least two Divisions were going to be put into the attack, and more if necessary ; further, that the attack had been practised behind the line on prepared ground, and the objective was a village unknown, which they were not only to go round, but to go through. Nice little pink forms arrived almost hourly from Division, giving further information of the forthcoming attack. Fifteen German tanks were to be used. Yellow Cro gas was to be flung in unsparingly. "Shepherd's Force" began to feel that the Germans were taking it far too seriously.

Finally, in the early hours of the 24th, just as the great bombardment had begun, the Division sent Major Shepherd a cheery little message, reading : "In continuation of my so-and-so of such-and-such a date, prisoner states that village of Cachy is their objective."

By this time Cachy had ceased to be a residential site, and had become a mere heap of road-mending material, for the bombardment was hot and strong.

Defensive measures against the tanks—of which this was the first use by Germans—had to be thought of. Arrangements were made to bring field guns forward to deal with them, but owing to the mist which was a constant early morning feature, it was realized that they would not be able to get on their targets. It was then decided to push up trench mortars, with orders to put down a barrage as soon as they saw a tank. It was not thought that this would do any damage, but it was hoped that it would scare off the tanks, as it was the Germans' first use of them.

The attack duly took place, the Germans broke through the troops in front and came down on "Shepherd's Force." A message came back to headquarters that two tanks were about 500 yards to our front, and that Germans were forming up around them. This attack was driven off, but one of the tanks came on until it was right on top of our wire. Then, to the general amazement, it turned round and tried to get away, but stuck fast soon afterwards, and was eventually brought into our lines. This was the first German tank captured by us, and "Shepherd's Force" very much wanted to adopt it as a mascot, but general opinion was against them. Drawings of it were afterwards distributed to units by G.H.Q., with "vital spots" marked for the benefit of all concerned.

Later on in the day the Germans attacked again with tanks and infantry, and got within 300 yards of our lines. It was beginning to look as though "Shepherd's Force" would shortly be struck off the strength of the British Army with some violence, when a dramatic thing happened. Seven of our own light fast tanks (whippets) came racing out of the Bois de l'Abbe and went all out for the Germans. By a happy coincidence these whippets were under the command of Captain Price, formerly of the 6th Northamptonshire Regiment, who has already been mentioned in these pages. The German attack was completely broken up, our fast tanks dashing to and fro among the Germans, shooting and crushing them down, and finally coming out of action covered with blood.

On the following night "Shepherd's Force" was relieved by a battalion of French Moroccan troops, and ceased to exist, its various parts rejoining their own units.

Now to return to the rest of the Brigade, which we left dug in between Gentelles and the Bois de l'Abbe. This position was occupied throughout the day, except that the 11th Royal Fusiliers were detached and moved into support behind the 58th Division, a little to the south of Gentelles.

At about 6 p.m. Captain H. C. Browning, adjutant of the Bedfordshire Regiment, and temporarily in command of the battalion, was summoned to Brigade headquarters, in a slit dug-out under a root-stack, and ordered to counter-attack towards the Villers Bretonneux-Aubercourt road, with a view to retaking our front line, which had been rushed by the Germans earlier in the day. This was, of course, the part of the line which had been pierced in front of "Shepherd's Force." He was told that the Australians would be on his left, and the West Kent Regiment on his right, and our barrage would open at 10 p.m.

He decided to attack with " C " Company on the right (commanded by Captain Kingdon, killed in the operation), " B " in the centre (commanded by Captain McBride, also killed), and " A " on the left (commanded by Lieutenant Trewman, wounded). " D " Company was held in reserve (commanded by Captain Lawrence, killed).

Having made his plans with his company commanders, Captain Browning pushed ahead with a runner to see where the Australians' right would rest, and to find the forming-up line. In attacking, the battalion would have the Bois de l'Abbe on their left, and Cachy to their right rear, with their objective directly ahead—a simple affair as regards direction, except for the darkness.

It was very heavy going through sticky mud all churned up by shell fire, and very dark, but luckily fine. On arriving at the line, locating it with some difficulty, Captain Browning found where his right and left were to rest (this gave him a front of about 900 yards), and proceeded to lay down the tape. Owing to the short notice at which the attack had to be carried out, he had brought no tape of his own, but borrowed about 300 yards from the Australians, and, cutting this into lengths, began to put this down on a sort of dot-and-dash principle— a piece of tape, a gap, a piece of tape, another gap, and so on.

Laying out a tape on a compass bearing, when you don't know where the enemy may be, is tricky work. The Australians had told him that the Bosches were somewhere around, so Captain Browning put out his runner about fifty yards in front with a rifle to act as a covering party, and bent to his job.

He had done about a hundred yards, and was stooping down, when someone bumped into him. He stood up and asked angrily—those of us who know him can imagine the glance of gentle indignation through the monocle!—where the first *H* in *H*alifax the intruder was coming to. Then he saw, to his annoyance, that it was a German—bother these Germans! they were always meddling with a fellow's job—and became acutely conscious that he himself was carrying only a stick. However, it was explained to the German that he was a prisoner, he was made to throw down his rifle, and thereafter he amiably strolled along with Captain Browning while the tape-laying continued.

Another 150 yards along five more Bosches were encountered coming from the direction of our lines. They fell in with the idea of the game at once, began " Kamerading " with all their hearts, threw down their rifles, and joined the procession. At this point Captain Browning thought it well to withdraw his covering party (one man), and use it as escort to prisoners (see Field Service Regulations *re* initiative of commander on the spot in arranging local protection). Six more Bosches were bumped into near the derelict German tank already mentioned, and added to the party, and when at last the tape-laying was finished, the whole party was handed over to the runner to be taken back. Just as he was on his way back with them another ten came up out of the darkness and surrendered.

It was now past 9.30 p.m., and when the assaulting companies were ready to get away, the barrage had already moved forward, so short had been the notice given for the attack.

Things were now getting very lively, the Germans throwing a lot of stuff about, twice blowing up the Bedfordshire Regiment's headquarters.

The assaulting companies moved off " into the blue "—or rather, into the black—with little information except that their objective was something over 2,000 yards ahead. Our line was very thin, the men being extended to five paces. Most of them were lads of under nineteen, some of the reinforcements hurried out from England when the Bosche started his push in March, but all were very keen and in good spirits.

The platoons came under machine-gun fire almost at once, and a number of officers and other ranks fell. But the rest pushed on, reached a belt of our own wire, trickled through, and dealt with a number of Germans in shell-holes and slits beyond, who promptly gave themselves up. Then in the darkness, lit up now and then by German star shells, the line pushed steadily on, till at last it was thought they were on their final objective, and orders were given to get down and dig in.

By this time only two officers were left, 2nd-Lieutenant W. Tysoe and 2nd-Lieutenant E. J. Scott, and they decided to halve the battalion front. 2nd-Lieutenant Tysoe was on the left, and in touch with the Australians; but 2nd-Lieutenant Scott could find nothing but Bosches on the right, so our flank on that side was in the air. 2nd-Lieutenant Scott therefore borrowed a platoon from the Australians, and then sent out a patrol on his right, who found the Germans working round behind us.

Ammunition was by this time running out, but one of our old dumps was found in front, and this was distributed. This piece of good fortune was largely due to Private G. A. Hughes, who was awarded the M.M. " He went forward [says the official account] to find an ammunition dump which was believed to exist about 150 yards in front of the line. He located it, and later took a party and succeeded in getting five boxes back to the front line when ammunition was urgently needed. When this was completed, he again went out on several occasions and managed to bring in wounded men, in spite of the heavy machine-gun fire which went on throughout the night."

Just before dawn Captain Browning managed to get up to the front line to see the situation for himself, and to mark the line on a map. He then returned, promising to send up rations and water.

At dawn 2nd-Lieutenant Scott came across to 2nd-Lieutenant Tysoe, reported his rather difficult position in view of the fact that the Germans still appeared to be working round his flank, and said he would go back for orders. He started off with his batman, but was wounded and taken prisoner on the way, and from this point 2nd-Lieutenant Tysoe was alone and in command of the whole situation.

For a time things were quiet, except for pretty constant sniping by both sides, the Bosche trickling reinforcements into his front line. 2nd-Lieutenant Tysoe took advantage of this comparative lull to reorganize the remnants of the battalion, dividing the men into thirties, just wherever they happened to be, and putting them under N.C.Os. as platoon commanders. By this time his " staff " consisted of Company Sergeant-Major O. H. Kirby (who acted as second-in-command) and a number of N.C.Os. who took command of the little scattered groups. These included the following, the details of their good work being quoted from the official accounts on which they were awarded medals :—

Sergeant G. H. Holloway, D.C.M., " was left in charge of a considerable part of the front line after a successful counter-attack in which nearly all officers became casualties. Owing to the attack on either flank being held up, the battalion was for a considerable time in a precarious position, and it was largely due to his great determination and personal example that the front line maintained its ground, in spite of several attempts by the enemy to cut it off."

Sergeant H. G. Robinson, D.C.M.: " After all the officers of his company and the company sergeant-major had become casualties, he took command of the men of his own and other companies in his part of the line, and organized the defence of the position gained, which they hung on to all the following day till relieved, though under heavy fire and almost surrounded.

Sergeant J. Boness, D.C.M. : " Time after time he rallied his men, keeping them together and inspiring confidence. Regardless of danger, he with a few men rushed a machine gun which was causing a good deal of trouble and put it out of action."

It now became of vital importance to report the situation to the rear, and 2nd-Lieutenant Tysoe sent two runners back to try and get a message through. Both disappeared, so two more were sent out. Later on one of them, Private A. G. Bailey, arrived back without equipment or helmet, and said that he had been attacked by Germans, and his companion killed or wounded. This was the first definite information that the battalion was surrounded. Private Bailey, who already wore the M.M., was awarded a bar for his work that day, the official account reading :—

" He left the line with a message for battalion headquarters. On the way he was attacked by a Bosche patrol, his companion being wounded. He shot three of the enemy in rapid succession, and in the confusion this caused escaped with his message."

Germans could now be seen moving all around, and the Australians on the left reported their left flank in the air and the Bosche in the wood.

At about 8 a.m. two Germans were seen approaching with a white flag, and it shows the confidence with which the Bedfordshire Regiment—nearly all of them mere boys, under a junior subaltern who, at any rate, was not of very advanced years—was holding out, though surrounded and cut off, that they actually thought the Germans were coming in to surrender. They were conducted to 2nd-Lieutenant Tysoe's shell-hole by a sergeant of the Machine Gun Corps, attached to the Bedfordshire Regiment, who took the opportunity to report that his flank was almost completely surrounded.

The party consisted of a German sergeant-major, who spoke good English, and a private as flag-bearer. On arrival they demanded of 2nd-Lieutenant Tysoe, to his great annoyance, that he should surrender to avoid further unnecessary bloodshed. The message from the German commander added that the little British force was surrounded by two divisions, and it would be blown out of the ground if it did not surrender. The German sergeant-major further confided that he had been promised the Iron Cross for this job.

2nd-Lieutenant Tysoe's reply was a refusal, but he added that if the flag party liked to be blindfolded, they would be taken back to battalion headquarters to ask if the line was to surrender. The Germans agreed, promptly produced handkerchiefs, and were sent back blindfolded under escort of Company Sergeant-Major Burles and his batman. Of the escort nothing more was heard of for some time, and they were reported missing until they were afterwards found to have been wounded and taken back through another division's area. The two

Germans were afterwards found wandering about our lines still blindfolded.

Another flag party was seen coming across some hours later, but 2nd-Lieutenant Tysoe refused to have anything to do with them, and they returned. He then crept from shell-hole to shell-hole, and reached the Australians, and agreed with them to hang on. About 12 noon an Australian Brigade attacked and captured the Bois de l'Abbe, and restored the situation on the left flank.

Owing to sniping, movement was very difficult, but Sergeant S. Walby volunteered to try and get back to battalion headquarters with news, and succeeded. In all, this N.C.O. made four journeys to the rear, under fire, two of them in broad daylight, and his information proved most valuable.

About 1 p.m. the Germans began heavy shelling, evidently a part of their threat to blow the little party out of the earth. Skipping from hole to hole to organize the defence of the exposed left flank, 2nd-Lieutenant Tysoe once fell into a slit on top of a Bosche who was reading a letter. Without apologizing for the interruption, he managed to be first with his revolver, and the German surrendered. He was sent back alone to the rear.

Just about this time Private F. Millward, a signaller, appeared with a sand-bag full of rations, and volunteered to distribute them. As a matter of fact the need for rations, which at one time had been rather acute, had now been overcome, the men having found iron rations and bottles of coffee in German equipment which had been hastily discarded when the enemy vacated the position. Millward did much good work that day, and was awarded the M.M., the official account stating that " he made continuous efforts to get in touch with battalion headquarters on the lamp, both by day and night, thus exposing himself to very heavy machine-gun fire. These efforts proving of no avail, he volunteered as a runner and took messages. Later he distributed rations along the front line in broad daylight, while machine-gun fire was continuously sweeping the line."

The shelling and machine-gun fire continued. Towards dusk much German movement was apparent on the right, and an attack appeared to be preparing at our rear. 2nd-Lieutenant Tysoe decided that something must be done, and formed a defensive flank with four of his roughly organized platoons, about 100 men in all.

At dark the Germans attacked this flank, but did not seem particularly strong, and our fellows, with splendid spirit, jumped up and went for them with the bayonet, driving them off.

About midnight a message came through from Captain Browning saying that the French would probably relieve the Bedfordshire Regiment, but the hours passed with nothing happening, except for occasional encounters with German patrols.

Towards 4 a.m. the Australians on the left moved off, after reporting that the French were formed up for a counter-attack behind us.

2nd-Lieutenant Tysoe then decided to get back if possible. It was still dark, but he took a compass bearing on the west corner of the Bois de l'Abbe, and got his men out by platoons, passing through three lines of French on the way.

For his fine work on that occasion 2nd-Lieutenant Tysoe was awarded the D.S.O., the official account stating that—

"He showed the greatest skill and ability in organizing and consolidating the line after a successful counter-attack. He was the only company officer left, and had command of the whole front line held by the battalion.

"Throughout the night of the 24th-25th he worked unceasingly under very heavy artillery and machine-gun fire, with his right flank exposed.

"During the evening of the 25th the enemy, after putting down a heavy barrage, launched an attack, and succeeded in advancing through the gap on the right of the battalion. 2nd-Lieutenant Tysoe at once counter-attacked on his own initiative with as many men as he could get together and drove the enemy back.

"This fine example of gallantry and leadership by this young officer was entirely instrumental in holding the ground gained with many young soldiers who were in action for the first time."

The Brigade was now withdrawn, and went into rest west of Amiens, until the war was resumed, so far as they were concerned, in a new sector.

Chapter XV

ALBERT

ON May 5th, 1918, the Brigade moved to the Albert sector, and for over two months returned to the old routine of trench warfare. The line was within about 500 yards of the western edge of Albert, and the battalion were on ground familiar to them from their earliest experiences in the autumn of 1915, the front line they now held having been a part of the support system in those far-off days. Ahead of them, beyond Albert, lay Fricourt, Montauban, Trones Wood, Thiepval, and many another place of proud memories.

It was a comparatively good sector, but, unfortunately, at the time of our arrival the retention of the spur (the high ground before Albert) had assumed considerable importance. Captured hostile maps clearly indicated that the enemy were of the same opinion. Officers from higher commands continually visited us, urged the importance of holding on, spoke of the honour of dying at one's post, and bade us an affectionate farewell.

The exact moment of the attack was said to be known, so we trembled and waited, and waited and trembled, later ceased to trouble, and eventually becoming thoroughly bored.

This boredom was considerably enlivened by the arrival of a general officer of cavalry, who rode with his staff up to a certain company headquarters in broad daylight. The true cavalry spirit of adventure appeared to be thoroughly ingrained in all his squadron leaders, who rode all over the sector, with hosts of retainers. These cheery and plucky visitors proved a trifle expensive, as the enemy noticed the show, and headquarters were soon afterwards completely destroyed by shell fire as a result.

Later on we moved across and took up a sector alongside the Australians holding Ville sur Ancre, where we renewed a friendship which had commenced so happily during the Villers Bretonneux attack. Small parties of American troops were attached to us during this period, and battalion commanders were instructed to offer them every facility for seeing and taking part in trench routine. This was evidently very thoroughly done, as one American officer, on return to Brigade headquarters, stated that he was now thoroughly acquainted with every missile which was fired from every piece of ordnance in the German Army.

During the Brigade's tour of duty in this sector battalions in reserve were camped in Henencourt Wood, and of a rest period of the Bedfordshire Regiment in this spot a story is told which may be received or rejected at pleasure.

One of the men got a little muddled through an error in estimating his powers of resistance in the matter of French wine, and lost his bayonet. Then, to his consternation, he found that there was to be an inspection by the General the next morning, so he made friends with one of the pioneers, who fixed him up with a wooden bayonet for the parade, forgetting the necessity of being able to obey the command, " Fix bayonets."

When this order came in due course next day, the unfortunate soldier was naturally discovered by his company commander as being the only man without his bayonet fixed. Sternly the O.C. company reprimanded him, and ordered him to get his bayonet fixed at once. With almost commendable quickness of thought, the man assumed a painful expression, and, with a break in his voice, said : " Sir, this is the anniversary of my mother's death, and I have taken an oath never to fix my bayonet on this particular day."

By this time the Brigadier had arrived, and it was evident that a crisis was imminent. With his usual rapid and comprehensive glance round the Brigadier at once fixed on the one weak spot, even though the man had been concealed in the rear rank of the rear platoon. A quivering company commander accompanied the General at once to the wretched bayonetless soldier. On interrogation once again, the man (with rather less confidence than the first time) replied with the same yarn concerning his mother. But the General had by this time seen what was the matter, and decided to work out the situation to its logical conclusion. " Fix your bayonet at once," he demanded, " and don't stand there discussing your home affairs. Now then, jump to it !"

But the man was not yet defeated, and his remaining presence of mind enabled him to play out his part to the end. Drawing his wooden substitute from its scabbard, he exclaimed : " Sir, I must obey your command, but may the Lord strike it into a wooden one !" As the wooden bayonet fell at the General's feet the man stood stiffly at attention, and must have felt the utmost relief when he saw the General unsuccessfully try to repress a suggestion of a smile. The man had won.

It was during this period that another change took place in the Brigade, the 7th (Service) Battalion Bedfordshire Regiment ceasing to exist, and being replaced by the 2nd Battalion, one of the line battalions of the regiment.

The reorganization of Brigades on a three-battalion basis had led to the disbanding of a number of service battalions. The 12th Middlesex Regiment had already gone (as mentioned in

Chapter XIII). Now it was decided that the Bedfordshire
Regiment must lose its junior service battalion, which happened
to be the 7th, and it was replaced in the Brigade by the 2nd Battalion, which up to this time had been serving with the 90th
Brigade of the 30th Division.

As a matter of fact, it was, so far as this Brigade was concerned, little more than a change of number. Practically all
the officers and other ranks of the old 7th remained, the officers
and other ranks of the 2nd arriving like a draft. To all intents
and purposes the 7th was simply renumbered as the 2nd, and
retained the commanding officer, second-in-command, adjutant,
and other officers under whom the service battalion had won
its spurs.

Apart from patrols and minor raids, the chief operation of
the Brigade in this sector was that undertaken against the German defences at the north-west corner of Albert, known as the
" Hairpin." This was carried out on the night of June 30th-
July 1st.

" The position [writes an officer who took part in the attack]
was peculiar. The front line trenches of both sides mainly
consisted of deepened remains of the old French defences.
Both front lines were almost on a level on the top of a small
hill. The standing corn amongst the trenches and partly in
No Man's Land largely concealed the view. In our own divisional area there was only one communication trench, on which
the Bosche 5·9's registered with remarkable accuracy. This
made the getting up of the large amount of stores, ammunition,
wire, etc., a lengthy business, and most of it had to be done
overland during the night. Fully a week was occupied in
forming the necessary dumps and camouflaging them, and this
was carried out successfully, no shell or trench mortar hitting
any dump or destroying the camouflage.

" The possession of the line given as the objective would give
us complete command of the northern end of Albert and the
Ancre Valley to the north, and would probably render the
enemy's positions east of the river untenable. It was therefore obvious that the enemy would put up a strong resistance,
and would probably sacrifice a great deal to retake his original
line, if lost."

The assaulting battalions were the Northamptonshires on the
right and the Bedfordshires on the left, and an elaborate scheme
for the attack, in which machine guns, trench mortars, gas,
smoke, and of course plenty of artillery, all played a part, was
drawn up. It was to be a night attack, and the novel plan was
adopted of keeping direction by means of flame tracer bullets,
Lewis guns firing these tracers on lines which defined the flanks
of the assaulting platoons.

The " Hairpin " system curved across our front in such a
way as to suggest an attack from the rear. Thus, while one

platoon of the Northamptonshire Regiment made a frontal attack, other platoons, from a point farther south, were to advance north-east, cross the trench, work along the east side of it, and attack from the rear. The Bedfordshire Regiment was to do much the same thing, the right of their attack crossing the enemy front line at a selected point, then left-wheeling and taking it in the rear.

Following closely on the heels of the assaulting companies were to be wiring parties, to wire promptly the far side of the trench, as a part of the consolidation scheme.

Orders issued by the Northamptonshire Regiment detailed " B " (commanded by 2nd-Lieutenant B. Martin) as the assaulting company, and " D " (commanded by Captain Gillott) as the wiring company. The Bedfordshire Regiment detailed " B " company for the assault and " C " for wiring.

Zero hour was 9.35 p.m. on June 30th. Gas had been put over on our right, to keep the enemy in that part of the line as much amused as possible, and smoke was put over that part of his front which we were to attack. This had the desired effect of making him put his gas-masks on.

Guided by the glowing lines of the tracer-bullets, the assaulting platoons pushed forward to their objectives, closely followed by the wiring parties. A few prisoners were taken and quite a fair number killed in the small mine-shafts the enemy had commenced in his trenches. The attack was evidently a surprise, as many of the Germans had their boots off.

The Northamptonshires secured their objective without trouble from the enemy, and their wiring company was extremely quick in putting out the wire, which was all in position before the smoke and dust of the barrage had cleared.

The Bedfordshire Regiment had rather a deeper objective, and met a good deal of machine-gun fire from their left flank, and some brickworks to their front, but the objective was reached. The wiring company were considerably hampered by machine-gun fire, and were unable to complete their work, although a good deal of wire was erected.

After 11 p.m. the front was again quiet, except for machine-gun fire, and the work of consolidation was pushed on. Companies of the Fusiliers were engaged in digging communication trenches between our old front line and the German line which we had taken.

Dawn on July 1st saw the beginning of a series of counter-attacks, which eventually led up to the enemy regaining complete possession of his old line.

Signallers had some bright moments while trying to keep touch with the assaulting companies. Touch having been lost with the Northamptonshire Regiment, Lieutenant C. H. Webb, Brigade Signal Officer, crawled up in the early hours of the 1st, and managed to establish lamp communication from a platoon within about fifty yards of an orchard held by the Germans. For this and other good work that day he was awarded the M.C., the official record reading :—

"He proceeded to the front line, having to crawl most of the way, and being continually subjected to grazing machine-gun fire. He established communication successfully. The same day, having ascertained the forward end of the 'loop set' [a portable wireless plant] had been damaged, he at once procured a spare set, and went up and re-established communication within thirty yards of the enemy."

It was too much to expect that the official account would give the best point of the little adventure. Lieutenant Webb had crawled up with his wireless, set up his wires above the parapet, and was feeling very full of heart and satisfied with the war, when a runner arrived breathlessly from the Brigadier and gasped out : " General's compliments, sir, and for goodness sake take that thing down ! You're within thirty yards of the enemy." So, amid a parting splutter of machine-gun bullets, the wires were taken down.

Private J. Stevens, of the Northamptonshire Regiment, did good work with the forward end of the "wireless" set which went over with the assaulting company. Under heavy fire he erected the station, and within half an hour after reaching the captured German trench was in touch with battalion headquarters. At one time our artillery was firing short, and the speed with which he was able to get off a message asking for the range to be altered undoubtedly saved many lives.

Lieutenant W. S. Oliver-Jones, of the Bedfordshire Regiment, was in charge of a party detailed to push beyond his battalion's objective to a sunken road, and clear out some dug-outs there. Owing to casualties, he had only six men with him when he arrived there, but he carried out the work successfully, personally blowing up the dug-outs before withdrawing. Several prisoners were taken and a number of Germans killed in the dug-outs, about fifty being accounted for in all. For this he was awarded the M.C. Similar awards were made to Lieutenant H. B. Steward (Bedfordshire Regiment) and 2nd-Lieutenant Martin (Northamptonshire Regiment), who led the assaulting companies.

All through the morning of July 1st the Germans made heavy bombing attacks on the captured trenches, and at dusk attacked under a heavy barrage of 5·9's and 8-inchers. Our Lewis guns succeeded in holding this up short of the old enemy front line, but he succeeded in regaining his old support line. Bombing blocks were established in his old communication trenches and held against bombing attacks during the morning of the 2nd.

Mixed fighting took place most of the day, in which large quantities of bombs were used, so that it was hoped the Bosche would not make another effort until dawn on the 3rd, by which time we should have been relieved by the 8th East Surrey Regiment. The hope, however, was not fulfilled, and again at dusk the enemy attacked under a heavy barrage. After heavy fighting he succeeded in regaining his old front line all along the front, except in a small portion of the 12th Divisional front (on our left). This was evacuated during the morning of the 3rd. The East Surrey Regiment had come up to relieve, but were sent back. The old line was held during the day, and then handed over to the East Surrey Regiment.

In view of the shortage of front and lack of depth in objective, our chances of success were problematical, for the enemy was known to be fairly strong in artillery, and in his counter-attacks used all guns within range.

Some good work was done in those trying days when the battalions were trying to hold on to the captured trenches.

Sergeant C. Clarke, of the Bedfordshire Regiment, won the D.C.M. On the evening of July 2nd he was sent up to take over a platoon which had just had its officer and sergeant killed. " On the way up [says the official account] he had to pass through an enemy barrage. He was blown up and buried by a shell, wounded in two places, and his helmet and rifle were destroyed. On being dug out, he procured another helmet and rifle, proceeded to his post, and took command of all available men near him. In the close fighting which occurred immediately on his arrival he showed a fine example of courage, proceeding at once to the threatened spot, organizing a bombing attack, and clearing a considerable portion of enemy trench. He refused to leave to have his wounds dressed till next morning."

During this period Captain P. J. Reiss won a bar to his M.C. " From 7 to 9 p.m. [says the official account] the new trench was very heavily shelled, and blown in in many places, followed by an infantry attack. During the whole of the bombardment Captain Reiss continued to encourage his men, and when the barrage lifted, he placed himself in the position of the greatest danger at the head of a communication trench. There with a handful of men he made a magnificent resistance, and held up a large number of the enemy. He threw over two boxes of bombs himself, and with the aid of his men was actually pressing back the enemy, when he was attacked from both sides, and forced to withdraw, being himself the last to leave."

Two good stories of this show are told by the signallers. The first concerns the final touch to the preparations. The scene is the Brigade battle post, and the time half an hour before zero. One of the heroes of the story tells it as follows :—

". The N.C.O. in charge was engaged in giving final instructions to the signallers manning the station. ' Don't forget these light signals, you chaps,' he said. ' A red and green pair of lights is the success signal, one red light is for artillery to lengthen range, one green is for artillery support, and we are to repeat all signals.'

" In a short time the General appeared, for it was from this tiny hole in the ground that he would direct operations. As soon as he appeared the signallers sprang to their instruments, and everything was ready. Suddenly, with a terrific crash, the bombardment opened. Soon various coloured lights began to light up the sky, to be instantly repeated at Brigade battle post. The battle had started, and the signallers were soon working at high pressure. Lamps flashed their messages to and fro, telling how the operation was proceeding. Private B——, who was in charge of all light rockets, arranged his stock to a nicety on the parapet.

" Suddenly from the front burst the red and green pair—the success signal. At once the General gave the order for the signal to be repeated, so that all the people who were co-operating with the infantry should know how the situation stood. B—— snatched a Véry light from the pile, then stopped. ' Hurry up,' whispered the N.C.O. ' I cannot fire two at once, corporal,' said B——; ' I have only one pistol.' The N.C.O. gave a groan. ' Do your best, then.'

" B—— fired, and then tried to fire again, but the first light had gone out before he could get the next off. With a smothered remark which may have been a congratulation, but was probably not, the General strode forward. ' Give me the pistol,' he ordered. B—— did so, and handed the General a light also. The General fired, and a green flare was the result. He snatched the second from B——'s outstretched hand and fired again. All eyes watched the tiny bead of light as it rose and then burst— *green* again ! An awful silence, then a gasp from the General. B—— turned sickly pale and his knees knocked. Then the General burst out with—well, at any rate, it wasn't a congratulation. The N.C.O.'s hair turned white in a single moment, and thoughts of suicide flashed through his mind. ' Cancel light signals,' the General shouted. The battle post instantly became a hive of industry. Lamps flashed, and an agonized telephonist bawled down his instrument. Soon order was restored, the General departed, and B—— began to breathe again."

The other story is thus told by the Bedfordshires :—

" The Bedfordshires were holding the line they had captured the day before, and the Bosche was strafing it pretty badly, but not sufficiently to justify our sending up the S.O.S. Still, we sent up the S.O.S., but not altogether according to plan.

" A private soldier was responsible for the mistake, and quite by accident set light to the rocket. Out rushed the company commander, exclaiming, ' My hat ! can I wash that signal out ?'—but he was too late in getting a ladder to fetch the rocket down. The result was an intense mutual strafe between our artillery and the Bosche, much to the dislike of the poor infantry."

The tour in this sector came to an end soon afterwards, and after a short rest to the west of Amiens, returned to the line at the end of July.

Chapter XVI

THE BRAY-CORBIE ROAD

WITH August began what the Army has agreed to call "The Hundred Days' Victory," which ended in the crowning mercy of the Armistice, as Napoleon's famous Hundred Days' Defeat ended in the crowning mercy of Waterloo.

Having relieved troops of the Australian Corps in the line on the night of July 30th-31st, the Brigade at the beginning of August was holding the front from the Somme, just west of Sailly Laurette, northwards to a point 500 yards south of the Bray-Corbie road—something a little over 2,500 yards. The Fusiliers were on the right, and the Northamptonshire Regiment on the left, with the Bedfordshire Regiment in reserve behind Sailly-le-Sec. Brigade headquarters were in the cliffs just north of the Somme, about 400 yards west of Vaux.

On the night of August 2nd-3rd the Bedfordshire Regiment relieved the other two battalions in the front line, the latter going into reserve to prepare for the proposed offensive to be carried out at a later date.

It was a period of heavy thunderstorms and much mud. The Australians, from whom we took over this sector, had been carrying out an aggressive policy for several weeks—"Them Aussies are real rough with Jerry!" as a private in one of the relieving battalions was heard to remark—and this did not tend to improve the trench system, for the Germans were still capable of hitting back quite in their old style. The Australian policy had been to allow the enemy to dig a front and support line, and when this was nearing completion to attack and capture it; and as an attack of this nature had taken place the night before we took over, the front was still in an active state. Our lines consisted of a great number of trenches, the forward ones only half dug, and by August 6th they were knee-deep in mud.

It is good to see the pleasures of trench warfare, now so soon to come to an end, from some other point of view than that of the P.B.I.—you can tell her that means "Poor Bloomin' Infantry"—so the following notes on this period by Captain R. Weir, M.C., of the 80th Field Company R.E., are of interest :—

"On August 3rd, 1918, the company received orders to construct brigade and battalion battle-posts on the south side of the Bray-Corbie road, to be finished in the usual incredibly short time.

"In the afternoon I set out with the Brigade Major to inspect the site of operations, armed with maps, hopelessly out of date ; but the General had said the dug-outs were to be ' just beside the old windmill,' and a trench map must surely be superfluous. As usual in a new sector, we seemed to take every wrong turning possible in the communication trench, and eventually arrived at what our maps said was the front line. If the front line, then someone must occupy it, so we turned northwards along a fairly decent trench.

"We had gone but a short distance before the trench suddenly came to dead end, and further careful consideration of the map became necessary. This helped but little, and we got out on top. We found that the trench started again about fifty yards farther on, and made a dive for it. It was fairly good, but after following it for 300 or 400 yards we became alarmed at the total absence of garrison. Not a soul had we seen since leaving Five Minute Valley, and the whole trench seemed to be littered with Bosche equipment, but not the slightest evidence that the British had ever been there.

"To meet the Bosche would be better than this loneliness, so we pushed on. We hadn't gone very far before coming to a cross-trench, with a very small dug-out on the corner. I suppose we had disturbed the occupant, for on going to the entrance an extremely sleepy sergeant looked out. Here at last was the garrison. ' Who are you ?' demanded the Brigade Major. ' Trench mortars, sir.' ' Where is the nearest company headquarters ?' ' Don't know, sir.' ' Well, don't ration parties pass this way ?' ' No, sir.' ' How long have you been here ?' ' Three days, sir.' ' Well, if you haven't seen anybody, how do you get your rations ?' ' Brought three days' with me, sir.' ' Where is the front line ?' ' This is it, sir, and the outpost is just in front.'

"We resumed our trudge, but had not made more than 300 yards when we got hopelessly tied up in a mixture of half-dug trenches, and as it was getting late we decided to return and get more definite information.

"Next morning I went off with a more up-to-date map that someone had discovered, and very soon had my men started on the new quarters. The sector was the most remarkable I had ever worked in. One could leave Five Minute Valley, visit the front line, tour its whole length and return, and not see a single soul beyond one's own working party. Happening to pay a night visit to the line on the 5th, the mystery was solved for me—the Brigade had resolved into a carrying party, taking ammunition, etc., to the most forward positions.

"The enemy attack on the morning of the 6th upset all the fine calculations. As is always the case in such affairs, the situation remained quite obscure until late in the morning, but it seemed fairly certain that any men working in the dug-outs at the time of the attack must surely be taken prisoners or killed. The shift on the job at the time consisted of twenty-two sappers and one officer. As soon as it became clear what had happened, I hurried off to the forward billets in Five Minute Valley. There I found every soul asleep, and totally unaware that the Bosche was within a few hundred yards. The working shift had not returned, nor had the officer, 2nd-Lieutenant Mackay. It was at once evident that the whole lot had been caught unawares and captured. It has since transpired that only one man was out on top at the time, and in going down to warn his mates was trapped with the rest.

"These forward billets were now, as billets, a little too forward, and, with the sanction of the G.O.C., the men were withdrawn. A motley lot they were, half asleep, each carrying a dixie, or such, and, not having sufficiently grasped the situation, terribly fed up. As luck would have it, the officer in charge of the new battalion headquarters had been wounded about midnight of the 5th, and was on his way to the casualty clearing-station instead of going to Germany.

"The battle of August 8th opened as all good battles should—with the sappers standing by ready to dig strong points whenever it became known that the infantry had advanced to their limit. We were to work for a strange Brigade, however, the 54th having been relieved by the 36th during the previous night.

"The 36th Brigade were so unfortunate as to be total strangers to this sector, and, to make things worse, the dawn broke in an extremely dense fog, and everybody was hopelessly lost.

"As time went on Brigade got extremely nervy ; no runner had arrived from the attacking battalions, tanks were coming back into ' stable ' as if the show were over, and not a man in Brigade headquarters dare go a hundred yards from his quarters for fear of losing his way. In the end the General consented to be guided, and off we went in search of the lost battalions. While doing this little tour the fog broke a little, and by the time we had interviewed everybody we met, and located the last battalion in the Quarry beside the Bray-Corbie road, things began to clear up a bit.

"Next day the Americans carried the line well on towards Bray, and to guard against accidents we erected a strong belt of wire along the crest just in front of the final line of the first day.

"The company rejoined the 54th Brigade at Hennecourt on the 10th."

It should be pointed out, in passing, that this area was familiar to the Brigade as the scene of their earliest experiences in the line, and from now onwards they were fighting over ground which they had known in 1915 and 1916.

But to return now to the doings of the rest of the Brigade.

A rather ticklish business was down for the night of August 5th-6th, and the Germans took a hand in no very helpful spirit.

The 54th Brigade (then represented in the front line by the Bedfordshire Regiment) were to be relieved by the 174th Brigade (58th Division), and were, in their turn, to side-step to the north and relieve the 55th Brigade astride the Bray-Corbie road. The Bedfordshires themselves were to be relieved by the 8th London Regiment, and then, side-stepping northwards, were to relieve the 7th East Surrey Regiment, with their left on the road. Obviously the latter relief could not begin till the Londons had relieved the Bedfordshires. This side-slipping relief by the Bedfordshires was ordered to preserve quite fresh the other two battalions of the Brigade for an assault on the 8th.

A relief is not an easy job at the best of times, and two reliefs in one night are just twice as bad. In addition, all the conditions were very unfavourable. The lines of approach which the relieving troops had to use had been systematically shelled for nights past, the ground was very muddy, the " going " very bad both in and out of the trenches, and the night was very dark.

In view of all this, O.C. Bedfordshire Regiment arranged for the relief to begin at 8.15 p.m., but heard late in the evening that the 174th Brigade had altered this to 9.30 p.m., and it was, as a matter of fact, exactly 10 p.m. before the guides were able to start. The relieving troops were very tired.

By 3.30 a.m. on the 6th this part of the relief was still incomplete, and O.C. Bedfordshire Regiment sent his adjutant to O.C. East Surrey Regiment to inform him of this fact, and to say that he intended to relieve the piquet, support, and reserve lines by daylight, which the mist and the formation of the ground allowed. The Bedfordshire Regiment's adjutant was actually with O.C. East Surrey Regiment arranging this when the German attack started. Matters were the more difficult as communication with the front line was very slow, owing to mist and mud, wires being useless owing to shelling.

The relief of the 11th Royal Fusiliers and 6th Northamptonshire Regiment was equally slow, and was not completed till about 4.30 a.m.

Shortly after 4 a.m., while the relief of the Bedfordshire Regiment by the London Regiment was still incomplete, the Germans introduced a quite unnecessary complication by putting down a heavy artillery and trench-mortar barrage, at the same time throwing gas shells in and around Brigade headquarters at Vaux, one falling between the General's and the Brigade Major's huts. This barrage was followed by a heavy hostile infantry attack, pushed with great determination, regardless of losses.

A great part of our outpost line was pierced and overrun, both on that part still held by the unrelieved companies of the

Bedfordshire Regiment and on the adjoining northward sector, held by the East Surrey Regiment, who were awaiting relief by the Bedfordshire Regiment. However, the Bedfordshires holding the piquet line stopped the German advance on their front, and, counter-attacking at once with their local supports, drove back the enemy to the original line, which was later handed over to the London Regiment.

A little later two companies of the Bedfordshire Regiment in support cleared up the situation in the rear of the East Surrey Regiment immediately south of the Bray-Corbie road, capturing two of the enemy, releasing several of our men who had been taken prisoners, and occupying the Cobar Trench in front of the cemetery and quarry.

Some good work was done at this stage by Lieutenant D. P. Cross, of the Bedfordshire Regiment, commanding the company in the first line. Although both flanks of the position were turned when the enemy overran the outpost line, he held his ground, offering such a stubborn resistance, and giving such vigorous assistance to our counter-attack, that he must be regarded as very largely responsible for restoring the line and arresting the German advance at this point. It was a good example of the value of small bodies of troops holding their ground even when surrounded, as the success of a local counter-attack is thereby materially assisted. This officer won the M.C. for his action on that occasion.

Another M.C. was won here by Lieutenant R. T. Oldfield, also of the Bedfordshire Regiment. " When the hostile barrage lifted off his trench [says the official account], he discovered the enemy occupying the trench on his left. He at once made a bomb-block, and moved a section of his platoon to prevent the enemy working farther round his flank. Shortly afterwards he was heavily attacked, but beat the attack off with rifle and Lewis-gun fire, and finally, by a series of small local enterprises, forced the enemy on his front completely out of the support system."

Other awards made in connection with good work at this stage are worth quoting as illustrating the desperate character of the fighting.

Corporal W. A. Ellis, D.C.M.: " About dawn on the 6th was in charge of the remnant of his platoon, which had already suffered serious casualties. When the enemy recaptured the forward posts, he went forward with a small party and a Lewis gun for an immediate counter-attack. His action was the means of restoring a large portion of our outpost line, and the capture of eighteen of the enemy and three machine guns. By his initiative, courage, and example he was able to carry his small command with him cheerfully through an exceptionally trying ordeal, and successfully beat off several attacks."

Corporal W. Pennycock, D.C.M.: "Ascertaining that the enemy had penetrated the front, he hurried back to his platoon, and so distributed them as to protect the left flank of his battalion. The enemy made three determined attacks on the position held by this N.C.O., and were beaten back on each occasion."

Sergeant F. M. Sims, D.C.M.: "Collected stragglers, rapidly organized them into a firing line, and held off the German advance on his platoon's front. Finding his left flank uncovered, he at once established and manned a block. Throughout the day the position held by the platoon under his command was repeatedly attacked, in addition to several minor bombing attacks. All these attacks were beaten off by rifle and Lewis-gun fire."

The Brigadier now sent to Lieutenant-Colonel Foster, commanding the 6th Northamptonshire Regiment, to push out battle patrols, each supported by one platoon. They had orders to fill any gap on the main road between the Bedfordshire and the East Surrey Regiments, to hold up any small bodies of the enemy who might be moving west along the road, and to send back all the news they could of the situation, which at this time (5 a.m.) was necessarily still somewhat obscure. As it turned out, Colonel Foster had anticipated this order, and had also moved up two companies along the south of the road. A little later the Brigadier moved his battle post to a point a little west of the cemetery, where he was in closer touch with the situation and his battalion commanders.

The prisoners captured a little earlier by the Bedfordshire Regiment had established the fact that the attack was being carried out by battalions of the German 120th, 123rd, and 124th Regiments, all of the 27th Division—a Storm Division which had been out of the line carrying out intensive training for over three months. This Division must have been put in specially for the attack, as it relieved the 107th Division two nights previously. It was evident that someone in Germany wanted to abolish the 54th Brigade.

By 6 a.m. the Northamptonshire Regiment was counter-attacking, and such good progress was made, in spite of heavy rifle and machine-gun fire, that by 8 a.m. much of the lost ground had been regained, and touch was restored with the left flank of the Bedfordshire Regiment. During the fighting Colonel Foster was wounded in the arm.

It was decided to counter-attack at dawn on the following day, in order to recapture the original front, and thus to secure the jumping-off place for the offensive planned for the 8th. Our support and front lines were shelled steadily with artillery and trench mortars throughout the rest of the day. Several small local attacks were made by the enemy against the Bedfordshire Regiment in Cummin's Trench and the Northamptonshire Regiment in Conamulla Support, but all were beaten off by rifle and Lewis-gun fire.

The counter-attack on the 7th was made by one company of the Bedfordshire Regiment on the right, one company of the Northamptonshire Regiment in the centre, and two companies of the Royal Fusiliers (" B " and " D ") on the left. The latter two companies were on the north side of the Bray-Corbie road.

Our barrage came down at 4.40 a.m. on Croydon Trench, and five minutes later moved on to Cummin's Trench. It had been drizzling rain all night, the trenches were all deep in mud, and the morning mist made visibility very poor. In spite of this, touch was kept between the assaulting companies.

The attack on the right and centre went forward successfully, the Northamptonshire and Bedfordshire Regiments gaining all their objectives. Twenty-five prisoners and thirty machine guns, including one heavy machine gun, were taken, and very heavy casualties inflicted on the enemy. As a matter of fact, the enemy was on the point of launching an attack, and his front-line and communication trenches were packed with troops, who had a very thin time when our barrage came down and our companies got among them.

In the meantime things had not been going so well on the north of the Bray-Corbie road. A company of the 8th East Surrey Regiment (55th Brigade) had been placed at the disposal of this Brigade, and was to be placed on the left of the Royal Fusiliers, to form the extreme left of our line.

Before our barrage opened, O.C. " B " Company, Royal Fusiliers, our left-hand company, was endeavouring to get in touch with this company of the East Surrey Regiment, but was unable to find it. Just before the attack began a further effort was made to find this company, but again with no result, and there was a gap of about 300 yards on the left of our line. Two platoons of Fusiliers were therefore put in to fill this gap.

When the attack went forward, the Fusiliers, after encountering and overcoming strong opposition in Croydon Trench, pushed on and captured Cloncurry Trench (which here formed the German front line), from where it crossed the Bray-Corbie road to just south of Cloud Trench. Meanwhile a platoon had fought its way up the latter trench and also reached Cloncurry Trench, where it turned south and joined up with the rest of the company.

On our extreme left O.C. " B " Company, Royal Fusiliers, who was engaged in prolonging his left when the barrage opened, in the endeavour to get touch with the East Surreys, or at any rate to fill the gap, now advanced with two of his platoons. Failing to get touch on either flank, however, he withdrew on Burke Street, without reaching his objective.

At 5.10 a.m. our protective barrage died down, according to programme, and at 6 a.m. the enemy launched four simultaneous counter-attacks for the recovery of Cloncurry Trench. All but one were beaten off. In the latter case the platoon holding a sector of the trench had used up all their bombs, and had to fall back fighting near Cloud Support. A bank running parallel to Croydon Trench greatly helped the enemy at this point.

Continual artillery, trench-mortar, and machine-gun fire was kept on our support trenches, the head of Cloud Support becoming untenable, and movement in the shallow trenches very difficult. A direct hit from a trench mortar knocked out a Lewis gun which had been doing good work near the Bray-Corbie road, and another strong attack gave the enemy a footing in another portion of Cloncurry Trench, along which he began to bomb his way.

" D " Company of the Fusiliers stopped these attacks till all their bombs were used up, and then fell back fighting on to Croydon Trench, where bombing blocks were established. This company now mustered one officer (Captain Baker, wounded) and three men.

Early in the afternoon further efforts were made to get in touch with the East Surrey Regiment on our left, and Lieutenant Wixcey, of the Fusiliers, with the remnants of two platoons of " B " Company, pushed up Croydon Trench and retook a part of Cloncurry Trench, proceeding to work north and south. After making some progress, these parties were heavily attacked, and after holding out very gallantly for about half an hour were forced back.

Under cover of heavy artillery and trench-mortar and machine-gun fire, the enemy launched powerful attacks against the Fusiliers about 3 p.m., and reached a part of Croydon Trench, but were stopped there by remnants of " B " Company and a Lewis gun.

The position now was that on the north of the Bray-Corbie road the enemy held all Cloncurry and Croydon Trenches. A hostile attack had gained a slight footing on Cummin's Trench just south of the road, and a Lewis gun team had been completely wiped out, but the Northamptonshire Regiment had regained this point. The line to the south of the road was now intact. A section of the trench mortar battery, with 100 rounds per gun, was sent forward to support the Fusiliers.

As the enemy were in great force on the north of the road, it was decided that no good purpose would be served by isolated attacks, and that a concentration of artillery and trench mortars should be brought to bear on the enemy, followed by a counter-attack at 9 p.m., after a heavy bombardment.

Unfortunately, this plan was upset by two very gallant young officers of the Fusiliers, who had done good work all day, and fell at the head of their men early in the evening, launching a counter-attack on their own initiative, before the plans for the combined counter-attack had reached them. This local counter-attack, and a portion of the reserve having been used up, the battalion was useless for further effort, and the Fusiliers eventually fell back to their original line.

In the early hours of the 8th the Brigade covered the forming up of the 36th Brigade on the Conamulla Support-Burke Trench line, and was then withdrawn. Although the counter-attack of the 7th did not wholly succeed, it held up the enemy, and contributed to the success on the 8th, when the Morlancourt Ridge position was carried according to programme. The 36th Brigade performed the task originally allotted to this Brigade, for which we were not available, owing to the hammering we had taken on the 6th and 7th. Those best qualified to form and express an opinion hold that, for the courage and initiative displayed by junior officers and N.C.Os. commanding platoons and other small bodies, the Brigade never had a more glorious day, in spite of its lack of complete success, as the day of bitter fighting astride the Bray-Corbie road.

Weight for weight, the Brigade probably never inflicted such heavy losses on the enemy with the infantry weapons—bomb, bayonet, and bullet. When the ground was walked over afterwards, the heaps of German dead bore testimony to the hard-hitting of our men when, driven back from their counter-attack, they stood stubbornly at bay and refused to let the enemy pass. The Fusiliers alone threw over a hundred boxes of bombs that day. Prisoners captured by the Brigade between the 6th and 8th numbered one officer and fifty-seven other ranks, and thirty-five machine guns were taken.

Three officers of the Fusiliers were awarded the M.C.

2nd-Lieutenant W. H. Measures, who commanded " C " Company in support, " considerably helped to strengthen the situation at two critical moments when immediate action was necessary, and gained most valuable information by personal reconnaissance."

2nd-Lieutenant W. Ross " was given charge of two platoons to support the attack in the evening. Seeing that their help was urgently needed, he at once brought them into action in a very skilful manner. Although subjected to intense machine-gun fire, he moved about the shallow trench freely, encouraging the men and superintending the bringing up of bombs. His example after a very trying day's fighting did much to hearten the men."

Captain P. Baker " was in command of the right company in the attack, and he displayed great initiative and dash in getting to his objective, in spite of unexpected obstacles. Later in the day, although both flanks were in the air, and he himself was wounded, he showed great determination in holding on to his position until only three men remained. He then crawled back to the next trench and at once reorganized its occupants, refusing to leave to have his wound dressed until ordered to do so."

A number of awards were also made to non-commissioned officers and men of the Fusiliers, including the following :—

Lance-Corporal G. H. Mallett, M.M. : " Finding the enemy bombing up a trench on his flank, hurriedly organized a party, and gathered all the bombs he could find. Though the men were badly shaken and disorganized through the loss of nearly all their company officers and N.C.Os., he succeeded in driving the enemy off, inflicting heavy casualties, and saving his flank from being driven in."

Private E. J. C. Burkes, D.C.M. : " Word was sent back that bombs were urgently needed. He immediately jumped on to the top, and, in spite of enemy barrage and machine-gun fire, collected all the bombs he could lay hands on, and rushed forward with them. ' When I came on the scene,' says his company commander, ' I found the men applauding him and cheering him on.' "

Private J. Leonard, M.M. : " Owing to casualties, he was the only company runner available. He constantly carried messages under heavy fire, and, although absolutely exhausted, insisted in carrying on until the battalion was relieved. On one occasion, although rendered unconscious by fatigue, he at once carried on with his duties on recovering."

Lance-Corporal M. Day, M.M. : " The attack was held up by fire from a machine gun. He promptly brought his Lewis gun into action, engaged the enemy gun, and silenced it, thus enabling the attack to be carried on to the final objective."

Private T. Maloney, M.M. : " Having his Lewis gun put out of action by shell fire, searched for and discovered another gun, took charge of it, and pushed forward with great energy and initiative, thereby greatly assisting his company in reaching their objective. His skilful use of the retrieved gun was of vital importance at a most critical stage."

On leaving the line at this point the battalions were marched back to bivouacs in Henencourt Wood. On the night of August 10th-11th they relieved the 141st Brigade in the sector extending along the railway from the Albert-Millencourt road on the north along the bank of the Ancre.

Chapter XVII

THE PASSAGE OF THE ANCRE-COMBLES

WE now come definitely to the great turning-point of the long campaign, for the period which opened with the crossing of the Ancre and the capture of Albert on August 22nd marked the transition from trench to open warfare. After that success it was clear that the Germans were beginning to crack up. It was not always easy to appreciate this fact at the time, for the enemy had still several good punches up his sleeve, and there were nearly two and a half months of fighting yet to come, with some very stiff fighting, before the Brigade reached Mormal Forest behind its last barrage. But the German resistance now took the form of defending one line after another. In fact, we were opposed by strong rear-guards.

This period began for the Brigade without incident on the night of August 10th-11th, when the line was taken over from the 141st Brigade along the railway at the north-west corner of Albert, near the site of the old Hairpin Trench. The Northamptonshires were on the right, the Fusiliers on the left, and the Bedfordshires in reserve in the Melbourne line. Brigade headquarters were in dug-outs in a bank on the northern edge of Henencourt Wood.

During this period there was plenty of work in reclaiming the forward trenches and dug-outs recently occupied by the Germans, especially in clearing deep dug-outs of gas and booby traps. Active patrolling was carried out nightly to ascertain how Albert was held by the enemy. It was found that the town was occupied by small machine-gun posts of the enemy in cellars and dug-outs, all very much on the alert. Our artillery was on many occasions given targets on which they fired, with a view to demolishing these posts.

On the night of August 18th the Brigade was relieved in this sector, and on the 20th relieved parts of the 129th and 130th American Regiments on the right of the divisional front, the line being the railway embankment from the village of Dernancourt northwards to the southern outskirts of Albert. Brigade headquarters were about half a mile south of the village of Bresle. The Northamptonshires were on the right, the Fusiliers on the left, and the Bedfordshires in reserve.

The 55th Brigade were on our left, in the western outskirts of Albert, and the 12th Division on our right. The enemy held the line of the Ancre in strength, with Albert as a bridgehead.

The general rôle allotted to the Division was that of covering the flank of the main attack of the Fourth Army by taking Albert and the high ground to the east of this town. It was the task of this Brigade to force the passage of the Ancre south of Albert, and join up on the above-mentioned high ground with the 55th Brigade.

The operation was one of some difficulty, as it involved the carrying up of bridging material to get both infantry and horse transport across the Ancre, which is here about 14 feet wide and 6 feet deep. The enemy had destroyed all bridges, and moreover the low ground on either bank was swampy and much cut up by shell fire, and the enemy held the farther bank, along the Albert-Meaulte road, in some strength.

The task of getting the bridges across the river was undertaken during the night of August 21st-22nd by the Northamptonshire Regiment and the Royal Fusiliers. The light trestle bridges were made by the Royal Engineers and brought up to the railway embankment, whence they were carried to the river and dropped across by the infantry. The fact that it was a bright moonlight night was a great drawback, and there was much cheerful chatter, promoted by the novelty and interest of the task, which drew a good deal of hostile attention. Every now and then you would meet a party returning from the river, and they would hail you with, " We've dropped our bridge in the river. Got to go back for another. Isn't it a lark ?" But with all the fun that the British soldier finds in such odd places, the job was carried through with splendid spirit. There was, for instance, the case of Private F. G. Hughes, of the Fusiliers, who was one of the bridging party. They came under heavy machine-gun fire at short range from the other side of the stream, and found it almost impossible to get their bridge across. Private Hughes at once jumped into the stream, seized the end of the bridge, swam and waded across, and got it into position under the fire of at least three machine guns.

Sergeant C. Robinson, of the Northamptonshire Regiment, did a very similar thing, jumping into the river and helping to get a bridge across under heavy fire.

During the night patrols succeeded in crossing the river, and gained a footing on the Albert-Meaulte road, between Albert and Vivier Mill, on our left. This greatly simplified the crossing of the assaulting battalions in the early hours of the next morning. It was not until 2 a.m. on the 22nd that it was definitely known that the ground which our barrage was to have swept at the opening of our attack was already held by us, and this necessitated amended orders being sent to the artillery and machine gunners.

The crossing of the river by the infantry took place in the early hours of the 22nd, and at zero hour (4.45 a.m.) the Royal Fusiliers and three companies of the Northamptonshire Regiment, forming the left of our attack, were formed up across the Ancre on the Albert-Meaulte road between Albert and Vivier Mill. This was to be their starting-point for the main attack of the day on the high ground at the south-east corner of Albert.

In the meantime one company of the Northamptonshire Regiment had crossed the river farther south, opposite Dernancourt, fought their way along the east side of the river, past Meaulte, and had now arrived to form the right of our attack.

At all the crossings there had been sharp fighting, which resulted in the capture of German prisoners and machine guns.

Among the prisoners taken at an early stage of the proceedings was a complete German battalion headquarters. In the dug-out was found one of our own men, taken prisoner while on patrol a few hours earlier, and he had the pleasure of escorting the German battalion commander to the cages.

Some gallant work was done at the river crossings. On the right a company of the Northamptonshire Regiment was held up for a time by heavy machine-gun fire. In the face of this, Company Sergeant-Major L. Radley and Sergeant A. Richardson succeeded in getting across, and the enemy then withdrew. The courage of this W.O. and N.C.O. was largely the means of enabling their company to get forward.

Lieutenant H. Beckingham, of the Northamptonshire Regiment, was in command of the first company to cross in his battalion's area, and took charge of the bridging operations under heavy machine-gun fire. He got his own company safely across, and so enabled the rest of the battalion to cross and reach the forming-up line.

Even when the river had been crossed, there was still a formidable belt of marshes to get over, especially in front of the Fusiliers, and the difficulties are best illustrated by the official accounts of actions for which medals were awarded. Here, as elsewhere, these are only selections from long lists of awards, and are given as throwing light on the operation :—

Sergeant Patrick Ryan, Royal Fusiliers, D.C.M. : " Two platoons were held up in the marshes. This N.C.O. at once went back under intense machine-gun and shell fire through a most difficult marsh, and succeeded in guiding them to the only path by which it was possible to reach the enemy's position."

Company Sergeant-Major A. W. Balchin, Royal Fusiliers D.C.M. : " The company was in a disorganized state, having had to wade through marshy ground, often over their hips. Company Sergeant-Major Balchin, seeing the effect that the death of the officers had on the men, at once went forward, reorganized, and led them forward under intense machine-gun fire. He succeeded in rushing the enemy's first position, thus enabling the rest of the company to make their way out of the marshes and reform."

Private Charles Smith, Royal Fusiliers, M.M., "was in charge of the company stretcher-bearers, and frequently took his party across the most difficult marsh ground under intense machine-gun fire. His coolness and example to the other stretcher-bearers was undoubtedly the means of saving many wounded men who would otherwise have sunk in the marsh and been drowned."

The river having been crossed, the assaulting battalions formed up on the Albert-Meaulte road, and at zero hour—4.45 a.m.—on August 2nd went forward with tanks under cover of a creeping barrage.

The enemy was holding his ground with a great number of machine guns disposed in depth along the whole front. Over eighty of these guns were captured and sent back, and many more were destroyed by shell fire or left on the ground.

By eight o'clock the Northamptonshires had practically reached their final objective for the day, and were consolidating their line. On the left the Fusiliers had met with severe opposition, and suffered heavy casualties, from the direction of Albert, Bellevue Farm, and Tara Hill. They were holding a line about 500 yards east of Bellevue, where they were afterwards relieved by the Bedfordshire Regiment.

Orders were now received from the Division that, on the final objective being reached, strong fighting patrols should be pushed forward by bounds, the ground thus reconnoitred being made good by companies following in close support. This was done by the Bedfordshire and Northamptonshire Regiments, and in the meantime the 8th Royal Berkshire Regiment, temporarily placed under the command of G.O.C. 54th Brigade, was moved across the Ancre to support the farther advance.

The Fusiliers, being unable to get forward on their left flank, which was in the air, until troops of the 55th Brigade who were pushing through Albert advanced to join up, had to dig in with their left flank thrown back to Black Wood. They were a little later relieved by the Bedfordshires, who attacked and captured an enemy strong point that had been causing some trouble.

During these operations General Sadleir-Jackson was wounded in the knee, having pushed into the front line, the better to control the situation. This bit of bad luck kept him away from the Brigade till after the armistice. Command of the Brigade was taken over on the spot, as a temporary measure, by Lieutenant-Colonel A. E. Percival, of the Bedfordshire Regiment, and was afterwards held by Brigadier-General J. A. Tyler and Brigadier-General O. C. Borrett, until the armistice. General Sadleir-Jackson rejoined us a little after that date.

The final stage of the operations on August 22nd were marked by some good work by a platoon of the Bedfordshire Regiment, led by 2nd-Lieutenant W. Ashton, who was awarded the M.C.

Says the official account:—

"This officer advanced with one platoon against heavy machine-gun fire, and managed to capture a trench on Tara Hill, from which enemy machine guns had been active all day, driving out the enemy and capturing a machine gun. He was entirely unsupported in this attack, which was carried on with great dash, and enabled the battalion on his right to advance, as from this position he could overlook any enemy machine guns that tried to engage them at close range. Though sniped at continuously, he established posts on his flanks, and a block in a communication trench, and held on till relieved in the evening."

Throughout August 23rd the Northamptonshire Regiment on the right and the Bedfordshire Regiment on the left maintained a constant pressure on the enemy, and succeeded in advancing the line another 1,000 yards by a series of rushes. Otherwise the day was uneventful so far as this Brigade was concerned, but the Brigade on our left carried out an important attack, which cleared the ridges dominating Albert, and left that shattered town finally in our hands.

The next few days saw steady progress. It was clear that the enemy was thoroughly disorganized, such counter-attacks as he made being desperate rearguard affairs carried out by any troops who happened to be on hand, without any general plan.

At 2.30 a.m. on August 25th the Brigade again attacked, with the Northamptonshire Regiment on the right and the Bedfordshire Regiment on the left, each on a two-company front, the intention being to secure as much ground as possible without becoming too heavily engaged.

Becourt Wood was soon cleared, and the leading companies then pushed up the hill and on towards Fricourt—scene of the Brigade's earliest experiences of the line, and now to be retaken by them. Opposition had now weakened considerably, and by the time our advanced patrols reached Fricourt the enemy was well on the run.

By the evening of August 26th the final objective of the Brigade had been taken by the Fusiliers, who were now fighting over the old German trench system where the Brigade won its spurs in July, 1916. This point having been reached, the Brigade was in reserve on August 27th and 28th, returning to the line on the night of August 28th-29th, when the whole of the divisional front was taken over and the advance on Combles continued.

Trones Wood, of proud memories, now roughly formed our front line, which ran along the eastern edge as far as the light railway, and was then thrown back towards the outskirts of Longueval. This line was held by the Northamptonshire Regiment on the right and the Bedfordshire Regiment on the left, with the Fusiliers in reserve near Caterpillar Wood.

Orders were to hold this line and to act as advanced guard to the Division when the line went forward. To assist in this, the 82nd Brigade R.F.A., " A " and " B " Companies 18th Machine Gun Battalion, " B " Squadron Otago Mounted Rifles, and one company 22nd Corps Cyclists, were allotted to the Brigade commander.

In the early hours of August 29th the Bedfordshire Regiment sent forward strong patrols, which, after meeting some slight opposition, were able to advance rapidly in the direction of Guillemont. By this time the 38th Division was well forward on our left, and accordingly the Northamptonshire Regiment took up the pursuit, the site of the village of Guillemont, of which no trace now remained, being passed by 7 a.m. with little or no opposition.

This having been reported, the Brigade was ordered to advance by bounds, and for the rest of the day steady progress was made, the leading companies in open formation, and the rest of the battalions coming along in column of route like a " sealed pattern " advance across the Long Valley at Aldershot. Field guns were up with the infantry, shooting over open sights at the Germans on the high ground beyond Combles. By 9 a.m. the Bedfordshire Regiment had reached Leuze Wood, meeting only slight rifle and machine-gun opposition, and taking a few prisoners, and by evening our line had reached the eastern outskirts of Combles, with the left flank bent back towards Bouleaux Wood.

That night, while the Bedfordshire Regiment was holding an outpost line on the edge of Combles, a motor-car occupied by a British staff officer dashed through the village, ignored or failed to hear the shouted warnings, and rushed on right into a German post. The Germans bombed vigorously, the driver was wounded, and the staff officer himself escaped by falling hurriedly into a ditch, from which he escaped to our lines some hours later. The car was still standing by the roadside, disabled, when our line advanced on the following day.

At this time Brigade headquarters were established on the slope of a hill, where the slightest movement brought down a German " hate." Accommodation was limited, and that night the two junior subalterns on the Brigade staff crawled into a hole in the back and fell asleep, cheerfully convinced that they would either be turned out or blown out of their shelter before daylight.

Early next morning they were awakened by guttural noises, and were startled to see a face under a Bosche helmet peering in at the entrance. They jumped up, grabbed their revolvers, and dashed out after the retreating figure, which proved to be that of the Brigade Major in a tin hat borrowed from a German prisoner. One wonders whether the Germans were playing practical jokes on one another at this stage of the war.

BATTLE FLAG OF THE 7TH (S.) AND 2ND BATTS. BEDFORDSHIRE REGIMENT.

To face page 176

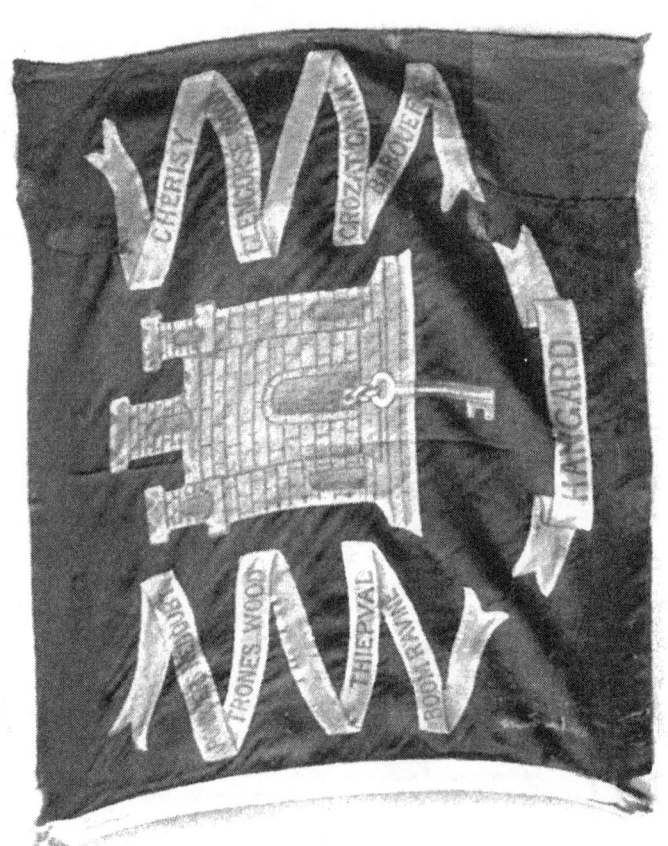

BATTLE FLAG OF THE 6TH (S.) BATT. NORTHAMPTONSHIRE REGIMENT.

It was decided to attack at dawn on the following day (August 30th), the Fusiliers to pass through the Northamptonshire Regiment, and the Bedfordshire Regiment to go forward on the left if this attack were successful. However, the attack made at 5.15 a.m. was met with heavy hostile fire, and although the general line of the Combles-Priez Farm road was reached, a stronghold at the latter point held out stubbornly. It was now apparent that the enemy was in strength on the Fregicourt line, and being steadily reinforced, and all our local efforts to get forward were beaten back. An attack by the Northamptonshire Regiment on the following day (August 31st) carried the line farther forward on our right, but the possession of Morvel by the enemy on our left still held matters up. The line as then reached was, with little variation, held till the Brigade was relieved on the night of September 4th-5th, and concentrated in the Leuze Wood area for rest and training.

Some idea of the successful character of the fighting which has necessarily been thus briefly summarized is shown by the record of prisoners taken by the Brigade. The total for August was 22 officers and 1,385 other ranks, made up as follows :—

Royal Fusiliers, 3 officers, 450 other ranks ; Bedfordshire Regiment, 2 officers, 198 other ranks ; Northamptonshire Regiment, 17 officers, 737 other ranks.

CHAPTER XVIII

THROUGH THE HINDENBURG LINE

THE next phase of the fighting concerns the capture of Ronssoy and Vendhuille, which resulted in the piercing of the much-vaunted Hindenburg Line.

On September 16th the Brigade moved up by 'busses from Guillemont to the neighbourhood of Gurlu Wood, and at dusk on the 17th moved up to the forming places for the attack of the 18th on Ronssoy and the high ground beyond, which gave good observation over the Hindenburg Line at Vendhuille and the canal.

For the purposes of this operation the 7th Royal West Kent Regiment was attached to the Brigade. The attack was to be carried out under a creeping barrage as follows :—

The forming-up line was on the east of St. Emilie. The Royal West Kent Regiment was to advance at zero and capture a line roughly two miles ahead, running north and south on the farther outskirts of Ronssoy. The Bedfordshire Regiment was then to go through the Royal West Kent Regiment, and continue the advance in an easterly direction to a line at the junction of the Bellicourt and Guillemont roads.

The Royal Fusiliers on the right, and the Northamptonshire Regiment on the left, had then to form a line facing north (that is to say, at right angles to the objective of the Royal West Kent Regiment) and attack northwards to a line that would include May Copse and Lempire. This was evidently a rather sticky proposition, and, as events proved, it did not succeed in reaching the whole of its objectives.

The next day of the attack began with very unpleasant weather. At 12.30 a.m. rain began to fall, and continued till about 9 a.m. It was very dark, and a strong wind was blowing. In spite of these difficulties, however, the Brigade reached the forming-up places in time, with the exception of the rear company of the Northamptonshire Regiment, which was ten minutes late, and in consequence suffered rather heavily from the enemy barrage.

At zero (5.20 a.m.) it was still pitch dark, but the assaulting troops got well away under our barrage, and the Royal West Kents reached their objective approximately up to time. The Bedfordshires, who were to leap-frog them, assisted them to clear the enemy out of a small copse at an early stage of the attack, and afterwards had almost continuous fighting, but passed through the first objective and reached their own objective about 7 a.m. They had captured large numbers of prisoners on the way, but it was some hours before the whole of the village was "mopped up," a job in which two tanks attached to the Brigade did splendid service.

By 7.20 a.m. the Royal Fusiliers and the Northamptonshires had reached their forming-up line, which ran east and west through the northern side of Ronssoy, and were facing north behind the new barrage which had now been put down to help them forward. They had already been engaged with small pockets of the enemy who had put up local delaying actions, especially in Ronssoy Wood, which was cleared by the Northamptonshires. Owing to the resistance encountered, and the nature of the ground in the village and wood, these troops were now somewhat mixed up.

It was at this stage that Lance-Corporal Albert Lewis, of the Northamptonshire Regiment, won the Victoria Cross. Unhappily, he was killed three days later while again doing splendid work. The official account reads:—

"On the morning of September 18th, 1918, this N.C.O. was in charge of a section which he had successfully kept together. He was on the right of the line, and the battalion started to advance to attack Ronssoy, where the east and west barrage opened.

"The battalion advanced to a point where the enemy machine-gun fire was so intense that it was a practical impossibility to get forward. The barrage went on, and the battalion was temporarily held up. This man, working with his section on the right amongst the ruins, observed two enemy machine guns opposite him enfilading the whole battalion. He crawled forward single-handed on his own initiative with bombs, got within bombing range, and successfully bombed the teams manning the enemy's guns. The enemy left their guns and ran out of the emplacement. Lance-Corporal Lewis thereupon used his rifle with good effect, and the whole team surrendered. He wounded six and captured four unwounded. By his courage and determination in putting out of action two enemy machine guns, he undoubtedly enabled the battalion to advance, and so contributed largely to the success that followed.

"Later, on September 21st, during another attack, this N.C.O. displayed splendid power of command. When his company was caught in the enemy barrage, he was the first to rush them through it, until they came under heavy fire from enemy machine guns, whereupon he immediately began to place them out in shell holes. While doing this he was killed."

During the morning these battalions attacked northwards, according to programme. The Northamptonshire Regiment reached Quid Copse on their left, and joined up with the Royal Fusiliers along Ridge Reserve. The clearing of the village in the rear of this line was still in progress. By the evening this had been done. At 5 p.m. the 55th Brigade attacked through the line we held, and some progress was made ; but the enemy put in a counter-attack, with the result that at dusk they were still in strength in Quenchettes Wood, X, Y and Z Copses, the north-east part of Lempire, Enfer Wood, and May Copse.

There was a good deal of shelling during the night, and at dawn it was found that the enemy had adjusted his line by withdrawing at some points. As a result, the Northamptonshires on the left occupied the line May Copse-Enfer Wood, and the Bedfordshires were able to send patrols into X, Y and Z Copses, which, however, were not yet clear of the enemy. That night the Northamptonshires and part of the Fusiliers were relieved by the 37th Brigade (12th Division), and concentrated in Ronssoy Wood.

It had now been established that Ronssoy had been held by the 1st Guards Grenadier Regiment (the Alexander Regiment), of the 2nd Guards Division. Six hundred prisoners from this Division and the 232nd Division were taken on the 18th. The stubborn resistance offered during these days showed the intention of the Germans to hold this ground at all costs as a bastion to the Hindenburg system, and this was confirmed by prisoners' statements. In all, the Brigade had taken about 900 prisoners up to this time. Three guns had been taken by the Northamptonshire Regiment and two by the Royal Fusiliers.

It was now decided to renew the attack on September 21st, with a view to capturing the remainder of the objectives of September 18th. In the larger scheme (which included an attack on the Knoll by the 53rd Brigade, and on Guillemont Farm by the 231st Brigade) this Brigade was to attack the intervening trenches. The Bedfordshires were to be on the right, and the Northamptonshires on the left, with the Fusiliers in reserve. The Knoll mentioned above was a feature of great tactical importance, as it commanded Vendhuille and the canal crossing at the village, and gave a view over the whole of the Hindenburg main line on the front of the 18th Division. The trenches to be attacked by this Brigade lay between the Knoll and the Farm.

Zero was fixed at 5.40 a.m. on the 21st, and the forming-up line (the Bellicourt road) was reached without incident. But the enemy appear to have been aware of our intentions, for they shelled the area heavily, and put down a barrage very promptly at zero.

The Division on our right (74th) got on well, but swung slightly to the right, leaving a gap on the right of the Bedfordshires, about Pot Trench, which caused difficulties. Some of the Bedfordshires appear to have reached Doleful and Duncan Posts, but could not maintain their position. The attack having been held up, and the enemy showing signs of a possible counter-attack, the Fusiliers, who were reorganizing in Ronssoy, were ordered at about 11 a.m. to be ready to move up at half an hour's notice. Soon afterwards the battalion was ordered to move two companies (organized as one company owing to casualties) to hold the line Shamrock Trench and a trench between Hussar road and Bellicourt road, and the remaining two companies (also organized as one company) were placed at the disposal of O.C. Bedfordshire Regiment.

By 12 noon touch had been gained with one company Northamptonshire Regiment, who had pushed on and gained Island Traverse, where they had both flanks in the air and were practically surrounded. During the afternoon they were forced to retire, but fell back fighting, bringing their prisoners with them, and inflicting heavy casualties. By 5 p.m. they rejoined the rest of their battalion near Holland Post.

Orders were now given for night attacks by the Northamptonshire Regiment on Doleful Post and the Bedfordshire Regiment on Duncan Post.

The company of the Northamptonshire Regiment that had previously fought its way to Island Traverse and out again was detailed for the Doleful Post venture, and we will follow their doings first.

The barrage came down at midnight, and at 12.15 a.m., with a little moonlight to show the way, the Northamptonshire Regiment storming party, about thirty strong, moved off. The attack was completely successful; the post was captured, about twenty of the enemy being killed and over forty captured, our own casualties being three slightly wounded.

Careful reconnaissance of the position before the attack by 2nd-Lieutenant R. Bland, of the Northamptonshire Regiment, had contributed very largely to this good result. He was awarded the M.C., the official account stating:—

" He was in command of a storming party, with orders to capture and consolidate a post held by the enemy. His skilful reconnaissance of the position enabled him to bring his party forward in extended order until each man was in jumping distance from the trench. At a given signal the whole party stormed the trench, captured the whole post and forty-eight prisoners, and killed about twenty of the enemy, with a loss of three casualties slightly wounded. The success was due to the personal courage of this officer, and to his skilful organization and reconnaissance."

For the same operation a M.C. was also awarded to 2nd-Lieutenant E. Marlow, who led his men into the trench, which he was one of the first to enter. There he shot two of the enemy, which caused some confusion and enabled the rest of the trench to be rushed.

The composite company of the Fusiliers temporarily attached to the Bedfordshire Regiment was sent over at 12.15 a.m., but through force of circumstances not under control of the officers swung too far to the right, and instead of capturing Duncan Post, captured Cat Post and parts of Dog Trench and Pot Lane, where they established themselves, and sent back twenty prisoners. This left the enemy in Duncan Post and Duncan Avenue, between this company of the Fusiliers and the Northamptonshires who were now in Doleful Post.

At 1 p.m. the artillery were warned that the enemy were dribbling forward in front of Doleful Post, as though preparing to counter-attack. Major Keep, temporarily commanding the Bedfordshire Regiment, had arranged an attack to clear the trenches about Duncan Post at 3 p.m., after a ten minutes' bombardment. However, this preliminary bombardment did not take place, as the artillery were standing by for the expected counter-attack on Doleful Post. One field gun alone was available, and opened fire over open sights at about 1,400 yards, with excellent results. The attack was carried out by Lieutenant R. T. Oldfield and 2nd-Lieutenant W. Pennington, of the Bedfordshire Regiment, with forty-four men, and was completely successful, the entire objective being captured. Between 150 and 200 prisoners were taken, and these, owing to the small numbers of our storming party, had to be handed over to the 74th Division. About 200 Germans were killed, 80 dead, and 30 machine guns being found in Duncan Post alone. About 100 of the enemy ran eastwards, and were pursued by the attached company of the Fusiliers.

Just as this capital little operation was being finished off, the Germans made the expected counter-attack on Doleful Post, with about one battalion. The S.O.S. was put up, and our barrage came down at once, unfortunately catching some of the pursuing Fusiliers.

The attack got within fifty yards of our line at Doleful Post, and was there completely stopped by rifle and Lewis-gun fire. As the enemy were unable either to advance or to return our fire, they returned through our barrage, which did tremendous execution. Some who took cover in shell-holes in front of the post were taken prisoners.

At 5 p.m. the enemy again attacked Duncan and Doleful Posts, but were again driven off with heavy loss, leaving about twenty prisoners in our hands.

The excitement of the troops who took part in the literal annihilation of the enemy during these counter-attacks was unprecedented, and morale and confidence were at the highest possible pitch. Companies of the Fusiliers and Northamptonshires both left their trenches in pursuit. During one of the counter-attacks a stretcher-bearer was seen running up and down the parados of the trench, throwing clips of ammunition to the defenders, and shouting, " Shoot, boys, shoot !" as if watching the exciting finish of a football match.

At dusk the line now held by the Brigade was consolidated with the assistance of the 80th Field Company R.E., under Captain Weir, and the 8th Royal Sussex Pioneers. That night the Brigade was relieved by the 55th Brigade and marched back to bivouacs around St. Emilie Quarries. On the 24th the battalions marched farther back to Nurlu.

About 400 prisoners had been taken in these operations of the past two days, and the Bedfordshires captured five 4·2 guns at Quenchettes Wood. A very large number of machine guns, trench mortars, and anti-tank rifles were also taken.

Of splendid individual work during the past few days there had been almost countless instances, and a selection from the official accounts on which medals were awarded can only aim at giving a few typical cases.

Among the Fusiliers, Captains G. E. Cornaby and W. Hornfeck were awarded the M.C. Of the former it is recorded that " on September 18th, owing to fog, the attacking lines of three battalions became greatly mixed. On arriving at Ronssoy, this officer, with absolute disregard to personal safety, and in spite of heavy machine-gun fire, exposed himself freely in order to get his men reorganized, and at once led them forward. This enabled his company to keep up with the barrage, which they would have otherwise missed, and to gain practically the whole of their objectives."

Captain Hornfeck, " in conjunction with Captain Cornaby, led his men forward, and, in spite of his exposed right flank, and heavy machine-gun and point-blank artillery fire from that direction, succeeded in gaining his objective, capturing two field guns and several trench mortars. On Captain Cornaby becoming a casualty, he took command in this area, reorganized round the principal strong points, and drove off two counterattacks."

Private F. T. Day, of the same battalion, won the D.C.M. at Duncan Avenue on September 22nd. " This man [says the official account], with his Lewis gun, frequently placed himself in most exposed positions, in order to engage enemy machine guns. On each occasion he put the enemy team out of action, enabling our waves to get forward. When his gun was eventually put out of action, he picked up a rifle and vigorously sniped the enemy, with excellent results."

Private Alfred Smith, also of the Fusiliers, was awarded the M.M. " On the 18th the officer and all N.C.Os. of his platoon had become casualties, and the men were badly shaken. He at once took charge of the remains of his platoon, and displayed qualities of leadership and extraordinary energy. His quick grasp of the situation enabled him to get on to the objective with the rest of his company, after having been cut off through the harassing fire of an enemy machine gun, which he eventually put out of action."

Corporal J. Hurst, who already wore the M.M., now won the D.C.M. when in charge of a party " mopping up " Ronssoy. " His keenness and good leadership accounted for at least five officers and forty men being captured. He also secured a signal station complete, shooting the operator who was sending a message."

Lieutenant R. T. Oldfield, whose work at Duncan Post has already been mentioned, was awarded a bar to the M.C. he won in August. Says the official account : " He was in command of an assaulting company which had been very much disorganized and reduced by enemy barrage and machine-gun fire. Realizing that both flanks were exposed, he rallied all men in his vicinity, and made a thorough reconnaissance of the country, locating the enemy's positions. He arranged for the co-operation of four machine guns, and led two successful bombing attacks, which enabled him to get into touch with units on both flanks, and surround a large body of the enemy who were duly cleared up. He reorganized and consolidated his position, and kept his men cheerful, despite the fact that they were very exhausted by four days' fighting."

The M.C. was awarded to 2nd-Lieutenant W. Pennington. " He took command of a company in action, when the position was very obscure, extricated his company, and proceeded to outflank an enemy strong point by marching through the next division and attacking from the flank. He manœuvred his company into position, commenced a whirlwind attack with all weapons at his disposal, and so disconcerted the enemy that he was able to get in at their rear and capture many prisoners."

A D.C.M. was well won by Private W. A. Suffolk, of the same battalion, at Ronssoy on September 18th. " His platoon came under heavy machine-gun fire, which seemed likely to impede seriously its advance. Private Suffolk advanced alone along the bank of a sunken road under heavy fire from two machine guns, and rushed the first, putting the team out of action. Then working his way round behind the second one, he sniped the team, killing them all, and thus allowing his platoon to continue its advance."

Captain A. J. Frost, of the Northamptonshire Regiment, won a bar to his M.C. on the 18th. " The battalion was held up by twelve machine guns and a field gun firing over open sights. He managed to get his company some 150 yards forward by short rushes to within about sixty yards of two machine guns. Seeing a tank come into view, he rushed the position and brought enfilade Lewis-gun fire to bear on the enemy line."

Private Ernest Mead, of the same battalion, won the D.C.M. on September 21st. " The company was far in advance of any other troops. The objective trench was seen to be occupied. Lewis guns being laid in position, the captain called for a volunteer to creep forward with him and try and hold up the enemy, and thus enable the company to advance. Private Mead, with his captain, crawled up and jumped into the trench, and while the enemy were holding up their hands the company occupied the trench."

An amusing story of the Fusiliers' attack on Ronssoy, on the 18th, is told by a sergeant of that battalion, who writes:—

"Having taken the village, we met with very heavy shell fire, both from our own and the enemy's guns. As things were getting very uncomfortable, our sergeant-major led us through the village out into open country, where we caught sight of the Bosche retiring for all he was worth. He then gave us orders to extend and open fire. As it became impossible for him to give any further orders by word of mouth, he had to fall back on the barrack-square system of extended order drill with whistle. Throughout the morning we kept advancing by the whistle, and, strange to say, our sergeant-major was escorted by a Jerry prisoner eating black bread and sausage. Several times he ordered him to go back, even threatening to shoot him, but he could not get rid of this docile prisoner until we finally reached our objective, when he was sent back under escort to the cage."

It was on the same day that the Brigade intelligence officer was detailed to return to rear Brigade headquarters, together with a few prisoners, and prepare for the return of the remainder of the staff. Tired and dirty, he picked out the best-looking Bosche, all of whom had their greatcoats on, and loaded him up with tin-hat, glasses, compass, and all the other useless things that one always drags into battle.

This particular Bosche did not seem over pleased, but stumbled back under the heavy load. Later in the day he was detailed for various unpleasant jobs given to prisoners of war, but in the middle of dinner, in the presence of the whole staff, he came in and remonstrated against a certain job. On taking off his greatcoat it was observed that he was a captain in the Prussian Guard!

After the same fight a certain staff officer of the Brigade was also walking back accompanied by a German prisoner, who was carrying, amongst other things, the officer's red-banded cap. There was a shout from a group of our men sitting by the roadside: "B'lime, Fritz, you got on the blinkin' staff, too!"

It was, I think, the same obliging prisoner who, when a shell burst rather near, came running up to the Brigade officer and handed him his tin hat—a thoughtful attention that was much appreciated.

After the strenuous days in and around Ronssoy, the rest at Nurlu was very welcome; but it did not last long, and on the night of September 27th-28th the battalions marched forward to a concentration area in bivouacs between Epetry and Guyencourt, with a view to taking part in an attack on the Hindenburg Line on the 29th.

While the Brigade was at Nurlu, General Lee, the Divisional Commander, addressed the troops, congratulating them on their splendid achievements, and informing them that the Army Commander had done the Division the honour of selecting it to remain in the Fourth Army to take part in the final breaking of the Hindenburg Line.

The main attack was to be carried out by the 27th American Division and other Divisions to the south. The 18th Division was to attack on the left of the Americans, with two objects :—

1. To protect the left of the American Division by gaining complete observation over Vendhuille and the canal, and by keeping constant pressure on the enemy in this direction. This task was allotted to the 54th Infantry Brigade. It was decided that the 11th Royal Fusiliers and the 6th Northamptonshire Regiment should attack on the left and right respectively, with the 2nd Bedfordshire Regiment in reserve.

2. To "mop up" Vendhuille as soon as American progress farther south permitted, and to prepare a passage for other Divisions to pass through. This task was allotted to the 55th Brigade.

A force known as the "liaison force" was also organized under the 54th Infantry Brigade, with a special mission. It consisted of two companies 2nd Bedfordshire Regiment, " B " Company 18th Machine Gun Battalion, 80th Field Company R.E., and a detachment of the 54th Infantry Brigade Signal Section. It was commanded by Major Patterson, M.C., 18th Machine Gun Battalion, and its task was to accompany the American attack on the southern side of the Macquincourt Valley, take up a position astride the canal, and prevent the enemy by fire from destroying the bridges. As soon as opportunity offered, the R.Es. were to push into the village to reconnoitre the bridges and report. Three sections of the 80th Field Company, with one company Bedfordshires as escort, were kept in reserve at Brigade headquarters for work on the bridges.

The Americans attacked and captured the Knoll (which overlooked Vendhuille) on the 27th, but were unable to maintain their gains. Another attack, in which this Brigade was to take part, was therefore arranged for the 29th, the Fusiliers (on the left) and Northamptonshires (on the right) being detailed for the operation.

The forming-up places were about Sart Farm (roughly on a line between Doleful Post and Lempire Post), and there was a good deal of shelling of this area, including gas, the enemy apparently being suspicious. Casualties, however, were not numerous, and the assaulting battalions got well away at zero (5.40 a.m.). The attack was to be made in a north-easterly direction, with the objective a trench line on the nearer outskirts of Vendhuille.

On the left the Fusiliers, having the Tombois road to guide them, kept direction without difficulty, in spite of mist, smoke, and enemy gas. On the right, however, the American troops appeared to lose direction slightly, and left a gap between the Northamptonshires and themselves. This caused the Northamptonshires to swing to the right, and some were carried on beyond and to the right of their objectives, and were lost.

However, the Fusiliers and the left of the Northamptonshires reached their objective up to time; the right of the Northamptonshires were engaged in heavy fighting on the Knoll, but eventually established a line roughly along the Knoll Switch. On reports that the American advance was proceeding well, the company of the Bedfordshires in reserve to the liaison force was moved forward to Dose Trench about 8 a.m., but was sent back to the battalion in Ronssoy Wood in the afternoon, when it was found that the liaison force would not be able to carry out its rôle.

Fighting continued throughout the morning on the Knoll, the enemy making several counter-attacks, which were all beaten off. Rifle and machine-gun fire from Guillemont Farm on our right, which was still held by the enemy, proved troublesome and hindered movement. In the afternoon enemy artillery was active, and the front line of the Fusiliers in particular came in for rather rough handling.

That night there was little activity on either side, and we took the opportunity to consolidate and reorganize on and around the Knoll. At dawn on the 30th the Brigade was disposed as follows: On the right, the Northamptonshires in Knoll Support and Switch and Tiger Trench; on the left, the Fusiliers in Tino Trench and Support, Spree Lane, Bell Avenue, and Tombois Trench. The 7th Queen's (55th Brigade), who had been placed at the disposal of this Brigade as counter-attack battalion, was in support in Lark Trench, Causeway Lane, Fog Trench, and London Road. The Bedfordshires were in reserve in Ronssoy Wood. What may appear a list of almost meaningless names in the foregoing will be of interest to those of the Brigade who were in the line at this important stage of the proceedings.

About 10 a.m. there were signs that the enemy were withdrawing on our front, and patrols reached Vendhuille without much opposition. Accordingly, by about noon most of the troops had moved forward to Vendhuille Trench, and the Fusiliers were pushed ahead to "mop up" the village. Rather acrimonious discussions with the enemy tended to hinder this work, and two companies of the Bedfordshire Regiment were ordered forward to assist, but the job had been completed when they arrived.

Orders were received from Division in the afternoon not to fight for the Vendhuille bridges, but to establish an outpost line along the west bank of the canal, and push patrols across if possible to locate the enemy. This line was accordingly established, but snipers and machine guns prevented the crossing by patrols.

That night the Bedfordshire Regiment relieved the Fusiliers and Northamptonshire Regiment in the line, and on October 1st this Brigade was relieved by the Scottish Horse (149th Brigade). On October 2nd the Brigade embussed at Guyencourt for Molliens-au-Bois, and there for a short time had a well-earned rest.

CHAPTER XIX

LE CATEAU AND THE ARMISTICE

MID-OCTOBER saw the Brigade moving forward again for what was to prove the last phase of the war.

Looking back on the war, it is very easy to regard the last days of October and the early days of November as a sort of triumphant procession, in which our troops marched gaily eastward in column of route, while a beaten and disorganized enemy hurried towards his own frontier without firing a shot. Such an impression is not only bad history, but is very unjust to the men who took part in the last operations. These may have been only a last desperate rearguard action, but the 54th Brigade will ever remember that the Germans on our part of the front had still a number of hard punches up their sleeves, and we were yet to lose many good comrades before the white flag came out of the enemy's lines. As a matter of fact, the Brigade's casualties in these last days were 26 officers and 675 other ranks, the heaviest in the Division.

On October 17th the Brigade moved up by train to the Nurlu area, and on the following day moved by 'busses to Serain, where we were destined to spend some time after the Armistice, and where the last Divisional review, referred to in Chapter I, was held. On the 19th the Royal Fusiliers and Bedfordshire Regiment went forward to Maurois (about four miles south-west of Le Cateau), and on the following day the Northamptonshires were sent up to Reumont in the same area.

On the night October 20th-21st the Brigade relieved the 199th Brigade in the line north-east of Le Cateau. The line here ran along the railway embankment of the Le Cateau-Neuvilly railway, and we had the enemy on the high ground directly to our east. The Northamptonshire Regiment remained at Reumont. The line was near enough to Le Cateau for the reserve companies to be accommodated there. It was not altogether a health resort, for the Germans were still shelling the place with plenty of high explosives and gas, and one recalls the neighbourhood of the big church tower as a specially unhealthy spot.

Life for those in the town became a matter of wandering about the streets by day, wondering where the next one would come to, and living in a cellar by night. One company of the Bedfordshire Regiment found itself a very comfortable headquarters in a house that had been a German officers' club from the early days of the war till very recently. There were a number of French civilians in the town, and they took things very philosophically, coming out each morning and cleaning their doorsteps as if there were no war on. Their satisfaction at the turn of events which had brought British troops back to Le Cateau after over four years of German occupation was only natural, and French flags, hidden away Heaven knows where through the weary months in anticipation of a day of deliverance, at long last now fluttered from the attic windows. Whether any of these flags could be seen by German observers is difficult to say, but several came down in the course of the evening " hates," when shelling intensified, and houses fell in all directions. These frequent crashes, when houses would suddenly flop across a street, and bricks and tiles fell in all directions, made the evening hours somewhat unpleasant. Happily, the German gunners, ever men of method and punctuality, stuck to the time-table idea to the last, so that, having once found that shelling was very light in the mornings, one was safe in carrying on sight-seeing before lunch.

Lieutenant-Colonel A. E. Percival has given me the following notes of the mingled excitement and humour of this period:—

" Soon after taking over the line I met the commanding officer of the battalion on our left, and he informed me that his men had captured and were holding the gullies by Richmont Mill, about 400 yards in front of the left of our line. As these gullies were in the front allotted to us, I told him I would take them over, and we went forward together to look at the ground.

" On arriving at the gullies we were surprised to find no men there, and on calling out we received no response. Shortly afterwards my runner made a dash with his rifle into a hole, from which he produced a live Bosche. As we were both unarmed except for walking-sticks we thought it was time we got back to our own lines ! We took the Bosche prisoner back with us, and got some useful information from him.

" The following day an amusing incident occurred. I sent my Adjutant, Captain Methuen, over to the headquarters of a neighbouring battalion to keep liaison with them. Captain Methuen was wearing a black waterproof of a nautical cut, and the Adjutant of the neighbouring battalion apparently regarded this with suspicion. There was the added fact that Captain Methuen had only recently acted as my Adjutant, and was not known personally to the officers of this other battalion. As a result he was closely followed back to our headquarters by a runner, who announced that he had been ordered to keep him in sight and see where he actually went to !"

The operations now to be undertaken were a part of the general advance. The scheme, seen " in the big," was that the Fourth Army, in conjunction with the Third, was to gain the western edge of the Forest of Mormal, and objectives farther north. The 13th Corps was to attack with the 18th Division on the left and the 25th on the right.

General Lee (18th Division) decided to attack with our Brigade (less the Northamptonshires) on the left, and the 53rd Brigade on the right, and having taken the first and second objectives to send the 55th Brigade, with 6th Northamptonshires attached, through to the final objectives, which were beyond Bousies. The attack was so timed that the 55th Brigade should get into the close country round Bousies about dawn on October 23rd. The distances to the first and second objectives, with which the two attacking battalions of this Brigade were concerned, were approximately 3,500 and 5,500 yards respectively. The Brigade arranged to attack with the Bedfordshire Regiment to the first objective, and the Fusiliers to the second.

Zero was at 1.20 a.m. on October 23rd. The early part of the night was wet, but the weather cleared later, and the battalions reached their forming-up places on and around the railway embankment without difficulty. This was the first time the Brigade had attempted a big attack by moonlight. Fortunately, there was a ground mist during the forming-up time, and this enabled the Bedfordshires, who were to be the first over, to get well out in front of the embankment without attracting too much notice. But the enemy were obviously very nervous, and indulged in a good deal of shelling, including gas, which caused some casualties.

The barrage came down well, and the Bedfordshires, although troubled by an enemy machine gun between them and the barrage, got well away, dealt with the machine gun, and pushed on, followed by the Fusiliers. The German replied promptly and heavily to our barrage, and we had a number of casualties in the early stage of the attack.

Some opposition was met with in three sunken roads near Richemont Mill, but this was speedily overcome, with the exception of one post, which remained in action after the Bedfordshires had passed over it, and was finally mopped up by the Fusiliers.

The moon was not putting in much work, and the attack pressed forward with the mingled advantages and drawbacks of darkness. This caused some confusion and lack of direction to many parties, and when daylight came the dead of our own Brigade and of the 33rd Division (on our left) were found lying together in one another's area. But the advance continued methodically. The enemy were in great strength, but our artillery inflicted heavy casualties, many prisoners were taken, and whenever resistance was offered our infantry killed large numbers.

The leading battalion had some heavy fighting at White Springs, rather more than half-way to the first objective, but managed to deal with this with the help of a half company brought up from Richmond Mill, and finally reached a road running directly across our front, some 500 yards short of their objective. Some companies of the Bedfordshire Regiment mistook this for their objective. As a result they halted, and the Fusiliers passed through and carried on the advance, shortly afterwards capturing eleven guns.

The Fusiliers now got well ahead, and one company (Captain Hornfeck), moving through the outskirts of Forest, reached its objective north-west of Epinette. There, however, it had both flanks in the air, and, fired on from all sides, was forced to retire behind the ridge at the north-east corner of Forest. Here it rejoined the other leading company, which, having lost its way, was digging in under the impression that it was on its objective.

It was now about 6 a.m., and the attack came to a temporary standstill till about 7.30 a.m., when the 7th Buffs (55th Brigade) passed through the Fusiliers according to programme, and without much difficulty went beyond the second objective in front of Epinette. Soon afterwards the Fusiliers and Bedfordshires moved forward to their original objectives, re-organized, and dug in. At the same time advanced Brigade headquarters moved to White Springs.

In the afternoon our Brigade took over the front from the 55th Brigade, the Northamptonshires, who had now returned to us, relieving the 7th Buffs. Brigade headquarters and the rest of the Brigade moved into Forest, and with orders to renew the attack at dawn on the following day we settled down for any rest that could be had.

The attack on the 23rd, which has now been briefly described, had gone through with all the smoothness the optimistic could expect. We took 14 guns (11 by the Fusiliers and 3 by the Bedfordshires), 6 trench mortars, 80 machine guns, and 3 anti-tank rifles, as well as 250 prisoners—not such a bad day considering that the total strength of the two attacking battalions that day was just under 800 officers and men. Our casualties had been—Fusiliers, 2 officers and 62 other ranks; Bedfordshires, 4 officers and 165 other ranks.

And now one comes up against the same old difficulty—at any rate this is the last chapter, and it will not bother me much longer—of attempting some selection from the numbers of instances of personal gallantry.

Take the Fusiliers first. I suppose it will be agreed that they had the nastiest moments in getting away from the forming-up line, for they followed the Bedfordshires, and the enemy, already jumpy, and very suspicious about the railway embankment, now plastered it with all the metal to hand.

At the beginning of this action the company led by Captain W. Hornfeck had to pass in single-file under the railway bridge and across a narrow footbridge. The enemy had this point well marked, and put down a heavy barrage on it as soon as our own guns opened. Seeing that the men in front faltered for a moment, Captain Hornfeck pushed forward to the bridge, and remained there under continual artillery and machine-gun fire until the last man was across, cheering them on by his fearless behaviour. It was his company that, as already mentioned, pushed forward beyond Epinette. There they hung on for over two hours with both flanks in the air. Five of the field guns taken by the Brigade were captured by this company.

Unluckily, Captain Hornfeck had one foot practically cut off by a shell while forming up his company for the attack on the following day. In spite of this he superintended the forming-up under heavy artillery fire, cheered his men on as they went forward at the right moment. His leg was afterwards amputated.

Good work was done by Sergeant A. Palmer on the 23rd. He was in charge of the right platoon of the Fusiliers. In the darkness touch was lost with the battalion on our right (53rd Brigade), and our right flank came under heavy machine-gun fire. Locating the gun which was giving most trouble, this N.C.O. pushed forward with two men over open ground, rushed the gun, killed one of the team and took two others prisoner, and so enabled his platoon to get forward. He then took out a patrol under heavy fire and succeeded in getting touch with the battalion on his right.

Of the work of the Bedfordshires that day Lieutenant-Colonel A. E. Percival has given me the following notes :—

"The battalion met with considerable opposition during the early part of the attack, especially " B " Company on the right, under Lieutenant Lang, and was held up at the start by a number of enemy machine guns. A very fine bit of work was done by Sergeant Rickard, who crawled forward, accompanied by a runner (Private Flute), and put a whole machine-gun crew out of action. They both received the D.C.M.

Meanwhile " C " Company on the left, led by Lieutenant Chester, had cleared the gullies after heavy fighting, enabling " A " Company (Lieutenant Hart) to pass through and attack the sunken road at White Springs. Very heavy fighting occurred at this spot, and many of the enemy were killed. " D " Company (Captain Rice) then took up the attack, and eventually reached the final objective. An inspection of the ground afterwards showed the very heavy nature of the fighting, which was proved by the large number of enemy dead and captured machine guns.

"The battalion moved into Forest just before dusk that evening, and settled down for the night, but at about 10 p.m. we were warned that we should have to continue the attack the next morning. It was not until 1.30 a.m. (on the 24th) that we received definite orders, and we had to be in position in front of Bousies, about two miles distant, ready to attack at 4 a.m. This did not leave much time, but rapid marching, and sending officers on in front to reconnoitre the village, got the battalion in position in support of the Northamptonshires about a quarter of an hour before zero. 2nd-Lieutenant Tysoe rendered valuable assistance by carrying out a reconnaissance of the village and surrounding country during this night."

With regard to the good work by Sergeant Rickard which Colonel Percival mentions, the official account of his action was as follows :—

" Shortly after the start his platoon was held up by an enemy machine gun, which had been pushed forward inside our barrage, and seven of his men were hit, including the Lewis-gun section. Realizing the danger to the rest of the battalion if this machine gun were allowed to remain in its present position, Sergeant Rickard took the Lewis gun himself, and went forward with one runner, who carried the drums. He got within six yards of the machine-gun post and then opened fire, putting the gun out of action and killing or wounding all the crew, ten in number. Followed by the rest of the platoon, he then fought his way forward, putting out of action several other machine-gun posts."

Private F. Flute, the runner who promptly picked up some Lewis-gun drums and followed Sergeant Rickards, is reported in the official account as having personally dealt with a sniper who was attempting to knock out the Sergeant.

The attack was continued at 4 a.m. on the 24th. Orders arrived from Division in the early hours, and were at once communicated verbally to the Royal Fusiliers and Bedfordshires, who moved off at once ; and a motor-car took orders to the Northamptonshires, who, it will be remembered, were now holding the line, having relieved the Buffs (55th Brigade). It was decided to attack with the Northamptonshires, who were to take the first objective, the other battalions then leapfrogging through to the final objective.

Our barrage came down at zero (4 a.m.), but was rather ragged and short, and caused a number of casualties in our own ranks. Our attack got well away, however, and the German reply was not particularly heavy. But the darkness and the close nature of the country proved a great hindrance. As a result our men soon lost the barrage, and a number of hostile machine guns began to give a great deal of trouble. The support battalions (Fusiliers and Bedfordshires) became involved in the fighting within the first 700 yards, but pushed on, and duly went through the Northamptonshires according to programme on the line of a road that runs south-east from Bousies Wood Farm.

The enemy had now pulled himself together, and though it was some comfort to know that he was only putting up desperate rearguard actions, it is just as unpleasant, and fully as fatal, to be killed in a show of this kind as in a full-dress battle. It must be remembered that the country rather lent itself to delaying actions, for after a spell over bare, open ground, not unlike our own South Downs, we were now among orchards, with thick hedges all strongly wired and very difficult to get through. More than ever the war had come down to the platoon and section commanders, and jolly well they rose to the occasion.

About dawn the Germans put in a couple of brisk little counter-attacks, one on the right company of the Northamptonshires, and one on the Fusiliers at Bousies Wood Farm, but both were driven off with loss. The Fusiliers now got forward, taking and passing the wired line in front of Bousies Wood Farm, but could not get across the top of the ridge, which was swept by machine guns from the little valley beyond. Trouble was also being caused on our right by machine guns in and around Renuart Farm, and others that had survived the attack of the 55th Brigade still farther on our right were enfilading our front line and making movement in the rear of it practically impossible. With these several hindrances the attack came to a standstill pending further artillery preparation.

This was arranged for with Division. Unluckily, the heavies took on certain German lines which were shown on aeroplane photographs, but which were now as a matter of fact held by us. As a result we suffered a number of casualties, and in addition, as some of the guns were shooting short, our support companies were shelled out of their positions.

During the afternoon Brigadier-General O. C. Borrett, C.M.G., D.S.O., was taken ill and evacuated, and Lieutenant-Colonel R. Turner, D.S.O., of the Northamptonshire Regiment, assumed temporary command of the Brigade.

About this time a fine piece of work by Lieutenant F. W. Hedges, Bedfordshire Regiment, attached 6th Battalion Northamptonshire Regiment, who was in command of the company now held up in front of Renuart Farm, enabled the advance to be continued. For this action he was awarded the Victoria Cross. The official account says :—

" His company was on the right of the Brigade front. He advanced a considerable distance to a point where his further advance was held up by about six machine-gun posts on the hill opposite the line. Early in the afternoon this officer made up his mind to clear out these enemy posts. Later, accompanied by one sergeant, and followed at some distance by a Lewis-gun team, he proceeded up the hill, under cover of a hedge, killed the first machine gunner, and took two other prisoners. He then worked his way along the crest of the hill, and dealt with three other machine-gun posts in a similar manner, taking the feed-blocks out of the guns, his total being four machine guns and fourteen men."

As a result of this fine piece of work the whole line, after being held up for some hours, was able to get forward. An advance was made at this point, and almost simultaneously the other three companies of the Northamptonshires, who had been held up around Bousies Wood Farm, turned the enemy position from the north. With these two tactical successes to our credit, the enemy resistance collapsed. At 5 p.m. the Bedfordshires captured Renuart Farm, the attack pushed forward, and by 6 p.m. the Brigade had reached a line near the Englefontaine-Robersart road, and had obtained touch with the flanks.

That night we were relieved by the 53rd Brigade, and by dawn on the 25th the Fusiliers and Northamptonshires had been withdrawn to Bousies, and the Bedfordshires to Epinette Farm.

In the fighting of the 24th the Brigade took 100 prisoners and 20 machine guns, the grand total for the two days being 350 prisoners, 14 guns, 6 trench-mortars, 100 machine guns, and 3 anti-tank rifles.

Among much good work this day (24th), that of two young Fusilier officers was rewarded by the M.C. The official accounts read as follows :—

Lieutenant G. E. Tyler " led his company forward with entire disregard for personal safety, rushing several machine-gun posts at the head of his men. He was badly shot through the lungs while consolidating, but continued to direct operations for nearly three hours until collapsing."

Lieutenant E. L. Moody " shortly after the start of the attack found himself in charge of three companies, the officers of two companies having become casualties. He did fine work in re-organizing them when held up, and afterwards in consolidation, walking about freely under heavy machine-gun fire. In the evening he took charge of the battle patrols going forward, and succeeded in gaining a considerable amount of ground."

It was, by the way, just about this time that the newest thing in hand-to-hand fighting took place—a duel with a Lewis gun, which is a very messy way of settling an argument. I think it was a Bedfordshire Lewis gunner, carrying his gun, who suddenly came on a Bosche in a shell-slit. The Bosche sprang out, seized hold of the Lewis gun, and attempted to wrest it from our man. A great struggle took place, in the course of which the German held the muzzle of the gun at his belt, and, clutching the barrel-casing, pulled as hard as he could. Let his fate be a hint to you, if you are ever quarrelling over the possession of a Lewis gun, for at this moment our man pressed the trigger, there was a sudden burst of fire, and—well, you can imagine that a German who has taken about twenty rounds all at once in his stomach is not a drawing-room ornament.

After forty-eight hours' rest the Brigade relieved the 55th Brigade, and each of our three battalions had a turn in the line. We held a two-battalion front till October 30th, when the right sector was taken over by the 50th Division, and our Brigade sector was reduced to a one-battalion front. This extended from the Robersart-Preux-au-Bois road northwards for about 1,200 yards. On November 1st the Royal Fusiliers relieved the Bedfordshires, who went into support at Bousies, while the Northamptonshires were in support in Epinette orchards. These dispositions remained unchanged until November 3rd, when the front of the Royal Fusiliers was extended a further 1,000 yards, in order to take in the whole of the Brigade front for the attack on the 4th.

This attack, which was to prove the Brigade's last show, was a part of a daylight attack on a large scale over a very wide front. So far as we were concerned, our objective was the village of Preux-au-Bois, on the western edge of Mormal Forest.

Putting the matter simply, we now held a line parallel with and a little west of the Robertsart-Englefontaine road, one of those straight-ruled roads of France, which here ran roughly north and south. From here to the centre of Preux was roughly 1,500 yards. The plan was for the Northamptonshires (less one company) to make the initial attack, and seize the ground on the north of the village. This done, the Bedfordshires, with one company Royal Fusiliers and the remaining company of the Northamptonshires, were to form up on the north of the village and attack in a southerly direction, mopping up the village. The rest of the Royal Fusiliers, still holding the line opposite the west side of the village, were in the meantime to keep the enemy amused with Lewis guns, rifles, and rifle-grenades, in the hope of deceiving him as to the real point of attack.

Zero was at 6.15 a.m. Our barrage came down well, and the Northamptonshires got well away, the enemy reply, though prompt, not being over heavy. Within the first 200 yards some opposition was encountered, but this did not prove serious, the only hitch in the proceedings being enfilade machine-gun fire on our right, from a point somewhere at the north-east corner of the village. This was a little troublesome just before the eastern objective was reached, but did not delay proceedings, and at 8 a.m., well up to programme, this part of the job had been successfully carried out.

The next attack, which had to start from the north of the village, on the ground just won, and push south, now formed up under the enfilade barrage, which was exceptionally accurate and good. The weather had been clear early, but soon after 6.30 a.m. a thick fog came down, which did not clear till about 9 a.m., and proved of some service.

While this southerly attack was forming up, about one company of the enemy counter-attacked down a little valley north-east of the village, but the Northamptonshires dealt firmly with this attempt to spoil a show that was going very well up to the present. Accordingly our second attack got away unhindered, but after the first 500 yards strong opposition was encountered. The company of the Fusiliers was now held up by machine-gun fire from near a house on the Robertsart main road, the two left companies of the Bedfordshires were heavily engaged near the cemetery and making but slow progress, and the company of the Northamptonshires taking part in this second attack was also held up by machine-gun fire.

Four tanks had been allotted to the Brigade, and were to accompany this southerly attack and mop up the village, one being attached to the Royal Fusiliers and Northamptonshires companies, and two to the Bedfordshires. However, they had by this time somewhat lost their way, and three of them were now operating with the two right companies of the Bedfordshires. These two companies were thus enabled to make good progress, and by about ten o'clock had fought their way through the village to near the church, where they gained touch with the 2nd Munster Fusiliers (30th Division), who had come up from the south, and proceeded to mop up.

By this time the enemy was well shaken, and except for isolated parties his resistance became weaker. By 11 a.m. the right company of the Royal Fusiliers (which had been holding our old front opposite the village, and had delivered a dummy attack at zero) was able, by keeping constant pressure on the enemy, to clear the cross-roads on the Robertsart-Preux road; and the company attacking from the north of the village, very ably led by Captain Hope, was able to clear the enemy from the point where machine guns had earlier proved troublesome, and to capture over 100 prisoners.

By this time one battalion 53rd Brigade had leap-frogged through the Northamptonshires and pushed ahead, so that early in the afternoon the Division had gained a line 2,500 yards east of Preux, and was still pushing on.

Our job was done. The battalions went into billets among the cellars and ruined houses of Preux, with orders to be ready at half an hour's notice on the following day to take up the pursuit. Not to make a long story any longer, the pursuit managed to do without us, an acquaintance of considerably over three years with Jerry had come to an end, and on November 6th we moved back to rest at Le Cateau, where we were when news of the armistice reached us.

Some mention, all too brief, has already been made of the good work done by the company of the Royal Fusiliers that took part in the southerly attack through the village of Preux. This was as a matter of fact a composite company, the remains of two others—" C " and " D "—and was commanded by Lieutenant (acting Captain) P. A. Hope, who for his courage and fine leadership was awarded the D.S.O. The official account states :—

" Although held up by machine-gun nests and the breakdown of the tank which was to deal with them, at the commencement of the attack, he eventually succeeded in breaking through with some twenty men. Without waiting for the remainder he at once pushed on with such effect that he succeeded in clearing up the whole area, capturing over 20 machine guns and some 200 prisoners, including five officers. The success of the attack in this area was entirely due to his leadership and determination, while the example of coolness and courage he set the men was beyond all praise."

Some good work was done with this company by Private D. Sale (" C " Company), who was also decorated. Says the official account :—

" The company was held up by heavy machine-gun fire. He at once pushed forward alone with his Lewis gun, and, although under heavy fire the whole time, got his gun into action and succeeded in silencing several enemy machine guns."

Captain R. B. Fawkes, M.C., of the 6th Northamptonshire Regiment, also won the D.S.O. that day. According to the official account, " he commanded the company taking the first of the battalion's objectives. This company met with considerable opposition from the start, but he led it successfully to the objective by skilful handling and fire tactics, and by the fine example he set his men, being absolutely fearless. The company won its way by rifle and machine-gun fire, captured a number of machine guns, and took over 100 prisoners."

The third D.S.O. won that day went to Captain R. L. V. Doake, M.C., of the Bedfordshire Regiment. " He was in command of one of the leading companies of the assault [says the official account]. The enclosed nature of the country called for special individual leadership on the part of officers and N.C.Os., and in this respect Captain Doake set a splendid example, being always in the thick of the fighting, and himself killing a large number of Germans. He led his company forward when the companies on either flank were held up, reached his final objective, and then sent parties out to either flank to help the other companies forward. This was completely successful."

Just one little personal narrative of this last fight of the Brigade. I quote from some notes kindly sent me by Lieutenant-Colonel A. E. Percival :—

" Some excellent shooting by Bedfordshire officers is recorded during this attack. In one case Captain Doake, commanding ' C ' Company, was moving through the orchards towards the village, accompanied by his batman, when he saw through a hedge a party of four Bosches with a machine gun not more than twenty yards away. He and his batman opened fire, and he claims to have brought down all the four Bosches with four rounds.

"Lieutenant Goben found himself face to face with a Bosche in a slit near the attack. The Bosche was armed with a rifle, and Goben had a revolver, and each side fired four rounds before Lieutenant Goben became the victor. His subsequent remark was that ' It would have been damned funny if it had not been so extremely dangerous.'

"No less than 1,400 civilians were liberated from the village, and also several Alsatian soldiers who had been in hiding there for a fortnight, awaiting our arrival. The civilians were very hospitable, and in many cases our men were enjoying cups of coffee in the houses before the enemy had been finally evicted from the village.

"One of the last sights seen by the battalion on this final day of active operations was a stout Frenchwoman chasing a big German down the street with a pitchfork in her hand."

So, roughly speaking, that Frenchwoman chasing a German out of Preux-au-Bois was the end of the war as far as this Brigade was concerned. There followed a short rest at Le Cateau, where the armistice was celebrated, a few weeks at Serain, and finally a move to Selvigny (Brigade headquarters and 2nd Bedfordshire Regiment) and Walincourt (11th Royal Fusiliers and 6th Northamptonshire Regiment), where we spent our last Christmas in France, carried on salvage and education, and gradually dwindled away as officers and men were demobilized. A very quiet, a very unexciting ending to it all—and yet not the end, for all of us, officers and men alike, made friendships and comradeships that we shall never willingly sever, and for many years to come it will always be a good introduction, when white-haired old veterans meet, to say : " Hullo ! Weren't you in the old 54th Brigade ? Shake !"

APPENDIX A.

BRIGADE COMMANDERS.

Brigadier-General H. Browse-Scaife (September, 1914—March, 1915).
Major-General W. C. G. Heneker, C.M.G., D.S.O. (March, 1915—December, 1915).
Major-General T. H. Shoubridge, C.M.G., D.S.O. (December, 1915—March, 1917).
Brigadier-General C. Cunliffe Owen, C.B. (March, 1917—October, 1917).
Brigadier-General L. de V. Sadleir-Jackson, C.B., C.M.G., D.S.O. (October, 1917—March, 1919).
*Brigadier-General J. A. Tyler, C.M.G. (August—September, 1918).
*Brigadier-General O. C. Borrett, C.M.G., D.S.O. (October—November, 1918).

* Commanded Brigade during absence of Brigadier-General Sadleir-Jackson, wounded.

BRIGADE MAJORS.

Major Rich.
Major O. P. L. Hoskyns.
Lieutenant-Colonel The Hon. C. M. Hore-Ruthven, D.S.O.
Major E. G. Miles, D.S.O., M.C.
Captain G. F. J. Cumberlege, D.S.O., M.C.
Captain G. D. Pidsley, D.S.O., M.C.
Captain The Hon. D. G. Fortescue, M.C.

STAFF CAPTAINS.

Major L. A. Newnham, M.C.
Captain H. B. Stutfield.
Major C. Runge, D.S.O., M.C.
Captain O. C. Johnson, M.C.
Captain L. W. Diggle, M.C.
Captain H. C. Browning, M.C. (acting Staff Captain).

COMMANDING OFFICERS.

11TH (S.) BATTALION THE ROYAL FUSILIERS.

Lieutenant-Colonel C. C. Carr, D.S.O. (September, 1914—September, 1917).
Lieutenant-Colonel A. E. Sulman, M.C. (September, 1917—July, 1918).
Lieutenant-Colonel K. D. H. Gwynn, D.S.O. (July, 1918—December, 1918).
Lieutenant-Colonel G. Blewitt, D.S.O., M.C. (December, 1918—January, 1919).
Lieutenant-Colonel C. F. Miller, D.S.O. (January, 1919—March, 1919).

7TH (S.) BATTALION BEDFORDSHIRE REGIMENT.

Colonel H. Martin, C.B. (September—December, 1914).
Lieutenant-Colonel E. D. Pickard Cambridge (December, 1914—March, 1915).
Major G. P. Mills, D.S.O. (March, 1915—April, 1915).
Lieutenant-Colonel Allenby (April, 1915—June, 1915).
Lieutenant-Colonel G. D. Price (June, 1915—October, 1916).
Lieutenant-Colonel G. P. Mills, D.S.O. (October, 1916—January, 1918).
Lieutenant-Colonel A. E. Percival, D.S.O., M.C. (January, 1918—May, 1918).

2ND BATTALION BEDFORDSHIRE REGIMENT.

Lieutenant-Colonel A. E. Percival, D.S.O., M.C. (May, 1918—March, 1919).

[NOTE.—Lieutenant-Colonel A. E. Percival was commanding the 7th Battalion when it ceased to exist, and took over command of the 2nd Battalion, which then joined the Brigade.]

6TH (S.) BATTALION NORTHAMPTONSHIRE REGIMENT.

Lieutenant-Colonel G. R. Ripley (September, 1914—October, 1916).
Lieutenant-Colonel S. H. Charrington, D.S.O. (October, 1916—February, 1917).
Lieutenant-Colonel Meyrick (February 3rd, 1917—February 17th, 1917).
Lieutenant-Colonel R. Turner, D.S.O. (March 1st, 1917—April, 1918).
Lieutenant-Colonel G. Buckle, D.S.O., M.C. (April 12th, 1918—May 3rd, 1918).
Lieutenant-Colonel Le Houquet (May 5th, 1918—May 13th, 1918).

Lieutenant-Colonel Walsh, D.S.O. (May 17th, 1918—May 29th, 1918).
Lieutenant-Colonel J. H. Foster (June, 1918—August, 1918).
Major J. H. Piper, M.C. (August, 1918—September, 1918).
Lieutenant-Colonel R. Turner, D.S.O. (September, 1918—January, 1919).
Major J. H. Piper, M.C. (January—March, 1919).

12TH (S.) BATTALION MIDDLESEX REGIMENT.

Brigadier-General F. A. Maxwell, V.C., D.S.O. (killed).
Lieutenant-Colonel G. C. Glover.
Lieutenant-Colonel Osborne.
Lieutenant-Colonel W. H. H. Johnson.
Lieutenant-Colonel J. H. Bridcutt.

80TH FIELD COMPANY ROYAL ENGINEERS.

Major H. G. Joly de Lotbinière (now Lieutenant-Colonel, Brevet-Colonel) (October, 1914—November, 1915).
Captain F. J. N. King (November, 1915—January, 1916).
Captain B. I. Chambers (January, 1916—March, 1916).
Major A. A. Chase, D.S.O. (March, 1916—January, 1917), (killed in action).
Major G. Bremner, D.S.O., M.C. (January, 1917—March, 1918), (killed in action).
Major G. Ledgard, M.C. (March, 1918—March, 1919).

152ND COMPANY ROYAL ARMY SERVICE CORPS.

Captain E. M. West, M.C. (September, 1914—March, 1919).

54TH FIELD AMBULANCE ROYAL ARMY MEDICAL CORPS.

Lieutenant-Colonel M. C. Beatty (July, 1915—April, 1916).
Lieutenant-Colonel D. C. Barron (April, 1916—February, 1917).
Lieutenant-Colonel G. Pritchard-Taylor, D.S.O., M.C. (February, 1917—March, 1919).

54TH TRENCH MORTAR BATTERY.

Captain H. M. Eldridge, M.C. (till August, 1917).
Captain R. Knight, M.C. (August, 1917—March, 1918).
Captain P. J. Payton, M.C. (March, 1918—February, 1919).

[NOTE.—The foregoing lists have been supplied by the units concerned, who are responsible for their accuracy.]

APPENDIX B

VICTORIA CROSSES

THE following officers, non-commissioned officers, and men of the Brigade were awarded the Victoria Cross. The ranks given are those held at the time the awards were made.

Sergeant William E. Boulter, 6th (S.) Battalion Northamptonshire Regiment.

For most conspicuous bravery. During the capture of Trones Wood, on July 14th, 1916, one company and a portion of another were held up by a machine gun, which was causing heavy casualties.

Sergeant Boulter, realizing the situation, with complete disregard of his own safety, and in spite of being severely wounded in the shoulder, advanced alone across the open in front of the gun under heavy fire, and bombed the team from their position, thereby saving the lives of many of his comrades, and materially assisting the advance, which eventually cleared Trones Wood.

2nd-Lieutenant T. E. Adlam, 7th (S.) Battalion Bedfordshire Regiment.

For most conspicuous bravery and gallant leadership during the operations at Thiepval on September 27th-28th, 1916.

On the morning of the 27th a portion of the village which had defied capture the previous day had to be taken at all costs, to enable the battalion to form up for an attack on the ridge beyond. This minor operation was held up by extremely heavy rifle and machine-gun fire from several strong points.

2nd-Lieutenant Adlam, realizing that time was all important, dashed across the open under the heaviest fire from shell-hole to shell-hole to collect his men for a combined rush. He collected a quantity of German grenades, and started a whirlwind attack on the enemy position. During this period he was wounded in the leg, so that at times he had to throw from a kneeling position. In spite of this he succeeded in out-throwing the enemy, and then, seizing his opportunity, in spite of his wound, he led a rush on the position and captured it, killing all the occupants of the trench. He continued with his men throughout the day, leading them with the greatest gallantry in smaller bombing attacks.

The following day he again displayed the highest courage in the course of the attack on Schwaben Redoubt. Though again wounded, this time in the right arm, so that he could no longer throw bombs himself, he continued to lead his men, with utter contempt of danger, until he was ordered to the rear.

Private Frederick J. Edwards, 12th (S.) Battalion Middlesex Regiment.

For most conspicuous courage, resource, and presence of mind displayed during the attack on Thiepval on September 26th, 1916.

His part of the line was held up by a machine gun. The officers had all become casualties. There was confusion, and even suggestions of retirement. Private Edwards grasped the situation at once. Alone and on his own initiative, he dashed towards the gun, which he bombed until he succeeded in knocking it out. By this gallant act, performed with great presence of mind and a complete disregard for his personal safety, this man made possible the continuance of the advance, and solved a dangerous situation. His was probably one of those decisive actions which determine the success or failure of an operation.

Private Robert Ryder, 12th (S.) Battalion Middlesex Regiment.

For most conspicuous bravery and initiative during the attack on Thiepval on September 26th, 1916.

His company was held up by heavy fire from the trench in front of them, and all his officers had become casualties. The attack was flagging for want of leadership. Private Ryder, realizing the situation, without a moment's thought for his own safety, dashed absolutely alone at the enemy trench, and by skilful manipulation of his Lewis gun succeeded in clearing the trench.

By this brilliant act he not only made possible, but also inspired, the advance of his comrades. It seems probable that this single heroic action made all the difference between success and failure in this part of the attacking line.

Private Christopher August Cox, 7th (S.) Battalion Bedfordshire Regiment.

For conspicuous gallantry and devotion to duty as a stretcher-bearer during operations in front of Achiet-le-Grand on March 15th, 1917, and subsequent days.

During the attacks on the 15th, under heavy rifle, machine-gun, and shell fire on an exposed crest, Private Cox worked continuously, carrying back wounded men on his shoulders. On the 16th and 17th he continued this work without rest, and with a complete disregard of his own safety.

This man has been in every engagement in which his battalion has taken part since July, 1916, and has always displayed the highest example of unselfishness, devotion, and personal courage.

2nd-Lieutenant Alfred Cecil Herring, R.A.S.C., attached 6th (S.) Battalion Northamptonshire Regiment.

For initiative, conspicuous gallantry, and devotion to duty on March 23rd and 24th, 1918.

On March 23rd the Germans crossed the Montagne Bridge, after some fighting, and gained a position on the south bank of the canal. 2nd-Lieutenant Herring's post was cut off and surrounded. He immediately counter-attacked with his post, and recaptured the position, taking over twenty prisoners and six machine guns.

The post was attacked continuously throughout the night for eleven hours, and all attacks were beaten off. This was entirely due to the splendid heroism displayed by 2nd-Lieutenant Herring, who continually visited his men during the night and cheered them up. The initiative and individual bravery of this officer were entirely responsible for holding up the German advance for eleven hours at an exceedingly critical period.

The late Lance-Corporal Albert Lewis, 6th (S.) Battalion Northamptonshire Regiment.

On the morning of September 18th, 1918, this N.C.O. was in charge of a section which he had successfully kept together. He was on the right of the line, and the battalion started to advance to attack Ronssoy, where the east and west barrage opened.

The battalion advanced to a point where the enemy machine-gun fire was so intense that it was a practical impossibility to get forward. The barrage went on, and the battalion was temporarily held up. This man, working with his section on the right amongst the ruins, observed two enemy machine guns opposite him, enfilading the whole battalion. He crawled forward single-handed on his own initiative with bombs, got within bombing range, and successfully bombed the teams manning the enemy's guns. The enemy left their guns and ran out of their emplacement. Lance-Corporal Lewis thereupon used his rifle with good effect, and the whole team surrendered. He wounded six and captured four unwounded. By his courage and determination in putting out of action two enemy machine guns he undoubtedly enabled the battalion to advance, and so contributed largely to the success that followed.

Later, on September 21st, during another attack, this N.C.O. displayed splendid power of command. When his company was caught in the enemy barrage he was the first to rush them through it, until they came under heavy fire from enemy machine guns, whereupon he immediately began to place them out in shell-holes. While doing this he was killed.

Lieutenant Frederick William Hedges, Bedfordshire Regiment, attached 6th (S.) Battalion Northamptonshire Regiment.

For conspicuous gallantry and initiative during operations north-east of Bousies on October 24th, 1918.

During the morning this officer, who was detailed to leap-frog his company to the final objective, handled his company in a very skilful manner, maintaining direction under the most difficult conditions. His company was on the right of the Brigade front.

He advanced a considerable distance to a point where his further advance was held up by about six machine-gun posts on the hill opposite the line. Early in the afternoon this officer made up his mind to clear out these enemy posts. Later, accompanied by one sergeant, and followed at some considerable distance by a Lewis gun section, he proceeded up the hill under cover of a hedge, and killed the first machine gunner and took two other prisoners. He then worked his way along the crest of the hill, and dealt with three other machine-gun posts in a similar manner, taking the feed-blocks out of the guns, his total being four machine guns and fourteen men.

The direct result of this officer's action was that the whole line, which had been held up since morning, was enabled to advance, thus having a great effect on subsequent operations.

www.ingramcontent.com/pod-product-compliance
Lightning Source LLC
Chambersburg PA
CBHW031141160426
43193CB00008B/207